To
John Popkin
With gratitude for
helping get the
of this book across

Cordially
Arnold Frost

Apr 1950

A MEASURE OF FREEDOM

AN ANTI-DEFAMATION LEAGUE REPORT————

A Measure
of Freedom

by Arnold Forster

DOUBLEDAY & COMPANY, INC., GARDEN CITY

NEW YORK, 1950

Contents

Acknowledgment

THIS BOOK is the product of co-ordinated research and writing effort by a large group of highly skilled people. No single person can truly be called the author of *A Measure of Freedom*. Trained specialists in the field covered by the book, in addition to participating in the original research, actually contributed the first draft of entire sections and in some instances entire chapters. More than fifty men and women worked on the project, thirty-five of them from their respective cities scattered throughout the United States.

Elmo Roper, his associate Dr. Julian Woodward, and the Roper Organization were responsible for the scientific polling and analyses recorded in the college opinion chapter. In addition, they did the study of the ten years of surveys on anti-Semitism reported in Chapter 6.

Of all those who helped build the book, a particular word of gratitude must go to the following: to Harold Braverman and Bernard Simon for their editorial research and writing assistance on the entire manuscript; Monroe Sheinberg, Jack Baker, Milton Ellerin, and their staffs for statistical research and analyses; Morton Puner and Arnold Scheuer for their editorial aid; Dr. Paul Hartmann and Herman Edelsberg for their legal and legislative research and analyses.

I am especially indebted to ADL's National Director, Benjamin R. Epstein, Nathan C. Belth and Harold Braverman, who participated in the daily planning and development of the book.

To all these and others goes whatever credit may come for producing *A Measure of Freedom*.

A. F.

New York, N.Y.
March 1950

Foreword

ON THE EVE of the founding of the Republic, one of the wisest Americans of his time said:

> "To get the bad customs of a country changed, and new ones, though better, introduced, it is necessary first to remove prejudice, enlighten ignorance, and convince [the people] their interests will be promoted by the proposed changes; and this is not the work of a day."

If we were to couple this sound advice of Benjamin Franklin with the oft-repeated but frequently neglected clarion call that "eternal vigilance is the price of freedom," the argument of this book becomes clear. For it seeks to change the "bad customs" of our country by awakening the people to the havoc that the prejudices in their midst create; it proposes to arouse Americans against those who fatten upon these prejudices to the nation's eventual destruction.

Anti-Jewish propaganda has corrupted the nation's bloodstreams in the past decade, coursing into big cities, small towns, and the farm country. It has had many names—the Black Legion, the Christian Front, the Gentile League, the Ku Klux Klan, the German-American Bund—and has often cloaked itself in a guise of respectability and patriotism.

It has even emerged as an organized political movement. In the United States the depression provided an unhealthy climate which nourished corrupt thinking, inflammatory speechmaking, and malevolent publications. In recent years it has become more apparent that anti-Semitism is only a part of the whole problem of prejudice and discrimination.

Freedom and liberty cannot be bought with complacency. Social and economic freedom can be maintained only by a continuing appreciation of the traditional American concept of democracy. Intelligent opposition must be generated against both the open and the hidden forces which seek to destroy it. And a militant unity among freedom-minded men is necessary to hit—and hit hard—at bigots.

True freedom precludes any compromise of democracy's principles, whether the pressures come from the fascist right or the communist left. The militant unity must be composed, therefore, of men and women who believe only in democracy, who will not sacrifice their principles by permitting any totalitarian invasion upon them for temporary gain. This is the creed upon which this book is written.

A *Measure of Freedom* sets down facts and figures gathered and evaluated by skilled researchers. It was not a simple task; it was a full year in the making. It represents a co-operative effort of all the resources of the Anti-Defamation League of B'nai B'rith.

No attempt was made to cover the entire field of prejudice. The study was limited to several areas of anti-Semitic manifestation and their relationship to civil rights. In surveying these areas the book does not dwell at length upon the problems of other minority groups; nor does it touch upon political activity except where politics has employed racial and religious bias.

A *Measure of Freedom* was undertaken at the direction of the Civil Rights Committee of the Anti-Defamation League: Jacob Grumet, New York, Chairman; Judge David A. Rose, Boston, Vice-Chairman; Leo Abrams, Alan Altheimer, Bernard Nath, Nathaniel Nathanson, A. N. Pritzker, and Benjamin Samuels, all of Chicago; Henry Epstein, Judge Martin M. Frank, Lester Gutterman, Judge Irving R. Kaufman, Samuel Kramer, Samuel Markle, Norman N. Newhouse, Louis A. Novins, Henry E. Schultz, and J. Irwin Shapiro, all of New York; Joseph Cohen, Kansas City; John Horwitz, Oklahoma City; Frank R. S. Kaplan, Pittsburgh; Charles W. Morris, Louisville.

The committee placed the task in the experienced hands of Arnold Forster, director of its activities. He first saw the value of such audits, established their scope, and has been directing them since their inception. For *A Measure of Freedom*, the fourth such report in as many years, Mr. Forster had the valued counsel of his friend and associate, Benjamin R. Epstein, National Director of the Anti-Defamation League.

We believe the American people want to know the weaknesses in our democratic fabric. From this knowledge will come an understanding of the need for correction and the inspiration to do the job. The Anti-Defamation League continues its work in the faith that the overwhelming majority of Americans are eager for a "more perfect union."

MEIER STEINBRINK
National Chairman, Anti-Defamation League

New York, March 1950

Chapter 1. Democracy's Dilemma

IN MAY OF 1949 the nine justices of the United States Supreme Court felt compelled to write four separate opinions in a single case. The case was the City of Chicago versus Arthur Terminiello; the constitutional principle involved was free speech; the issue, how far could a rabble-rouser go in inciting an audience in a public hall against a religious group. Four justices dissented from the majority opinion; but even they disagreed among themselves. Two arrived at their conclusion on the fundamental question of free speech; the other two on technical grounds.

Here was clear evidence that the free speech controversy raging in the public forum has even divided the justices of the land's highest court. It is a controversy made acute by the development of modern propaganda techniques and new means of mass communication.

The majority position of the court, which can be summed up in the phrase "Let them get it off their chests," finds support from normally opposing interests. On the one hand is the liberal American Civil Liberties Union, which comes to its position out of an ardent desire to defend the most extreme limits of free speech. On the other is the Chicago *Tribune*, which comes to the same conclusion from a most conservative orientation.

There is another section of opinion—as vitally concerned with the preservation of American democracy as the ACLU—which asks the question: "Haven't we learned from the tragedies of Nazism that you must protect the people against the dissemination of completely false and vicious appeals to religious hatred?" It is the only way, says this group, to safeguard freedom from destruction.

This is not an academic question. It reaches directly into our daily lives.

Rejecting a concept of law which would prohibit such incitement as Terminiello's speech, the majority of the court declared that one function of free speech under our system of government was to invite dispute. "It [free speech] may indeed best serve its high purpose when it produces a condition of unrest, creates dissatisfaction with conditions as they are, or even stirs people to anger." Deciding that the case at hand evidenced no "clear and present danger of a serious substantive evil that rises far above public inconvenience, annoyance, or unrest," the majority held that the speech in question was protected against censorship or punishment.

Speaking for himself and Mr. Justice Burton against the majority viewpoint, Mr. Justice Jackson eloquently stated the philosophy of those who look askance upon unbridled right of free speech:

This Court has gone far toward accepting the doctrine that civil liberty means the removal of all restraints from . . . crowds and that all local attempts to maintain order are impairments of the liberty of the citizen. The choice is not between order and liberty. It is between liberty with order and anarchy without either. There is danger that, if the Court does not temper its doctrinaire logic with a little practical wisdom, it will convert the constitutional Bill of Rights into a suicide pact.

Unbridled speech or the temperate exercise of control—which?

Last year there was a controversy over the British film *Oliver Twist* that is also typical of the problems upon which these differing interpretations of free speech touch. When it was first announced that the J. Arthur Rank production of the Dickens classic was on its way to the United States, many Americans were disturbed by the description of the characterization of Fagin in the film. Here was a page from Hitler in film strip; here was Streicher come again to destroy; here reborn, was the distorted stereotype of the Jew.

American movie distributors refused to become involved in the distribution and exhibition of the motion picture after the Anti-Defamation League and others expressed the fear that the film was harmful. The Rank Organization withdrew the picture in the United States.

Immediately the cry went up. Censorship!

Censorship? Was the publicly expressed opinion that the movie had a harmful potential in and of itself an exercise of censorship? The extremists argued that it *was* censorship if, as a result of such opinions, the movie was withdrawn from exhibition—*even though no such demand had been made*. But others argued that freedom of speech establishes the right to say publicly what one believes (in this case, about *Oliver Twist*) without being accused of an undemocratic attempt at censorship irrespective of its effect on the exhibition of the picture.

Here was the principle of free speech clashing with itself. Untrammeled freedom undoubtedly includes the right of the producer to exhibit his product. The same untrammeled freedom clearly guarantees the right of anyone to express his opinion—even though a direct result of that opinion may be the refusal of theaters to exhibit the motion picture.

The clash among adherents of free speech in the *Oliver Twist* controversy might be resolved if there were basic agreement on the question pointed up by Justice Jackson in the Terminiello case: Freedom to speak or freedom to destroy a religious or racial group? Can we protect the first and stop short of the second? Certainly. There must be a middle ground; perhaps a concept different from any thus far suggested, one that will safeguard free speech against both censorship and its own excesses.

Whatever Americans eventually choose will determine the road to be taken by human relations agencies intent upon extending to all, within a constitutional framework, the benefits of democracy. This much can be said with certainty: Only an anti-democrat can espouse serious and substantial restriction upon the rights of free speech, assembly, press, religion and the other guarantees of the Bill of Rights. An honest respect for democracy dictates full support of these freedom principles.

However, unfettered license to say and do as one pleases does not limit the right of others to condemn what is said or done as inimical to the country's welfare. If Gerald Smith has the absolute right to call together a thousand Americans and tell them Jews are a menace in America, Jews have the concomitant right to label him an anti-Semite and declare it from the rooftops. If the KKK has the right to condemn Catholics for allegiance to the Vatican, Catholics have an equivalent right to label the hooded order un-American. If Congressman John Rankin proposes that American Negroes be deported to Africa, it is right for these Negroes to label him a racist.

Yet it is with real reluctance that freedom-minded men label an utterance or a viewpoint as bad for America. For the implication may be that to condemn it as anti-democratic may be to silence it forever. And there, once again, we are confronted by the same clash of free speech.

There can be no doubt that democracy has a right to defend itself from its enemies inside its borders and in foreign lands. How best to do it with the weapon of speech is a serious problem. Until the multiple questions arising out of this free speech issue are resolved within a democratic framework, one must use the weapon of public condemnation with intelligence and caution.

When World War II ended, the United States was plagued by racists, bigots, fascists, who had become expert in the weapon of the word and had embarked upon a program against democracy. A Nazi trick they had learned to use artfully was to divide racial and religious groups by lies.

One reaction to this device was the full flowering in America of human relations agencies: organizations created to develop ways and means of counteracting the bigot and building better intergroup relations.

At the beginning, some leaders in human relations work believed that the wisest way to handle racial and religious conflict was to ignore it as a passing phenomenon. Others wanted to close their eyes to the ugly facts of discrimination because they were convinced that to talk openly and frankly about the amount of prejudice burdening the nation was to create a kind of bandwagon atmosphere which would serve only to increase the number of bigots. There is also a small number which even now suffers embarrassment from frank talk about racial and religious bias—akin to that once provoked by frank discussions of venereal disease.

Today there is little argument about the wisdom of exposing democracy's enemies. It is recognized, too, that no wall can successfully be built to keep the facts of prejudice from democracy's citizens.

Nor is there controversy any longer about the indivisibility of racial and religious freedom. It is all one problem; no group or class is safe while any single one among them is insecure. A United States Supreme Court judgment which renders unenforceable the restrictive covenant in real estate protects more than the minority member in the free right to choose his home; it also guarantees the majority against the development of slum-ghettos.

Obviously, human relations agencies reflect many and varied opinions as to the best methods of solving intergroup problems. Like religions, they travel different roads but seek the same end.

Clearly, one responsibility devolves upon all of them and upon all interested in preserving democracy: to encourage those who are helping the nation, and to expose those who are trying to destroy it with racial or religious hatred. This book is intended to carry out only the second task. It is not a blueprint for freedom. It offers no solutions or panaceas. Devoted to a description of corroding prejudice in America, it tells, in a sense, a negative story.

Nor is an attempt made to examine every facet of the contemporary record of prejudice. Only several of the vital areas have been chosen for detailed coverage; such important fields as discrimination in employment, discrimination in housing, social accommodations, etc. have been touched upon only in passing. On the other hand, discrimination in education is dealt with intensively, as is the field of professionally organized anti-Semitism. A study is offered of the prejudice tests conducted in the last ten years—an analysis by scientific poll takers. Prejudice in sports is covered in a full chapter. The misuse of political and economic tensions which grip the American people, provoking the expression of otherwise latent prejudice, is also described.

The detailed analyses, unfortunately, appear to result in undue emphasis upon the bigotry around us. The intent, however, is constructive. The report is written in the conviction that one way to help ensure a healthy America is to drag out into the merciless light of public attention the activities of those in our country who are designing its destruction. One can only hope that in reporting the negative side alone, A Measure of Freedom does not convey the impression that all is wrong in our great country. The ensuing pages stem from an ardent desire to protect America's democratic way of life from what are believed to be serious sources of danger that should be warning signals for Americans.

Chapter 2. The Knight Riders

RADIO LISTENERS who were tuned in to the Mutual Broadcasting System on the evening of September 2, 1949, were introduced to a new manner of demagoguery. They heard a vacuous and ungrammatical defense of Ku Kluxism by a sixty-five-year-old preacher and semi-professional politician whose bizarre affectations—like wearing his white hair shoulder length—matched the unorthodox name of Lycurgus Spinks. As the self-anointed "Imperial Emperor" of the Knights of the Ku Klux Klans of America, the Reverend Dr. Spinks, a Baptist minister without honor among Baptists, was chosen by the producers to be the feature of a "Meet the Press" broadcast. Normally, on this program, a newsworthy personality—a congressman, a labor leader, a cabinet minister, a scientist—is interviewed by Washington newspaper correspondents. Into a glamorous limelight, which had focused upon such front-page figures as Robert A. Taft, John L. Lewis, Eleanor Roosevelt, Earl Browder, Thomas E. Dewey and Whittaker Chambers, there now swaggered the aging and argumentative Dr. Spinks. His title of "doctor," according to the *Atlanta Constitution's* editor, Ralph McGill, was acquired "when Doc used to be one of those fellows who lectured on sex, hiring halls and talking to 'men only' and then a matinee for 'ladies only.'"

To the hostile newspapermen who fired pointed questions, and to the millions who listened in, the Imperial Emperor revealed himself to be a charlatan, a boastful liar, a fraud and a buffoon. A consummate gall insulated him from the contempt of his questioners. He was not at all perturbed by his admission that he once scrounged for a living posing as the reincarnation of George Washington; "I made a good job of it," was his proud rebuke. Drew Pearson, one of the four interviewers, openly suggested that Spinks had been involved in a South Carolina bank embezzlement, escaping extradition from Mississippi through the good offices of the then Governor Bilbo. The Emperor disdainfully brushed aside Pearson's documented evidence. For the most part, he ignored all embarrassing questions, hiding behind an arrogant claim that he was leading a widespread revival of the Ku Klux Klan.

There was mixed public reaction to Spinks' momentary reprieve from obscurity. Some persons applauded the broadcast on the theory that it gave the Klan, in the burlesque figure of Spinks, an opportunity to expose to a nation-wide audience its bigotry, its ignorance and its unsavory character; and that Spinks had succeeded very well in that purpose. Others challenged the wisdom of permitting Spinks to spew his nonsense on a reputable forum. They argued that by implication it raised the Klan to respectability and gave credence to Spinks' boast that the night riders were mobilizing in great numbers.

Whatever its impact, the broadcast was an illuminating footnote to Ku Klux Klan activity in 1949. That there *was* such a broadcast highlighted the fact that the Klan was very much in existence—and in the headlines—during the year. Certainly there were more magazine articles, newspaper exposés and legislative inquiries pointed at the Klan during the twelve months of 1949 than at any time since the prewar days when Kluxers were photographed picnicking and parading with German-American Bundists in the shaded fields of New Jersey.

What confounds many Americans is how to interpret this sudden abundance of publicity. Do the shocking stories of cross burnings, floggings and midnight terror really mean that the Klan is again on the march? Or is the Klan staggering under the weight of public censure and the opposition of an aroused and enlightened South which has placed anti-mask laws and other roadblocks in its path?

The selection of Lycurgus Spinks as a spokesman was, in itself, a commentary on the confusion that exists about—and even among —the Klan. Spinks is little more than a garrulous nonentity in the Klan, addicted to a ten-gallon hat and a chestful of fraternal emblems and most competent as a marksman who can ring the cuspidor dead center across half a room. He ran for governor of Mississippi in 1947, getting 4,344 out of the 350,000 ballots cast and had scored about as well in two prior campaigns for state tax collector. But Spinks has a flair for booming oratory flavored with magnolia figures of speech, and an overdeveloped imagination provided him with a vision of 265,000 members in his Klan. All of which, it appears, spurred his entry to radio.

The homage surprised even Spinks. And it both amused and amazed a lot of Mississippians. Spencer R. McCulloch, a St. Louis *Post-Dispatch* reporter, summed up their sentiments with the comment of a Delta native, who chuckled, "Grant may have taken Richmond, but old Spinks sure took Washington."

The estimate of one dissident and indignant Klan leader—that Spinks was Imperial Emperor "over himself and one other guy"—

was very much closer to the truth than the count of 265,000 arrived at by Spinks' wild arithmetic. In fact, before the year ended, the Emperor had abdicated, consolidating his meager forces with those of Sam Roper, former head of Georgia's Bureau of Investigation, who had also joined the scramble for Klan leadership.

Today the term Ku Klux Klan is more properly a synonym for a kind of mass dementia than the name of a single terrorist organization. The historic Knights of the Ku Klux Klan was founded in 1865 in Tennessee by a group of Confederate soldiers as a weapon against Negro suffrage. General Nathan Bedford Forrest was its first Imperial Wizard and it remained active until 1869, successful in its objectives of limiting the Negro vote and repelling so-called carpetbaggers. The Klan was revived by a bumbling, naïve character, William J. Simmons, who with some cronies journeyed atop Stone Mountain on Thanksgiving night, 1915, and there re-established the pattern of mysticism and secrecy that was to become the Klan's strongest ally. The outfit was incorporated July 1, 1916, in Atlanta, with a lot of high-sounding principles that were abused and perverted by hooded terrorists, lynchers, publicity-shrewd exploiters, and political opportunists. Within a few short years following World War I, the Klan rode to heights of mobocracy and corruption unparalleled in American history. Its membership was estimated to have been as high as 4,000,000 extending into almost every state in the Union, and its income mounted into the millions, largely from property, publishing, membership dues and the sale of ceremonial robes manufactured in the Klan's own factory.

Public revulsion against the Klan's unbridled criminality ultimately destroyed the organization's nation-wide strength. The Knights of the Ku Klux Klan finally ceased to exist as a legal entity in 1946 when the federal government levied a $685,355 assessment upon it for unpaid taxes. To avoid payment the Klan surrendered its corporate charter and dissolved.

The wild and furious outbursts of the current Klan—fifty-one incidents of mob violence, including a lynching, were recorded in Alabama, Tennessee, and Georgia during a three-month period in 1949 —dramatizes the sorry fact that the hooded order, with its bigoted philosophy and vicious practices, is still a serious menace to democracy and to the security of millions of Americans.

But it is a menace which the South no longer ignores nor fears. The postwar Klan lacks the tight, mystic unity, the strength and quality of membership, the dynamic leadership and—most significant —the climate of public acceptance, which had made it an awesome and frightening power in the 1920s. Instead, buffeted from without by an aroused and organized Southern populace and eaten away internally by jackals fighting to control it, the current Klan is a fragmentized and insecure movement, groping for direction and existing largely off its past reputation.

It is now also a productive racket for a gang of confidence men. Since the tax defeat of the once all-powerful KKK, as many new Klans have sprung up to succeed it as there have been money-grubbing promoters ready to claim the $10 klektokens (initiation fees) which simpletons have been willing to pay in return for being assured that the color of their skin makes them superior human beings. Once banded together, a mob spirit and the burden of tradition-weighted prejudices impel them to lawlessness and violence.

So feeble has become the internal structure of the Klan that it is a common practice for enterprising kleagles (organizers) to go their independent ways, collecting initiation fees for non-existent Klans. Ten dollars is the prevailing klektoken demanded of the man who wants to join a Klan, and there are many who do for no other reason than to find an outlet for their limited social life. In many rural areas the Klan is "the poor man's club." Its precepts are the natural outgrowth of social and economic patterns which existed and were solidified long before the twentieth-century Klan came into existence.

The traffic in $10 klektokens—in some instances the fee is higher —is organized along straight commercial lines. The contact man, or organizer, takes his cut first, about three dollars. Five dollars goes to the local klavern. The remaining two dollars is supposed to be forwarded to the Klan's national headquarters. Most distressing to Klan leaders, however, is the defection among many local bosses when it comes to parting with the two dollars.

Editor McGill, a constant scrutinizer and critic of the Klan, provides an apt description for the Klan's organizing technique. The kleagles, Mr. McGill writes, "look up some fellow who was a member in the '20s and get him active. They try to name a well-known man as Exalted Cyclops. A Cyclops, in mythology, was a one-eyed monster and some of the Klan's Cyclopses have been monsters. Then they find someone whose handwriting can be read and he is the Kilgrap, or secretary. A Klabee is the treasurer. If they can persuade a preacher to serve, he is the Kludd.

Dr. Samuel Green, the Atlanta obstetrician whose mild, spectacled eyes and baggy appearance masked his practical cunning and his strength as a volatile and articulate Klan leader, evaded the government's tax demands by incorporating a new movement, the Association of Georgia Klans. For the changeover, Green used the old KKK application blanks, stamping on the new Klan's name. He appointed himself Grand Dragon at a salary of $10,000 a year, later changed his title to the more imposing Imperial Wizard. He also seized control of klaverns in South Carolina, Tennessee, Florida and Alabama.

The Association of Georgia Klans carries on as spiritual successor to the Klan of the 1920s. It is the most powerful of seven Klan splinter groups. That the Klan musters its greatest organized strength in Georgia is the natural outgrowth of a political anachronism unique in the United States.

Primary elections in Georgia—and the Democratic Party primary is the only election that has meaning—are not determined by popular vote, but by the county unit system which gives six primary votes each to the eight largest counties in the state, four votes each to the next thirty, and two votes each to the remaining 121 counties. (Twentieth in size, Georgia has more counties than any other state in the Union with the exception of Texas.) "The eight large counties," the New York *Herald Tribune* reported [June 7, 1949], "represent 270,000 of the state's one million voters. Thus, more than 25 per cent of the voting strength of the state is in eight counties with forty-eight unit votes, a little more than 11 per cent of the unit vote. In a primary election, one vote in a small county—Chattahoochee, for instance—is worth 106 votes in Fulton (Atlanta) County. Yet Fulton County pays the state over a million and a half dollars annually in general property taxes while the smaller county pays $1,000."

Under such conditions, in which the rural vote controls the outcome of state elections, it is understandable why Green found a hospitable atmosphere in Georgia. Federal judges have ruled that Negroes cannot be denied the right to register; lily-white primaries are unconstitutional. But Klansmen in the farm counties are able to exert the pressures that frighten Negroes and liberal whites from the polls. Their success with this maneuver was demonstrated during the 1948 elections. In the town of Wrightsville, for example, the Klan staged a parade of intimidation on election eve. Next day, not one of the 400 Negroes who had registered dared to vote.

The present governor, Herman Talmadge, was helped to election with this type of Klan support—which, in turn, explained the presence of Dr. Green as lieutenant colonel and aide-de-camp on the governor's staff. Young Talmadge's father, the red-gallused Gene Talmadge, won the governorship shortly before he died despite the fact that one of his opponents, James V. Carmichael, got a clear majority of the popular votes. He, too, was the beneficiary of Klan support in his political endeavors. Ol' Gene used to say, "I don't care if I don't carry a single county that has a streetcar in it—I can still win the election."

Floggings, cross burnings, night raids and marches up Stone Mountain for klonvocations and mystic initiations symbolize Klan bigotry. Sometimes the more violent incidents are without official Klan sanction, escapades of uncontrolled zealots acting on their own initiative. But the effects of such marauding have been to lower the boom of public wrath upon the heads of Dr. Green and other Klan leaders. Yet, whether violence is ordered by a bedsheeted gang leader or is prompted by the unchecked impulses of self-righteous hoodlums on the search for "sin," the methods of terror, intimidation and brutality are in the "grand" tradition of the Ku Klux Klan.

The corrupt political and financial purposes of the Klan are often diverted by brutal-minded Klansmen who find their organizational paraphernalia, the hood, the robe, the whip, useful instruments for satisfying grudges. Their after-dinner diversion, firing an oil-slicked cross, is sometimes directed against a white, gentile, Protestant, native-born American—whom some Klansman doesn't approve of for personal reasons. It is not difficult to rally fifty or a hundred other malcontents to participate in the orgy. They are rewarded with the vicarious thrill of power that is the essence of mob rule; it recharges their false sense of superiority.

During 1949 cross burnings flared up in Georgia, Louisiana—where a six-foot cross was fired on the campus of Tulane University—Alabama, the Carolinas, Tennessee and Florida. Virtually free of concentrated Klan terrorism in recent years, Florida suddenly became a focal point of nightshirt activity. Three crosses blazed at the Miami Shores Community Church on the night of February 19 as an expression of the Klan's resentment toward a white congregation that dared to invite a Negro minister to preach there.

Two young Georgia attorneys who filed an injunction suit against the Klan were answered by a flaming cross set off in the yard of their residence, while four bullets were pumped into the house. A fiery cross appeared in front of Jere Moore's home in Milledgeville,

Georgia, because Moore, the local editor, had defied the Klan in the columns of his paper. J. W. Atkins, editor of the Gastonia (North Carolina) *Gazette,* got a similar threat after denouncing attempts to revive a klavern in that town. In Talladega, Alabama, three crosses blazed outside the homes of local residents at whom the night raiders, about fifty in number, shouted threats from beneath the cover of hoods. The identifying numbers of their automobile license plates were carefully shielded; some of them were armed with guns. At the height of the furor, a twelve-year-old boy kicked down one of the crosses and doused its flames in a water hole; the mob dispersed and drove away. Dr. Louie D. Newton, one of the South's distinguished Baptist leaders, has censured the blasphemous terrorism. "The cross is to be borne, not burned," said he. But for Klansmen, the burning cross is a useful weapon of intimidation. (There also were cross burnings north of the Mason-Dixon line. In Athens, Ohio, a panic-stricken Negro family looked on helplessly while the sanctity of their home was violated; in Union, New Jersey, a group of local citizens who had assembled to protest the death sentence of "the Trenton Six"—six Negroes convicted of murdering an aged white man—were similarly warned with a blazing cross.)

A mob of 100 Kluxers was needed to assault two Chattanooga war veterans who refused to kneel before a burning cross. In Lytle, Georgia, Klansmen viciously lashed a steel worker because, the Klan piously explained, the victim had "cursed his mother." In Dolly Pond, Tennessee, a hooded mob invaded Little Holiness Church and blackjacked six men "for not looking after their families." These were incidents involving white victims; the deeds needed "public" explaining. Not so, of course, with Negroes; it is not an extraordinary event for colored persons to be terrorized, abducted or mauled into insensibility—mostly in pretended defense of "Southern woman-hood."

For many Klansmen the danger of retribution is lessened not only by the anonymity under which they operate, but also by the friendly co-operation of law enforcement officials. In some rural communities the Klan and the sheriff's office are synonymous, a situation which, one might suspect, tends to unbalance the scales of justice. Frank Bettis, an Atlanta feed-and-flour merchant, got hopping mad when the Klan staged one of its bedraggled parades in his neighborhood. Mr. Bettis said as much to the police authorities, who acted promptly. They arrested Mr. Bettis for "driving while drunk." A court case and jury verdict were needed before the trumped-up charge was dismissed. At that, the outcome was in the nature of a defeat for the Klan. In its halcyon days the Klan would have been virtually assured of a conviction.

The present Klan, for all its lawless activity, has a far greater hatred and fear for the law than had its high-riding predecessor which, by contrast, was itself the object of fear among law enforcement officials. Southern opposition to the Klan last year was distinguished by grand jury investigations and scores of indictments. Trials were held in Birmingham, Chattanooga and in several Georgia towns, and if convictions were rare, still it was heartening to find local prosecutors willing to oppose the Klan in open court, though they had to contend with intimidated witnesses and Klan-sympathizing juries.

The threat of federal intervention likewise has prompted many Southern localities to clean house. A subcommittee of the House of Representatives Judiciary Committee made a gesture toward investigating the Klan, even holding a preliminary hearing in Birmingham. It was deterred by the plea of anti-Klan witnesses who urged that the state of Alabama be granted time and opportunity to settle its own problem in its own way.

The Department of Justice set a precedent, however, when it brought ten men to trial in a Rome, Georgia, federal court for conspiring with a mob to violate the civil rights of seven Negroes who were flogged on April 2, 1949, near Trenton, Georgia. The victims had been falsely arrested, then handed over to a hooded gang. The trial was unique in that the defendants included, in addition to six Klansmen, Sheriff John W. Lynch and three of his deputies. It ended with a hung jury. The Klansmen did not escape unscathed; each defendant had to scrape up about $1,000 for his legal defense and they still must face a re-trial. The case was the first attempt by the federal government to prosecute both law enforcement officers and Klansmen in the same civil rights proceedings. It attracted considerable attention from the national press, special correspondents arriving in Rome to cover the story. A close-up study of two of the Klan defendants compelled a Chicago reporter to write, "If they are representative members of the Klan it seems probable that a Chicago policeman, armed with a whistle, could have restored law and order in a minute."

A good deal of the Klan's energies was dissipated in 1949 in unspectacular meetings and parades. In an effort to mobilize supporters, Klan leaders whipped up a number of local demonstrations throughout the South. (Since 1949 was not important as an election year, the Klan had little cause to march in defense of white primaries.) A motorcade of forty automobiles filled with sheeted Kluxers rode through the campus of Talladega College, Alabama, an incident interpreted as a warning to the students that they were not to participate in the Alabama Students Conference on Civil Rights. A fifty-car caravan put on the same kind of show in the Alabama towns of Brighton and Bessemer. On February 9, 1949, the citizens of Denmark, South Carolina, watched with uncloaked amusement while a parade of Klansmen, some carrying red flares, marched through the streets. This was supposed to have been a special demonstration; Dr. Green himself put in an appearance and he promised the presence of no less than 1,500 supporters to fill out the ranks.

By actual count, 269 misguided malcontents paraded. They were a sad-looking lot. Onlookers who lined the streets—many of them Negroes—were openly unimpressed and unfrightened, and quite free with their insults. Shouted one white woman: "I hope you get pneumonia and die." Another taunted, "When do the real Klansmen come?"

The marchers just shuffled along in embarrassed silence.

Negro spectators also chimed in and the classic remark for the occasion was attributed to an old Negro woman who jeered at the mortified Dr. Green:

"Give us your sheets and we'll wash 'em!"

In an effort to piece together the shreds of Klan dignity, Green mobilized a second march in West Columbia, South Carolina. Here the line of paraders added up to a meager 282 Klansmen, about one third of them women. Green was heckled by students from the University of South Carolina who tossed stench bombs and ignited firecrackers while the Imperial Wizard was holding forth on the virtues of white supremacy.

"If you let President Truman ram the civil rights bill down your throats, it will be legal for a Negro to come up on your porch and ask for your daughter's hand in marriage," the exasperated Dr. Green shouted.

"She can always say no!" roared the students.

Perhaps the most spectacular Klan demonstration in 1949 occurred on January 27 in Tallahassee, Florida. It was a well-organized move to invigorate the long dormant Klan in that state. A motorcade of 437 automobiles bearing Florida, Georgia and Alabama license plates rode through the streets of the capital city, its appearance of strength enhanced by the presence of an official police escort. Floridians bitterly disapproved of the raucous scene; their outspoken governor, Fuller Warren, described it in these words:

The hooded hoodlums and sheeted jerks who paraded the streets of Tallahassee made a disgusting and alarming spectacle. These covered cowards who call themselves Klansmen quite obviously have set out to terrorize minority groups in Florida as they have in a nearby state. [He meant Georgia.]

The numerical strength of the Klan has always been a closely guarded secret. To refute a statement that its membership was dwindling to insignificant numbers, Dr. Green, in an interview in May 1949, claimed control over 140 klaverns in Georgia, twenty in South Carolina and fifteen each in Tennessee, Alabama and Florida. He said that there were a minimum of 100 members in each klavern. This adds up to at least 20,500 dues-payers enrolled in the Association of Georgia Klans, a count which Southern observers are inclined to weigh with skepticism. Still, Green's statistical claims were not as exaggerated as those of other, less fortunate Klan leaders. In August 1949 a federal tax investigation estimated the Georgia Klan's enrollment at "not more than 10,000."

Green's purpose was to stabilize the Klan as a political tool. Such extracurricular incidents as lynchings, "morality" raids and indiscriminate cross burnings displeased him, not for any particular offense to his moral conscience, but because the cumulative effect of such outrages tended to magnify public opposition to the Klan.

The glib little doctor, who loved parades, secret handgrips, mystic meetings and the other hokum that make up Klankraft, nourished a desire to remake the Klan into a "respectable" Southern institution. It angered him that the Department of Justice had included his group on the government's list of subversive organizations and, as though to offset the curse, he began uttering such nonsense as, "no real Klansman could hate a colored man because of his color or a Jew because of his religion."

Green foresaw the adoption of anti-mask laws in Southern communities, a prescience which prompted him to issue his famous edict of August 8, 1949, directing Klansmen not to wear masks. Green's control over individual klaverns was not absolute, but to show he meant business the Imperial Wizard disciplined three klaverns which were involved in lawless outbreaks.

To underscore his new approach that the Association of Georgia Klans was, first and foremost, a fraternal and benevolent organization, Green introduced a weird public-relations program. Newspapers throughout the country published a photograph of hooded Alabama Klansmen, one of them dressed to represent Santa Claus, presenting a radio as a birthday gift to a 107-year-old former Negro slave.

Another stunt is for Klansmen, robed and hooded, to march into a church, listen patiently to a sermon, then fill the collection plate with a presentable contribution. This is not a new idea; it was first used by Edward Young Clarke, the clever press agent who took over the Klan in the early 1920s and lifted it from obscurity.

Georgia Klansmen have tried other gimmicks. The Columbus klavern posted a $350 reward for the apprehension of the lynchers of Roy Mallard, a Negro who was murdered by hooded men because he was "uppity." Another group, with much fanfare, distributed $364 worth of food among needy whites and Negroes. And twenty suits of underwear, each stamped conspicuously with the initials KKK, were sent to the inmates of an Atlanta old folks' home.

On August 18, 1949, Sam Green dropped dead of a heart attack while working in the garden of his Atlanta home. The final year of his reign had been a burden for the Imperial Wizard. The press, the pulpit, civic officials, veterans and labor organizations and other forward-looking elements in the South were becoming more and more outspoken in their opposition to the Klan and its vicious practices. Green had been a shrewd operator, a successful demagogue wise in the ways of the fanatics and opportunists whom he had gathered in the folds of his embroidered sheet. Since organizing his Association of Georgia Klans, the ambitious little man had been its dominant and unifying personality. But his authority was far from absolute, and when he died, the visible cracks of disintegration that had threatened the tottering unity of the Klan now split wide open. Petty organizers wrangled with one another, each seeking to inherit the spoils of Green's legacy.

That all was not harmony in the Klan, even in its native Georgia habitat, was evident more than a year before Green died. Dissident klaverns in the towns of Columbus and Manchester broke away from Green's rule and established themselves as the Original Southern Klans, Inc. Founder of the group was a twenty-three-year-old war veteran, Alton E. Pate, who was granted a charter in Muscogee County Court on June 30, 1948.

The split really stemmed from a behind-the-scenes struggle for power between Green and "Parson Jack" Johnston, rabble-rousing minister and newspaper publisher who had operated in Columbus as Green's lieutenant. Johnston was dissatisfied with the way Green divided Klan profits; he and Fred K. New, a politico-lawyer in Columbus, became the real leaders of the Original Southern Klans. Green petulantly dismissed the rebellion as "bolshevik Klans who pulled out because they could not run things for themselves."

Johnston and his partner publicized an ambitious program. They intended to operate a radio station, a newspaper printing plant and a textile factory to manufacture ceremonial robes. They also planned to publish magazines, produce motion pictures and operate a death benefit insurance fund. And, to assert their militancy, the rebels loudly rejected the fiction of "we-don't-hate-anybody" fraternalism which Green was attempting to sell to an unbelieving public. Instead, they frankly declared their new Klan to be anti-Semitic, anti-Catholic, anti-Negro—and a profit-seeking business, too.

In less than a year, the Original Southern Klans proved to be all sound, little substance, collapsing under the weight of its grandiose ambitions. Except for publication of two issues of its official organ, *The Klansman,* none of its plans materialized and the impact of the group was negligible. The few local meetings it sponsored were poorly attended and its efforts to organize a chapter in Atlanta failed. All the fury of Parson Jack's campaign spent itself without profit and by February 1949 he "pulled out." (Subsequently, Johnston and New fell ill and both have since ceased to be active in Klan circles.)

Johnston later admitted that the combined opposition of churchmen, editors and other civic leaders of Columbus had effectively prevented the Original Southern Klans from securing a stable following. At this writing, the Columbus office of the Original Southern Klans is closed. For the time being, perhaps permanently, the rebels who defied Dr. Green have suspended organized operations in Georgia.

Sam Green had hardly been interred before the patient citizens of Alabama found themselves confronted with no less than three competing factions of the Klan. (Alabama also has an abundance of small Klan-like movements under a variety of names: Knights of the White Camellia, True Americans, etc.) A struggle for membership and power between Green's Association of Georgia Klans and another offshoot of the parent Klan, the Federated Ku Klux Klans of Alabama, Inc. had been in progress since the KKK tax defeat of 1946. The Federated group was started by a Birmingham roofing contractor, William Hugh Morris, who incorporated it on July 21, 1946. Dr. E. P. Pruitt, a Birmingham physician, was designated president; Morris installed himself as secretary-treasurer, later called himself "Grand Wizard."

On August 23, 1949, five days after Green's sudden death, the third Klan entry in Alabama appeared in the picturesque form of Lycurgus Spinks. He stepped out of the shadows to announce that he had heard the call and had organized his Knights of the Ku Klux Klans of America with headquarters in Montgomery. Spinks added that all Klansmen—whether they were aware of it or not—swore allegiance to his imperial leadership.

The multiple-chinned Mr. Morris was beset with too many troubles of his own to pay much mind to Spinks. For one thing, he was in jail. Fourteen of his Klansmen had been indicted for mob violence and when Morris, testifying before the Jefferson County (Birmingham) grand jury, refused to produce a list of Klan members, the judge cited him for contempt. Later he was freed in $500 bail on his promise to produce Klan records. Instead, he told the court that the records had been "stolen" from his home. Back into a cell went Morris, to remain there a total of sixty-seven days. He was finally released by Circuit Judge Robert J. Wheeler on the ground that he had "purged" himself of contempt by submitting a Klan roster "from memory."

The imprisonment of a Klan potentate and the arrests and indictments of lesser fry scared many rank and file Klansmen. They hastened to resign, fearful that Morris would reveal their identities. Enactment of an Alabama anti-mask law, the first such statewide legislation against the Klan in the South, also cut deeply into the Klan's strength. Klansmen didn't see much sense in being Klansmen if they were expected to violate the law with their faces uncovered.

Dr. Pruitt, anticipating the legislature's attitude, rushed forward with Sam Green's futile gesture: he ordered Klansmen to "discard" their masks. That didn't appeal to Morris, then sitting out the hot summer days in the county jail. The Grand Wizard charged that Pruitt had "overstepped his authority." From his cell, he "accepted" Pruitt's resignation.

Morris claims that his Federated Ku Klux Klans has a membership of 30,000 in 65 klaverns. Spinks believes that this is a fair estimate—if Morris is willing to count each Klansman fifteen times. Whatever his strength, it appears that Morris has attracted a large number of violence-minded "moralists." Their midnight maraudings filled the headlines during the summer of 1949 and events got so out of hand that Governor Folsom went on the air to tell Alabamans, "Your home is your castle; defend it in any way necessary." He issued an executive order directing state law enforcement officials to arrest all terrorist groups.

Any sort of misconduct which might scandalize the community, whether real or fancied, becomes pretext enough for zealots to cover themselves with hoods and robes, grab their bull whips and take the law unto themselves. They dragged a forty-two-year-old white woman, a grandmother, from her home, threatened to burn her at the stake, then forced her to watch in trembling fright while a cross was burned on her front lawn. They had heard that she "rented rooms" to high school students.

Another Birmingham mother was flogged because the Klan did not approve of the "company" one of her daughters was keeping; the suitor and two other men, one a cripple, also were abducted and beaten up. A navy veteran was taken from his home and clubbed because, said the Klan, he neglected to support his family, and a gang raid on a Brookside café was justified on the grounds that the cafe owner was catering to both white and Negro patrons.

The wild outbreak of criminal outrages made Birmingham residents, spurred on by editorial criticism in the local press, more angry than frightened. It didn't please them much either when the disclosure was made that of fifty deputies assigned by Sheriff Holt A. McDowell to investigate a flogging, no less than thirty were either Klansmen or, at least, sympathizers.

Dr. Pruitt made a big show of denying that his Klansmen were responsible for the violence; he offered a $50 reward for proof to the contrary. (Trial evidence later established the identity of the whip-holders as members of the Alabama Klan.) But the campaign in Alabama by newspapers, ministerial groups, veterans, and others organized to expose Klanism as disreputable, un-American bigotry had gathered momentum. Instead of the "martyrdom" which he said would bring him 100,000 followers, Wizard Morris discovered ruefully that his tenure in a cell only pointed up his organization's lack of respectable public support.

There were indications that, in the early days, Morris had the support of some businessmen and industrialists who saw in his outfit a useful, labor-busting weapon with which to combat unionization drives spreading throughout the South. But most of these cynical gentlemen soon abandoned Morris when they found that "morality" violence is of little help to an anti-union crusade.

Morris propels his drive for power on the prejudice of his followers against the Roman Catholic Church and something he calls "the whiskey trust." But the victims his Klansmen flog are, often as not, white Protestants. Before the year was over, the pudgy, balding Morris, trapped between public antagonism and the jealousies of his rivals, was ready to compromise his ambition to become enthroned as king of a new nation-wide Klan. He shopped around for a merger with other splinter Klans.

Florida suffers at least two Klan organizations. The older one, The Ku Klux Klan of Florida, Inc., was chartered in September 1944, with headquarters in Orlando. Its incorporators and directors are listed as A. B. Taylor of Orlando, A. F. Gulliam of Clarcona and H. F. McCormack of Apopka. This outfit operates in the central part of the state as an affiliate of the Association of Georgia Klans, but except for a few, scattered cross burnings and an occasional anti-Negro demonstration nothing much was heard from it. That is, until July 1949, when it precipitated a wild three-day reign of terror in the Negro quarter of Groveland that was not quelled until a National Guard detachment marched in. Beginning on the evening of July 16, the Klansmen rode high and wild, burning and pillaging Negro homes and threatening the lives of hundreds of innocent, fright-stricken persons. Excuse for the orgy was the alleged rape of a white woman. Four Negroes were accused of the deed. Three were tried and convicted in a charged atmosphere reminiscent of the famous Scottsboro trials. The fourth was shot and killed by a white posse.

The second Florida Klan appears to be the personal promotion of a publicity-seeking, Tallahassee plumbing contractor named Bill Hendrix. Like several other Klan leaders he proclaims "the threat of communism" as the *raison d'être* of his outfit. It was chartered in March 1949—six months after Governor Warren had demanded the outlawing of the Klan as an "un-American mob"—under the name of Original Southern Klans, Inc. Presumably it had a tie-up with the Johnston-New group in Georgia. Application for Hendrix's appointment as resident agent for Florida was filed by a W. H. Crodser, Jr., who listed himself as "president" of The Original Southern Klans and gave his address as "Columbus, Georgia."

Collapse of the home office in Georgia forced Hendrix to go

into business for himself. He staged a parade and hooded initiation ceremony on June 11, 1949, at which an estimated 1,000 Klansmen from Florida, Georgia and Alabama observed the induction of 250 members into this newest realm of the Invisible Empire. Hendrix also changed the name of his organization to The Northern and Southern Knights of the Ku Klux Klan; he then hastened to the newspapers to out-Spinks even the fanciful Lycurgus with extravagant claims of membership.

Following a "secret klonvocation" August 28, in Jacksonville, Hendrix announced that he had been elected "national adjutant." He also gave his dues-payers the hokum they adore: an anonymous "Permanent Emperor, Samuel II" had been chosen, he declared. Samuel II proved something less than permanent, however, and was shortly replaced by an "Imperial Wizard" to whom Hendrix gave the cryptic designation, "Number 4-006800." This Wizard issued a proclamation advising members to await new instructions on how to preserve "the American way of life" because "a state of emergency exists in the Invisible Empire."

The stated aims of Hendrix's group include awakening Americans "to the fact that the fantastic taxation by the federal government, already upon us, and regimentation by the federal government already in force and proposed, will bring in a communist state in the United States of America within a few years." Hendrix boasts that his group has 302 chapters in fourteen states, including New York and New Jersey, and that its membership totals 650,000. The figures, of course, are preposterous.

Application blanks distributed by Hendrix (P.O. Box 4914, Jacksonville) include a statement that the organization is not anti-Catholic, anti-Jewish or anti-Negro, but that its membership is restricted to "native-born, white, gentile, Protestant citizens of the United States." The disavowal of racial and religious prejudice does not square with the contents of an unofficial mouthpiece, *The Southern Gospel*, a monthly published at River Junction, Florida, by A. C. Shuler, pastor emeritus of the Jacksonville Central Baptist Church. Shuler, who made an unsuccessful attempt in 1946 to organize a Jacksonville chapter of the fascist-patterned Columbians, has no qualms about libeling "kike Jews" in his publication.

Hendrix has labored mightily to maintain the fiction of his anti-Communist crusade. He tried to join the anti-Robeson forces following the riot in Peekskill, New York, with a proclamation for a week of cross burnings throughout the country "to light up the skies of

America in protest of Communism." This got him front page attention in the Miami press; but the fiery protest sputtered badly, six crosses were burned, five in Florida and another in Voldosta, Georgia. Some observers are cynical enough to believe that, whatever the threat of communism, Hendrix gets most of his inspiration from the $16 yearly dues each of his followers is obligated to pay.

The most important Klan leader to emerge in 1949, following the death of Imperial Wizard Sam Green, is the least known and least publicized of the ambitious men competing for Klan power. He is Samuel W. Roper, fifty-four, a calm, poker-faced former Atlanta city detective whose twenty-five years on the force has made him wise in the ways of local politics. During the governorship of Eugene Talmadge, Roper had ascended to the peak of his police career when he served as director of the state's bureau of investigation.

A reticent man, seemingly lacking in the fiery emotionalism that is the stock-in-trade of the garden variety demagogue, Roper has a reputation for planning his moves with calculated force. The absence of bombast in his makeup does not imply a lack of fervor for the career of Klan boss he has staked out for himself; more likely it is part of a preconceived plan. Roper is shrewd enough to understand the temper of the South and its audible wrath against the shocking conduct of the Klan. A fire-spitting clown shrieking "nigger, nigger!" might win the hearty approval of the wool hatted poor whites, but Georgia "crackers" are not the kind of members Roper wants with which to rebuild the Klan to its ancient "glories." Like Sam Green, whom he had served faithfully and well, Roper strives for "respectability." He, too, has applied for membership in the anti-communist movement. He regards the federal civil rights program as another hateful specter with which to rally those substantial elements of the community who prefer their white supremacy maintained in genteel fashion: no nightriding, no violence, no bloodshed.

Roper is a long-time Klansman, having joined the movement in the early twenties. He moved upward in the hooded hierarchy to become "Exalted Cyclops" of the Oakland City klavern and was Green's chief investigator with the title of "Imperial Nighthawk." He slipped in quietly as successor to Green, becoming the new Imperial Wizard of the Association of Georgia Klans, complete with gold-red robe, blue cape and a gold hood upon which his title is stitched in blue.

Except for these gaudy raiments, Roper has little to show in the way of Klan wealth. Indeed, the stocky policeman has fallen heir, comparatively, to a pauper's legacy. There is even some doubt that Roper will receive the $10,000 salary or the private automobile which Green, who ruled in a period of Klan decline, nevertheless managed to allot for himself. During its era of supremacy the Klan operated from ornate surroundings, in its own expensive building, with all the funds it needed; now Roper finds himself reduced to penny-pinching operations in a dreary two-room office tucked away over a poultry market on the west side of town.

Roper's immediate program is twofold: to consolidate the various Klan fragments into a unified group under his leadership, and to continue the pretense that the Klan is now a friendly, benevolent organization dedicated to good deeds and civic betterment and not at all interested in hiding its identity beneath a hood. "We are an educational outfit," Roper said. "Why, we give baskets of food to needy families every Christmas. Sure, we give some baskets to Negroes. The Ku Klux Klan is the best friend the Negro has."

As an afterthought, to dispel any unwarranted confusion that the sudden benevolency of the Klan might cause among his racist-minded supporters, Roper carefully added the postscript:

"Of course the Negro must be segregated. That is the way God intended it."

In his program for unity Roper has proceeded with an "I-can-get-along-with-anybody" policy. He extends the open hand of friendship to all other Klan leaders. Lycurgus Spinks was the first to grasp it—presumably because there was little else Spinks' eager hand could get at—and Roper has assumed a dual role as both Grand Dragon of the Associated Klans of Georgia and Imperial Wizard of The Associated Klans of America, the title given to the amalgamation of the former group and Spinks' Knights of the Ku Klux Klan of America.

Roper is confident that he can draw other Klan factions into this new orbit. He sees the possibility of a "United States of the Ku Klux Klan" a superstructure under which the various state-wide Klan groups would federate; the swallowing of Spinks' group was the first move in that direction. In November, Roper reported further progress; he had reached "a working agreement" with Morris and the Alabama Klans. He expected that the "agreement eventually will lead to consolidation."

At first Morris appeared to be of the same mind. But it later turned out that the "working agreement" wasn't working—a dispute arose over the division of power. In December, Morris held council in Montgomery, Alabama, with Florida's Bill Hendrix and a Leesville, South Carolina, grocer named Thomas L. Hamilton. The trio conveniently ignored Roper and mutually agreed that they would act as "the governing body" of a national Klan movement.

Hamilton enters the picture as a Johnny-come-lately. He is Grand Dragon of an added starter called the Federation of Carolina Klans which popped up to speak for all Klansmen in North and South Carolina.

The emergence of the Carolina group upset Wizard Roper's plans. As part of his organizational drive Roper had personally appointed Hamilton Grand Dragon for South Carolina, entrusting him with the job of enticing Klansmen in that state into the Roper fold. "But as soon as he got acquainted with all the klaverns Hamilton attempted to pull them out," Roper ruefully admitted.

Such defections are irritating problems to Wizard Roper. They are by no means his worst. Roper is forced to operate under the cloud of an insistent gentleman named Marion H. Allen, United States collector of revenue for Georgia. Mr. Allen casts a long shadow; it is he who struck the original Klan group the fatal $685,355 tax blow in 1946.

On August 24, 1949, a few days before Roper seized control, Mr. Allen levied a $9,322.40 tax assessment against the Association of Georgia Klans. This lien, the collector reported on September 12, was paid by the Georgia Klan "under protest." Mr. Allen has since come forth once more, this time seeking an additional $8,383.72. At this writing, Wizard Roper still hasn't made payment—with or without "protest."

The postwar Ku Klux Klan, for all the frenetic activity which gave it a surface resemblance to its oligarchic forebears, is hardly more than a shell of its former self. If pomp is still there, the power of the Klan is weak. In the 1920s—when it could muster 50,000 masked men for a mammoth parade through the main avenues of Washington, D. C.—the Klan was a supra-government all unto its own, as frightening an example of organized mob rule as this nation has ever known. By contrast, the 1949 Klan did not evoke stark terror and mass subservience.

To regain their lost stature, Klan leaders have tried to hitch a ride on the Dixiecrat political wagon. The rebellion of Southern political leaders against the civil rights campaign was embraced by Dr. Green and his ambitious friends as a tailor-made opportunity for herding the flock once more. But it hasn't worked out that way. Even staunch defenders of the South's *ante bellum* mores reject the Klan as a means of sustaining their white supremacy traditions. The Klan has fallen into such disrepute that many of its ablest opponents are themselves former Klansmen.

Like any other fungus, the Klan cannot grow and flourish except in a specialized environment. The favorable surrounding it once found in the South is rapidly disappearing. The once "silent people" of the South have found their voice; they no longer fear to strike back at the Klan. Exponents of states rights accept in some measure the corollary of state responsibility to uphold the law and protect all citizens.

All of which has forced the Klan on the defensive. The South is answering masked raids with a rapid series of local anti-mask laws that destroy much of the secrecy which is the Klan's best protection. On November 3, 1948, Wrightsville, Georgia, claimed the honor of being the first Southern community to legislate directly against Klan hoodlumism when it passed an ordinance prohibiting demonstrations by hooded or masked groups. A month later, the Macon City, Georgia, council, jolted by public criticism of the rental of the city auditorium for a Klan convention, approved an ordinance prohibiting the wearing of masks and hoods on city streets. On March 8, 1949, Columbus, Georgia, headquarters for the Original Southern Klans, banned the burning of crosses. Atlanta, historic center of Klan operations, on May 2, 1949, likewise banned the wearing of hoods and masks. So did Tallahassee, Florida, reacting quickly to the mammoth Klan motorcade which rode through its streets. Miami, Coral Gables, Miami Beach and other Florida resort towns did the same. By the end of 1949, twenty-five Southern communities had defied the Klan with this kind of legislation.

The successful technique of getting anti-mask laws on the statute books, town by town and city by city, was organized by anti-Klan groups—among them the Anti-Defamation League—after Georgia's legislature had rejected an attempt to make the law state-wide. Those Georgia legislators who owed their seats to Klan support rose in mass protest when Representative John Greer first introduced the bill, arguing long and loudly that the Klan was a Southern tradition. Representative Vaughan Terral of Floyd County, showed a novel concern for civil rights. The anti-mask bill, he protested, would interfere with the religious freedom of Moslem women. (Another representative took time out to explain to Mr. Terral that Georgia law would not be applicable to the Far East.) On January 20, 1949, the measure was indefinitely tabled by a vote of 89 to 65.

Governor Warren also failed in his efforts to have the Florida legislature ban not only the wearing of masks, but the Klan itself. In Tennessee two proposed laws died in committee, but an 1869 statute which makes it unlawful to "travel through the country masked and disguised to the disturbance of the town and to the alarm of the citizens" was recently invoked against a Chattanooga Klan leader involved in a flogging incident.

"Mobs, hooded or unhooded, are not going to rule Alabama," Governor Folsom told newspapermen. "We are going to stop these gangs." An anti-mask law was enacted shortly thereafter.

The immediate impact of the South's anti-mask laws was to spoil the dramatic effect of Klan parades. Their faces bared, the quality of the men and women attracted to the Klan hardly assumed an awesome caliber. They looked—and felt—downright silly.

An eyewitness report of a Klan motorcade held October 14, 1949, in Augusta, Georgia, a town protected by an anti-mask ordinance, dramatizes the asininity to which the once fearsome Klan has descended. This was intended to be an important Klan demonstration, marking the consolidation of forces between Roper and Spinks. Both men participated in the cavalcade. The observer wrote:

Proceeding single file through Broad Street, winding through the Negro quarter, were 138 automobiles, and 12 trucks carrying about 125 Klansmen. All the trucks and most of the cars bore South Carolina license plates.

The Klansmen wore robes and hood that covered most of the face, except for the mouth, nose and eyes. Many hid behind dark glasses and false handle bar mustaches, others painted themselves with lipstick and rouge for fear of being recognized. The parade had a police escort and was conducted with the approval of city and police officials who had issued a permit providing that no masks would be worn.

The childish disguises made the paraders look ridiculous in the eyes of spectators who watched and heckled. Many white persons lined the streets of the Negro section to jibe at the sheepish marchers.

"You can't start a new fire on wet ashes."

With this laconic comment, Dr. Hiram Wesley Evans, an old, feeble one-time active dentist, now living in quiet retirement in Atlanta, dismisses the Ku Klux Klan as an organization without a future. He reigned as Imperial Wizard when the Klan's corruptive powers were uncontrolled and its grasping hand reached into almost every state in the Union. A shrewd and cynical organizer and a dynamic leader, he understood the psychology of the Klan. To his mind, the Klan is on the way out. Or, as he put it, "The Klan can't live without the mask."

That is the hope of a lot of Southerners. But whether the Klan continues to flounder toward eventual oblivion or, conversely, attracts the leadership and support that can make it a serious menace once more, is a question that only the South can really answer. The present war against the Klan is of the South's own making; of its church leaders, its editors, its labor organizers, its veterans, its civic-minded leaders.

The South by no means has abandoned the traditional principle of white supremacy. The South has opened new economic and educational opportunities for its Negro citizens, but the shifting social patterns travel in slow, unspectacular motion and the line of racial demarcation remains largely inviolate. In that sense, klanism remains an acceptable Southern tradition.

But the Klan itself does not. It shrivels in the light of constant exposure as a dues-collecting racket preying upon uneducated dupes.

Informed observers recognize the possibility of increased outbreaks of Klan activity in 1950 paralleling the national elections and the expected drive for federal civil rights legislation, although the volume of incidents may be restricted in those communities which have anti-mask or similar protective laws. But the possibility of unity among the Klans—that is, a unity that can develop into a sizable, strong movement—is deemed remote. Besides the jealousies which sunder the handful of Klan leaders, there is still the problem of the tax debt with which a revived Southwide Klan might have to contend. The late James A. Colescott, who succeeded Evans as Imperial Wizard, last year revealed to a newspaperman that when Sam Green was awarded all rights to the old Klan it was on the condition that the klaverns operate only on a state-wide basis. Consolidation, said Colescott, would give the government an opportunity to bring up the tax matter.

The Klan of Dr. Evans rose to heights of evil power largely because of ignorance and public indifference. Once entrenched, its fingers manipulating the strings of marionette politicians, the organized mob was not easy to dislodge. An enlightened South that shows neither fear nor favor to the hooded fools or their racketeer leaders can prevent any real recrudescence of the once-powerful menace.

Chapter 3. Patrons of Patriotism

THE PETTY hate merchants and their followers take their cues from a handful of top professional propagandists who operate in a number of different settings. These "leaders," wittingly or otherwise, are the real philosophers of the hate movement. They interpret current events on the domestic and international scene in accordance with their own prejudiced ideologies, and issue a "line" which is promptly absorbed by a group of followers.

Most of the professional super-patriots work with each other—invariably arriving at similar points of view. Their conclusions regarding any given issue of the day can always be precisely predicted.

Each of these molders of prejudice is an anti-Semite, but to portray any one of them simply as an enemy of Jews would be a distortion. Their anti-Jewish animus is just one facet of an anti-democratic philosophy.

While their goals are virtually the same, each cloaks himself in different garb; one as an economist, another as a writer, another as a politician. In the following pages an effort is made to place each in proper focus against the background of his total activity.

GERALD L. K. SMITH: Bigotry is big business with Gerald Lyman Kenneth Smith. He makes it pay big dividends. In 1949 his total "take" exceeded $150,000, and he repeated his successful 1948 invasion of the West Coast, drawing listeners by the thousands.

Gerald Smith is a successful failure; he makes a very good living, but fails to win any serious following for his crackpot Christian Nationalist Crusade. A decade of raucous hate-mongering has made Gerald Smith almost a fixture on the American scene. His incessant invective against Jews and other minority groups has been so blatant and has appeared with such monotonous regularity that a tendency has developed to discount its effects. There has also arisen, in some responsible quarters, a kind of indifference to Smith's perennial crusade of bigotry. This is a mistake; constant vigilance may be relaxed only at serious risk. An examination of his activities reveals how serious.

St. Louis, Missouri
September 27, 1949

Dear Friend,

I am dropping a line to my very best friends because it involves an embarrassment. I would be ashamed for the enemy or those outside the inner circle of our loyal supporters to know that we faced a serious financial crisis just on the eve of our Convention.

The last general letter I sent out failed to bring in the necessary money to pay our bills and plan our future. People responded with gifts but they did not respond with large enough gifts to meet the need. It is a source of great concern to me. Sometimes I wish I could be proud and vain and did not have to beg the friends of the movement to give the money necessary to pay these heavy bills, but there is nothing else I can do.

I hope it is not asking too much for you to make as large a gift of money as you can, put it in the enclosed very special envelope and rush it in by return mail. If necessary and if possible, use an air mail stamp.

Letter from Gerald L. K. Smith discussed on page 38.

I know you will not fail me. You never have when you realized just how serious the situation was.

We are expanding rapidly and getting new supporters, but our responsibilities are bigger, broader and wider.

I am all set to leave for Washington, D.C., right after the Convention and will report to you concerning our activities, but I cannot even start unless we can get in more money with which to carry the load. If I could call on someone else I would do it, but I have no place else to turn except to you. Please make the most sacrificial gift possible.

The future of this victorious fight hangs on what you do now. Hundreds of movements in this country, such as ours have died and quit because their leaders were too proud to raise the money to pay the bills!

I love this cause enough to give all that I have to it, and I love it enough to ask you to do the same thing. Please, I beg of you, do your best at this critical moment.

Sincerely yours,

Gerald L. K. Smith

Smith's 1949 efforts, his income, and his background go a long way in explaining the man. His financial manipulations first, because money seems to be of first importance to Smith.

Donations to Smith's political front, the Christian Nationalist Party, totaled $90,543 in 1949. Smith attested to that amount in a sworn statement filed with the Clerk of the House of Representatives in accordance with the provisions of the Federal Corrupt Practices Act. In 1948 the rabble-rouser reported a larger amount, $114,253. Smith, of course, is required to make no report of his income from other sources, which is estimated to have brought his 1948 and 1949 incomes each to more than $150,000.

The Federal Corrupt Practices Act requires that only individuals who have made contributions in excess of $100 to a political party be listed by name. One hundred twenty persons were identified in the Christian Nationalist Crusade year-end financial statement. Twenty-five gave $200 or more; they are:

G. W. Dickinson, Waterbury, Conn.	202.00
J. C. Jetter, Chicago, Ill.	297.00
R. Bjoraas, South Bend, Ind.	223.00
H. B. Woods, Ligonier, Ind.	425.00
W. Anders, Detroit, Mich.	200.00
M. Gordon, Leslie, Mich.	270.00
F. C. Lee, Grand Rapids, Mich.	212.00
J. Lipnitz, Moran, Mich.	270.00
B. Tschirhart, Ferndale, Mich.	270.00
J. Berglund, St. Paul, Minn.	217.00
C. Berkins, St. Paul, Minn.	208.00
L. Ellison, Minneapolis, Minn.	243.00
O. Nesbit, South Bend, Ind.	204.00
J. G. Hasenbank, Lake Elmo, Minn.	277.00
G. M. Schmidt, Akron, Ohio	260.00
D. T. Mitchell, Mahaffey, Pa.	534.00
A. J. Stauffacher, Wolsey, S.D.	210.00
Courts Cleveland, Granbury, Tex.	596.00
Mrs. H. G. Reinsch, Tacoma, Wash.	308.00
G. B. Chandler, Atascadero, Calif.	399.00
E. W. Fawkes, Chico, Calif.	296.00
A. A. Kantell, LaCanada, Calif.	305.00
K. Osborn, Los Angeles, Calif.	200.00
H. Wagner, Anaheim, Calif.	230.00
L. Worthington, Bakersfield, Calif.	350.00

The source of the balance of Smith's reported receipts was not indicated. Presumably, it was collected through mail solicitations or at his meetings.

Regardless of the actual state of his exchequer, Smith habitually pleads poverty; it is part of his fund-raising technique. Hardly a mailing goes out from his office that does not dwell upon his dire need for money. Typical was his September 27 letter (facing page 36).

When Smith gets out a heartrending appeal for money, the effort takes priority over all other work at his headquarters. Everyone on the staff quits his regular routine and pitches in. For example, on October 17 Smith's staff of fifteen worked around the clock folding, stuffing, sealing and stamping envelopes. The next day 3,500 special pleas were sent to a select list throughout the nation. At the same time 15,000 regular appeals for contributions went to his general mailing list, 4,000 to California alone.

The mailing list of the Christian Nationalist Party consists of forty drawers of addressograph plates; Smith's unverified claim is that it contains more than 200,000 names. This much is known definitely— the California group is made up of 17,000 names.

Almost as much mail comes in as goes out. Two days each week are devoted to incoming correspondence. One day is consumed preparing answers, the other is devoted to filling orders for literature, when an average of 500 kits of material, each bearing 15 cents in postage, is sent out. The returns are well worth the effort.

Attendance at Smith's 1949 meetings varied from fifty to 2,000, depending upon locality and the intensity of his planned publicity. Circulation of his monthly magazine, *The Cross and the Flag*, remained virtually constant, approximately 25,000, and he issued his usual quota of pamphlets and newsletters. His program, his brand of outrageous prejudice and particularly his vituperative anti-Semitism have changed little in the last decade. In 1948 they were set forth in the "political platform" adopted by the Christian Nationalist Crusade's first "national convention"; in 1949 Don Lohbeck, Smith's thirty-year-old lieutenant and editor, keynoted the program at the second national convention.

The 1949 gathering, held at the St. Louis Kiel Auditorium (September 27–30), was an even more ridiculous failure than the preceding year's. Attendance was as low as thirty and never exceeded 150. (In 1948 the convention drew audiences of 350.) In other respects, it was a carbon copy of the previous meeting: the same transparent speeches by Smith and his henchmen, the same participants (including the "guest appearance" of featured speaker General Van Horn Moseley), the same official pronouncement of bigoted philosophy.

A highlight was young Lohbeck's speech reiterating the 1948

eight-point Christian Nationalist platform and elaborating on its anti-Communist, anti-Negro, anti-Jewish planks. Again the Jew was portrayed as the arch-enemy of civilization. The official Christian-Nationalist "line" included:

THE NEGRO: The Christian Nationalist Party favors the complete and absolute social and political segregation of the black and white races in the United States of America—because that is the only way that we can survive as the leader of Christian Civilization.

The organized Jew is the burden on the neck of the Negro in America. As soon as we can show this to the Negro—then, in the ranks of Communism, the Jew must stand alone.

COMMUNISM: Just read the screaming hysterics of the Jewish Press (I mean the papers for the Jews) and you can see that they live in terror of the day when to all Americans it is evident that Communism is a Jewish product, a Jewish plot, a Jewish trick. . . . The power of the Jew Communist in our Federal Government is almost beyond belief.

ISRAEL: The Zionist movement is an un-American movement, and we Christian Nationalists demand the deportation of every Jew who has worked for or supported this foul conspiracy to make our people slaves, economically and politically, to the anti-Christian Jewish master.

THE INTERNATIONAL JEW: The economic life of our country is completely in the hands of Jewish financiers—and our people are held in slavery to the Jews through the fear of poverty and economic insecurity. . . .

But we know, and in his heart the Jew knows, that throughout the length and breadth of white Christian civilization there is an awakening stirring in the hearts and souls of the people that will not be stilled until this alien element—this mongrel element that can only pervert and corrupt and destroy that which our brothers have built—an awakening is stirring that will not be stilled until all of Christendom is freed for all time from the menace of Jewish intrigue and Jewish control.

Smith has developed a successful formula for squeezing out the maximum financial profit for his Crusade. In 1949 he concentrated his frenzied meetings in the Los Angeles area, where he had a Midas-like success in 1948. During his stay in California, the self-styled patriot spoke (mostly in the Los Angeles Embassy Auditorium) before several overflow audiences of 2,000. In other sections of the country he drew an average of less than 300.

On May 29, in one of the small halls of the Embassy Auditorium, the well-heeled agitator blamed the Jews for his inability to rent a larger meeting place. The following month (June 15 meeting) he asked his wealthy listeners to purchase a building with an assembly hall large enough for Christian Nationalist meetings, offering to guarantee an annual rental of $1,000.

A by-product of Smith's rewarding visit to the Coast was a new front, the California Anti-Communist League, organized in June with the Reverend Wesley Swift, one of the West's most successful professional bigots. Smith's objective was the reinstatement of State Senator Jack B. Tenney as Chairman of the California Joint Fact-Finding Committee on Un-American Activities. Smith said he was mobilizing his forces "to work with the Los Angeles Civic Association in the fight against Communist infiltration in California." There is no evidence that Senator Tenney gave any support or encouragement to Smith's group. Six hundred and fifty persons attended the California Anti-Communist League's September 9 meeting at which Swift promised the Senator would speak. Tenney did not appear.

Hardly a year passes without Smith becoming involved in the creation of some veterans organization. Nineteen forty-nine was no exception; in the fall, he lent a hand in the formation of a "Nationalist Veterans of America" whose offices were established in the St. Louis headquarters of the Christian Nationalist Party. The first meeting of the group was held October 7; by November 8 five had been held. The officers of the organization are old Smith stand-bys —John Hamilton of Boston, George Vose of Kalamazoo and Opal Tanner, Smith's personal secretary for many years.

The Nationalist Veterans of America is no different from the usual Smith enterprise. Its charter aims include: the preservation of America as a white Christian nation, the limitation and restriction of immigration to the white Christian people of Europe.

Smith's arrogance toward co-workers constantly causes defection in his camp. The latest recalcitrant is Jonathan E. Perkins, former Smith writer, advance agent and leg-man. Perkins broke with Smith following a violent disagreement over money matters and, subsequently, wrote an exposé of his former employer, *Gerald L. K. Smith Unmasked*. (Smith has had similar disputes with Arthur Terminiello and Elizabeth Dilling, two professional propagandists.) Kenneth Goff, long-time Smith henchman, while on a tour during the summer, complained bitterly that the petty American fuehrer was exploiting him; that he was forced to put up with third-rate hotel accommodations while the leader and his wife invariably stopped at the best hotels.

In the fall of 1949 Smith came East on one of his periodic junkets which included brief stops at Cincinnati, Philadelphia, Pittsburgh and Huntington, West Virginia. He arrived at the nation's capital in October.

Smith made no attempt to hold public rallies in Washington, D. C., announcing instead that he would "meet the press" on October 23, at which time "Mr. Smith will release the result of his thorough investigation of Drew Pearson—proving him to be a blackmailer and a perjurer." A far better publicity gimmick!

The agitator's charges against the famous columnist later formed the basis of a new booklet, *Drew Pearson—Blackmailer*, which Smith issued late in November. Pearson has refused to dignify the scurrility by answering it.

Smith's publicity-potent interest in prominent personalities on the Washington scene is reflected in another Christian Nationalist publication, *Suicide*, which appeared at approximately the same time as the Pearson pamphlet. Modestly billed as "the most sensational manuscript ever to appear in print dealing with Washington, D. C.," it was written by a "Mr. X." The macabre nineteen-page booklet is replete with "highly sensationalized inside stories" about the deaths of President Roosevelt, John Winant, Wendell Willkie, Huey P. Long and others. In the demise of each Mr. X sees the sinister machinations of a "hidden hand"—later identified as part of the "underground conspiracy of the Zionist Jews to rule the world."

Presidential assistant David Niles is singled out for special libel as "the anonymous Secretary of Minorities" and "the most dangerous man in Washington."

Smith's fraudulent Christian Nationalist Crusade skillfully exploits the Communist menace and benefits handsomely. Despite his blatant bigotry, Smith never fails to depict himself as the arch-defender of the "Christian" way of life, and the arch-enemy of "the reds." A talented and experienced demagogue, Gerald Smith is a successful racketeer who earns a magnificent income from his mischievous and disruptive preachings. Despite the preposterous exaggerations about the number of his followers—"more than three million"—Smith undoubtedly makes some impact upon the more unstable elements in some of the communities in which he appears. Gerald Smith is still a problem for democracy to solve.

JOSEPH P. KAMP: In one important respect the suave Joseph P. Kamp is a greater nuisance than the crude Gerald L. K. Smith;

Kamp has succeeded in deceiving a greater number of important people regarding his real nature and true purpose.

As 1949 drew to a close, the pince-nezed, frock-coated Kamp was in imminent embarrassment of going to prison. If eventually he is jailed, it will be something more than a temporary respite for Americans from his sixteen years of well-paid activity in undemocratic propaganda. It will be a source of chagrin and pain to a number of his saddened friends, some of them highly placed, some notoriously low.

Indicted in December 1944 by a federal grand jury for self-righteously refusing to reveal the officers and contributors to his Constitutional Educational League, Kamp, a former process-server, has thus far avoided serving his four-month sentence by a long drawn out series of legal maneuvers. A petition to the Supreme Court for a review of his case is now pending. Should this petition be denied, the propagandist will have exhausted his bag of legal tricks and, as a self-avowed martyr, unhappily begin to serve his long-delayed sentence.

In his desperate efforts to keep out of the penitentiary, Kamp has not hesitated to use Congressional influence. On March 23, 1948, Representative Clare Hoffman of Michigan addressed a letter to U. S. District Court Judge Ben Moore who was preparing to impose sentence upon the pro-fascist pamphleteer. It was written in the hope that the Judge would accept it "in the spirit in which it is offered—a desire that you know something of Joe's work."

Congressman Hoffman was apparently aware that there might be some question of propriety involved in sending the letter. He introduced his plea for mercy with:

Dear Judge Moore: If, pending sentence, it is not in order to call your attention to certain characteristics of Mr. Kamp, you will, of course, consign this to the wastebasket without reading it. If communications like this are in order, then your attention is more humbly and respectfully solicited.

While preoccupied all through 1949 with an impending jail term, Kamp, a glib patrioteer, found ample opportunity for his propaganda work as "acting chairman" of his Constitutional Educational League. The several pamphlets he produced were consistent in point of view with the half hundred others he has issued in the last decade. These writings have netted him a not unsubstantial, or unwelcome, income.

Two new titles published in 1949 which he considers of outstanding importance are *Hitler Was a Liberal* and *Frame-up in Steel.* He released the first pamphlet in March, the latter in October. Neither is anti-Semitic.

Frame-up in Steel, a reprint of a speech made by Congressman Hoffman attacking President Truman's Steel Fact-Finding Board, brought Kamp $2,000 in sales and contributions in the first twenty days following its release. But more important than the pamphlet or the money is the person with whom the convicted promoter was dealing at the time. No less a figure than Charles M. White, president of the Republic Steel Corporation!

Kamp's relationship with White is on a "Charlie-Joe" basis. The steel pamphlet resulted from an arrangement the two friends worked out in the summer of 1949. Kamp sold White on the idea that he could document what he considered the leftist leanings of the members of President Truman's Steel Fact-Finding Board. Kamp asked White to underwrite his expenses up to $500. Later, when Kamp decided to reduce his "findings" to pamphlet form, he kept the industrialist apprised of the negotiations surrounding its printing and distribution. In the meantime, Kamp helped Representative Hoffman gather material for his speech attacking members of the Board. He made several trips to Washington and was in the Capitol on September 29 when Hoffman delivered the speech on the floor of the House.

Ostensibly, the Congressman wrote the speech himself, but several passages bear a close resemblance to Kamp's style—particularly that portion dealing with the background of a Jewish board member, David Laurence Cole:

Another circumstance that suggests suspicion of undue pro-labor bias is the fact that Mr. Cole, who graduated from Harvard Law School as David Cohen, studied under, and was exposed to the influence of, Justice Felix Frankfurter . . . Also of significance is the fact . . . that . . . Mr. Cole . . . was a "friend of Sidney Hillman."

The Hoffman-Kamp relationship goes back many years. In 1945 the Michigan legislator admitted that his congressional office had been used to distribute the League's literature. Since then Kamp has kept in close contact with his friend "on the hill"; a framed, autographed picture of the congressman was prominently displayed in Kamp's New York headquarters. On October 10, 1949, Hoffman wrote his good "Friend Joe," telling him about a man "who has plenty of money and who usually contributes to one or more patriotic organizations such as yours."

The president of Republic Steel and congressmen are not the propagandist's only highly placed friends. Nor has Kamp hesitated to call on them for help in his trouble. In a "Dear Charlie" letter, dated April 1948, Kamp urged White to intercede for him with the Speaker of the House and other key representatives to support a resolution rescinding the contempt citation. Congressman Ralph Church of Illinois had introduced the resolution.

Kamp revealed to White for his "confidential information" that several of his friends had already talked with some congressional leaders; he named Sam Pryor and General Wood as two of his spokesmen. In this same letter Kamp revealed that Congressman Cox was "working" on members of the Rules Committee of which the congressman was "a ranking minority member." Kamp explained that he had arranged, at the same time, for "hundreds of letters and resolutions" to go to leading members of the House from influential people and organizations in every part of the country. "However," he concluded, "it is personal contact that counts."

There is another, an uglier, side to Kamp's professional life and work which makes him a proper subject of interest in any essay on full-time bigots. It is the record of a personal anti-Semite's close working relationship with such people as Gerald Smith, Elizabeth Dilling, Gerald Winrod, Merwin Hart, and virtually every other known professional hate-monger in America.

Kamp's record of anti-democratic propaganda is long and loathsome. It began in 1933. For three years thereafter he was executive editor of *The Awakener,* a semi-monthly that offered a thinly disguised fascist line. Associate editor was Lawrence Dennis, professional proponent of American fascism, and one of its contributors was John Eoghan Kelly, a Christian Fronter who was jailed in 1943 as an unregistered agent of Franco Spain.

Some of Kamp's early efforts earned him the approval of World Service, official Nazi news bureau which operated from Ehrfurt, Germany. *Join the CIO and Help Build a Soviet America,* written by the propagandist in 1936, was "recommended" by the Hitler news agency in 1938; it was also sold at the German-American Bund's Aryan Book Store in Los Angeles.

In 1937 Kamp took over the Constitutional Educational League and became its executive vice-chairman—a position he still holds in addition to his acting chairmanship. The League's presses immediately began to issue a torrent of anti-democratic propaganda. The pamphleteer's basic theme that this country was in imminent danger from the "reds" and "foreign-born" was repeated with endless variations. Not long afterward he added all-out attacks upon liberal groups and prominent individuals—especially those with "Jewish" names.

From the outset Kamp's propaganda was favorably received by professional anti-Semites. The November issue of Gerald Winrod's *Defender* magazine hailed Kamp's pamphlet, *The Fifth Column in Washington.* That same month *The Fiery Cross,* official publication of the Ku Klux Klan, ran a laudatory editorial on *The Fifth Column in the South,* another Kamp product. Joe McWilliams, then New York's number-one pro-Nazi, sold Kamp's literature at his meetings, as did Christian Front organizations in the New York area. And the frenetic Elizabeth Dilling sent postcards to her followers urging them to buy his booklets.

Kamp associated with individuals known for their open antagonism toward Jews, among them the late Major Alexander Cloyd Gill who was research director of the Constitutional Educational League. Gill was reputedly the author of the fraudulent *Benjamin Franklin Prophecy* and a key figure in the 1936 Asheville, North Carolina, conference of professional anti-Semites. Kamp was also intimate with Allen Zoll, whose record is described in ensuing pages.

In the early days of World War II Kamp openly expressed his admiration for the notorious General Van Horn Moseley and supported Merwin Hart's pro-Franco views. Bitterly anti-New Deal, Kamp's irresponsible attacks on high government officials, coupled with his destructive propaganda on this country's war activities, finally got him into difficulties. In July 1942, and again in January 1943, his Constitutional Educational League was named as an organization used as a tool by groups of persons indicted by federal grand juries for conspiring to undermine morale in the armed forces.

(Kamp's personal conviction, now the subject of an application by him for review by the Supreme Court, stems from a citation originally handed down by a congressional committee investigating campaign expenditures in December 1944. Late in March 1948 the indictment came to trial, and Kamp was convicted of contempt of Congress and sentenced to four months in jail. In December 1948 the United States Appeals Court turned down Kamp's appeal, and a year later the same court denied the propagandist's move to reargue his appeal. The only maneuver left was a petition for a writ of certiorari, which he filed with the Supreme Court.)

In 1942 Kamp published *Native Nazi Purge Plot,* a purported exposé of "alien-minded super-collectivists' of varying scarlet hues" whom he accused of plotting to establish a "New Order." High on the list of human relations agencies involved in this alleged conspiracy was Anti-Defamation League. Characterizing the ADL as a "fountainhead of malicious misinformation," the pro-fascist publicist charged that it was a "low racket which promotes hate, breeds intolerance, fosters suppression and boycott, and engages in defamation of the vilest sort."

Native Nazi Purge Plot declared that the twenty-eight Washington sedition defendants were victims of "Maloney's 'Moscow Trial.'" (William Power Maloney was the first government prosecutor assigned to the case.) Kamp conceded that "a handful of those indicted might conceivably have had such a fantastic idea" [plotting conspiracy], but he portrayed the majority as "fanatic Americans [with] enthusiastic loyalty to this country and its institutions. . . ." The avowed anti-Semitism of virtually all of the defendants was airily dismissed with the comment: "Unfortunately some of them are also anti-Semitic."

Kamp is known to be a confirmed anti-Semite though he expresses himself cautiously in most private conversations. Usually, he is content to make snide remarks which show his fundamental hostility toward Jews. For example, when Israel was admitted to the United Nations, Kamp observed: "They will soon take that over [too]."

Although Kamp is in frequent communication with many professional anti-Semites, he officially "disapproves" of their open prejudice. In 1948 he wrote Mrs. Jessie Welch Jenkins of the National Patrick Henry Association (a violently anti-Semitic organization in Georgia) to advise her that her work "would be more effective" if she "would campaign against the Communists instead of 'the Jews.'" "I pull no punches in exposing the Jewish Gestapo, or any Jew who happens to be a Jew . . ." wrote the propagandist, "but why continue to hurt your own movement by being too inclusive in identifying 'subversives'?"

Another correspondent who wrote Kamp regarding the authenticity of the anti-Semitic *Benjamin Franklin Prophecy* received a cautious but revealing reply. Kamp did not think that it was "advisable" to circulate the document. "There is no way to prove that Franklin said anything of the kind. I don't say he didn't say it, I just want you to know you cannot prove it. . . ." Admitting that "several articles" had been written denouncing the Franklin forgery as a

fiction and a fraud, Kamp went on to explain to his correspondent
that she was free to believe or not, as she preferred, the report that
the Jews had "paid to have these articles written."

Kamp's transparent caution with regard to Jews is reflected in
his pamphlets. He avoids open anti-Semitism, preferring indirection
and innuendo. A favorite device is to label as Communist individuals
with apparently Jewish names. In instances where his prey have
Americanized their names, Kamp, the patriot, provides his readers
with their "real" names.

How to Win the War . . . and Lose What We're Fighting For?
written by Kamp in 1942, exemplifies this technique of bigotry.
Among the New Deal "Communists" attacked was motion picture
star Melvyn Douglas, then publicity chief of the wartime Office of
Civilian Defense. Kamp made his point by incorporating an attack
upon Douglas attributed to Representative Leland Ford:

> He is a former Communist and his name is not Douglas, it is Melvin
> Hesselberg. Do we always have to have men who have changed their
> names, and whose past activities are questioned, in high places of govern-
> ment?

Similarly, *Famine in America,* written by Kamp in 1943, is sprin-
kled with charges against "Russian-born" individuals in government
employ. Joseph Weiner, then head of the Office of Civilian Supply,
is identified as "an associate of Ben Cohen, an ardent exponent of
the Frankfurter school of radicalism." The following comment, attributed to Congressman Karl E. Mundt, is offered:

> "Who is this Joseph Weiner? . . . [I] looked him up and . . . found
> that he was born . . . in Don Borodus, Russia."

Walter Winchell, who publicly branded Kamp a "fascist," was
the subject of a vicious pamphlet, *With Lotions of Love* published
in 1944 (reprinted and widely distributed in 1948). Much space is
devoted to a discussion of the columnist's alleged "real" name
(originally pinned on him in jest by humorist Harry Hirschfield, and
then maliciously spread by Fritz Kuhn). Walter Winchell *is* his real
name. Characterizing Winchell as the "press-agent stooge" for "the
satellites, the sycophants and stooges of the Smear Bund," Kamp
offered the "real names" of various civic organization officials (including some in ADL) who he claimed constantly provided the
newspaperman with his "choicest morsels."

Kamp continued his foul campaign against Jews in his next

pamphlet, *Anything but the Truth,* published in 1945. The Office of War Information's short-wave research department was characterized as "run by Frances Keene (Ratensky)"; the chief of the Foreign Language Division was identified as "Karr, or Katz [who] was trained as a shipping clerk and a brush peddler."

The postwar years saw no letup in Kamp's efforts to malign Jews. *Communist Carpet Baggers in Operation Dixie,* published in 1946, contained the usual quota of offensive charges against "Communists" whose names are unmistakably Jewish. Joseph Gaer, a leader of the CIO's Political Action Committee, is described as "born in Russia —his real name is Fishman." The administrative head of PAC is identified as "Clarence Low (Lowenthal)." A group of "alien-born and alien-minded garment workers in New York" are charged with meddling in Southern politics, and frequent references are made to the "New York agents of a Semitic Smear Bund."

Professional anti-Semites are among the Constitutional Educational League's best customers. Bulk purchasers of pamphlets have included George E. Deatherage, once indicted for sedition. In 1948 Gerald Winrod ordered 10,000 copies of *Open Letter to Congress* and 2,000 copies of *With Lotions of Love.* In 1949 Winrod negotiated for a 5,000 bulk lot of Kamp's *Frame-up in Steel.* Elizabeth Dilling also buys thousands of copies of Kamp booklets, as does Gerald Smith.

Smith and Kamp have maintained a close working relationship in the use of each other's arrant literature. Nearly every week since early in 1948 there has come to Kamp's desk a bulk-purchase order from Smith for copies of *With Lotions of Love.* Smith sometimes seeks Kamp's help in locating printers, and in turn offers criticism of Kamp's published material.

In March 1948 Smith, writing in one of his "Dear Joe" letters that he was "highly pleased" with a Kamp book, asked what the cost for them would be "per thousand." He congratulated Kamp "for taking the complete dive," and invited Kamp to join him in the Southwest "where the percentage of white men is a little higher than in your metropolis."

The sale of pamphlets provides the Constitutional Educational League—and Kamp—with a comfortable margin of profit. Printing costs are only a few cents per copy, and the booklets retail at ten, fifteen, and twenty cents each, with varying discounts for bulk orders. The pamphleteer claims to have a key list of more than

50,000 names and an additional list of several hundred thousand persons who have written him at least twice for literature.

A substantial part of the League's income comes from "subsidies" and contributions which Kamp promotes from large industrial organizations and wealthy individuals interested in his anti-labor, anti-democratic propaganda. Kamp has a list of 500 such contributors. He personally communicates with the large donors; lesser fry are handled by a small number of salesmen who work on a 25 per cent commission basis. Two men, Frank Murphy and Chester Hanson, are the backbone of Kamp's sales force and have been with him for years. Murphy seems to be the heaviest producer; for October 1949 he earned more than $1,000 in commissions.

In the past two years Kamp has continued the publication of defamatory pamphlets. His Constitutional Educational League was especially active in 1948 and two new pamphlets appeared, *Behind the Lace Curtains of the YWCA* and *Open Letter to Congress*.

Open Letter to Congress, subtitled *Gentlemen: Are You Mice or Men?,* is another irresponsible attack upon ADL and other human-relations agencies. In it Kamp demands that Congress investigate the "Jewish Gestapo and the Smear Bund" and the "Jewish Ku Klux Klan" which he complains are "smearing" him and other "patriotic" Americans. Among the "crimes" with which the "Jewish Gestapo" is charged are "suppressing free speech . . . promoting the class war . . . agitating the Negro question . . . [and] stirring up anti-Semitism." Kamp concluded his diatribe by urging Congress to "investigate this menace that smears you, sneers at you, and defies you while it threatens your country."

Open Letter to Congress was widely applauded by the nation's hate press. Gerald Winrod's *Defender* endorsed the booklet in March 1948, as did Gerald Smith's newsletter of the following month. Other anti-Semitic publications recommended Kamp's pamphlet to subscribers, including W. Henry MacFarland's *National Progress,* the *Ohio Pioneer,* and Lawrence Reilly's bigoted *The Eleventh Hour.*

Fifty thousand copies of *Behind the Lace Curtains of the YWCA,* which charges that the nationally famous women's organization is infiltrated with Communists, were mailed free at a cost of approximately $5,000. Kamp sent complimentary copies to leading newspapers, members of Congress, chambers of commerce, American Legion officials and various religious organizations. Mrs. Arthur Forest Anderson, president of the YWCA National Board, characterized the professional patriot's booklet as "a sorry compilation of inaccuracies, insidious half-truths [and] perverted facts. . . ." Notwithstanding, the publication received uncritical publicity in sections of the nation's press and helped foster the illusion that the Constitutional Educational League is a worthwhile and truly patriotic organization.

Busy scurrying back and forth between New York and Washington in his endeavor to keep out of jail, and though engaged in the production of his nauseating literature, Kamp finds time to act as go-between for other professionals in the field. When Upton Close and Merwin Hart had their falling out in 1947 (described later in this chapter), word spread through their circle that Hart had cheated Close miserably. Up until the break between the two men, Hart's organization, the National Economic Council, had been sponsoring Upton Close as a commentator on a national network broadcast.

The report of the split reached Elizabeth Dilling in Chicago and on the letterhead of her "Patriotic Research Bureau" she wrote to Kamp, addressing him by his first name. Describing the report that reached her from California "that Merwin K. Hart absconded with about $80,000 of money collected to keep Mr. Close and others like him on Mutual network," Mrs. Dilling expressed serious concern. "What about it? Is it true?" she wanted to know.

Kamp drafted a response and submitted it to Merwin Hart for approval. For some obscure reason Kamp did not reveal to Hart the identity of his correspondent; he simply referred to her as "an influential friend in the Middle West."

Hart did not approve of the precise language of Kamp's proposed reply, and in a June 1947 letter to "Dear Joe" suggested that Kamp amend his letter to Mrs. Dilling to indicate that Close was "paid more than $30,000 for his year's services. Do you know of any other anti-Communist getting that kind of money?" At Hart's further suggestion Kamp added to his letter that "less than $8,000 of the total of some $230,000 that was raised was applied to expenses." Requesting his friend Kamp to write that the job was done "as a public service," Hart had Kamp also insert the statement that "neither the Council nor Mr. Hart received anything for services."

Kamp's reported yearly income is only a fraction of that of his star salesmen. His official salary as League chairman is modest—about $50 a week—but his scale of office operation and his mode of living indicate that this is probably only a small part of what he spends.

For the past ten years Kamp's New York headquarters has been a well-equipped three-room office at 342 Madison Avenue, which he shares with his wife, Mildred, and Lambert Fairchild, the Constitutional Educational League's chairman. (Fairchild's activities as paid chairman—he receives a small weekly salary—are evidenced only by an occasional flowery foreword to a Kamp booklet.)

The propagandist and his wife maintain an expensively furnished three-room apartment in Manhattan's fashionable East Fifties, a combination which is difficult, if not impossible, to maintain on Kamp's announced income.

No wonder this great promoter of patriotism constantly complains to intimates that he is overworked! He spends endless hours chatting with essentially the same visitors day in and day out. He keeps irregular office hours; his writing is done only under the pressure of deadline. In search of new material he spends much of his time poring over reports of the Un-American Activities Committee or perusing lists of "subversive" organizations.

In addition to Kamp and his wife, his office staff uses the three-room headquarters. The staff consists of a secretary and a New York University journalism student who acts as a part-time office boy. For long stretches of time there is no apparent activity in the League's headquarters. Nevertheless, the office boasts an impressive assortment of business machines. A twenty-trunk switchboard—only four lines of which are connected—stands prominently alongside a large addressograph machine, a Sound-scriber, and five typewriters.

Among Kamp's visitors in 1949 were Robert Donner, wealthy Colorado anti-Semite, Lawrence Dennis, and J. B. Matthews, one-time director of research for the Dies Committee.

Kamp's fancier friends rarely get to visit with him at the headquarters. Frank H. Lee, Jr., owner of Lee Hats in Connecticut, maintains the connection through the mail and away from the office. Kamp takes credit for motivating Lee's decision to discontinue sponsorship of Drew Pearson's Sunday night radio broadcast.

In March 1949 Kamp wrote to "Dear Frank," complaining because the "S.O.B." was being permitted on Lee's program "to say what he pleases." While Kamp disavowed suggesting that Lee should censor Pearson, he did add that Lee "ought to give Drew a good dressing down." Kamp enclosed his newest booklet in the letter and asked

Lee to telephone when next he came to town. "I would like to talk with you soon . . . With kind regards . . ."

Kamp's operations are still small time in comparison with such a professional as Merwin Hart; less effective than an Upton Close. But over the years he has attracted a steady following of misguided individuals who are continuously subjected to the impact of his bigoted thinking. In time many, no doubt, come to accept his oblique anti-Semitism as a matter of course—some, perhaps without being aware that the Jews are being especially singled out for attack. This makes Kamp a serious nuisance, which he will continue to be so long as he is able to attract financial support for his propaganda activities.

UPTON CLOSE: On Saturday night, October 29, 1949, in an hour-long speech at the annual banquet of the Milwaukee, Wisconsin, branch of the Steuben Society of America, Upton Close, the former radio news analyst, declared that he was a bearer of "good news" and that his text for the evening was: "The nation is showing signs of returning to sanity."

Thereupon the commentator reached back into history and, in an emotional tirade, accused Roosevelt and the Jews of removing him from the national radio networks in 1944. He castigated F.D.R. for succeeding himself three times. He pleaded with his audience to expose "the pressure politics" which, he said, were imported from Europe. He urged a fight on displaced persons legislation. He declared that several members of President Truman's official family had already "jumped out of windows," and they would be followed by others who had a choice only between suicide or the American courtroom which "they had tried so hard to corrupt."

In other words, Upton Close's "line" in 1949 changed little since he shifted from professional broadcaster to professional bigot—and started on the road to disrepute.

Some people say that Close has long been suffering from a persecution complex and that he has unfortunately focused on the Anti-Defamation League of B'nai B'rith as his tormentor; this is too simple an explanation. In the course of his Milwaukee harangue he repeated his usual fantastic attacks upon ADL: "I blame B'nai B'rith and the Anti-Defamation League as the organization that is responsible for these happenings and partially responsible for Roosevelt having me taken off the air." His absurdities included the charge that ADL was spending six million dollars a year to investigate and persecute people who disagreed with it; that the League "had over 20,000 paid investigators scattered throughout America."

He revealed his distraught state when he charged that within two hours after he was admitted to a hospital, "agents for the League," disguised as nurses at the institution, were investigating him. He concluded with the accusation that the B'nai B'rith and the Anti-Defamation League have "infiltrated" the movies and theaters with their propaganda.

Though Close is the kind of bigot who always finds it necessary to deny his anti-Semitism, he experiences difficulty in concealing his real feelings once he is on his feet and hypnotized by his own voice. In the Milwaukee speech he referred to Jews as "God's chosen children," and ended his disturbed presentation with: "Thirty million Americans of German descent should arise united and fight the present administration and the B'nai B'rith and Anti-Defamation League."

Close's career, which began in the early 1920s, gave no clue in its formative years to the role he eventually was to play. An obscure lecturer and author who had traveled widely in the Orient, Close eked out a living during that period by speaking before ladies' clubs on such innocuous topics as "Cherry Blossoms and Pear Orchards." Twenty years later the same Upton Close, by then a national network news analyst, was being denounced as a fascist and anti-Semite.

The commentator's metamorphosis became evident in the early forties. A die-hard isolationist, he had cast his lot with America Firsters and extreme nationalists like Charles Lindbergh, Merwin Hart, and General Wood. He was one of those, too, who minimized the threat of Hitler and the Japanese war lords. Concomitantly, he developed an antagonism toward Jews who, he claimed, were pushing the United States into war. In 1941, in a San Francisco speech, Close declared: "The Anglophiles and the Jewish people on the umbilical coast east of the Hudson River" who were being "taken for a ride in a taxicab of sympathy for England or hatred for Hitler" were involving the nation in another European conflict.

Close's interpretations of current events involved him in an almost continuous storm of controversy. Over the air, in July 1944, he openly championed the notorious Tyler Kent, United States Embassy employee in London, convicted in 1940 by a British court for delivering information to the Axis. (A short time later Close discontinued broadcasting for NBC.)

As the war in Europe drew to its finish, Close became more and more antagonistic toward what he termed "Jewish pressure groups" and "other alien minorities." On January 14, 1945, broadcasting over the Mutual Network, Close complained on the air:

We have now in our midst secret groups . . . [who] use the most vicious and secret pressures to destroy voices who dare to oppose . . . [They] use the cloak of religious liberty and racial equality . . . to hide their character-destroying . . . methods against those they want out of the way.

The following month Close told his radio listeners:

I have seen Jewish opportunists on the one hand taking advantage of the fears of their own people and, on the other hand, increasing the prejudice of those who tend to be narrow-minded.

In July 1945 the news analyst intimated that New Deal pressure had forced the *Saturday Evening Post* to cease publishing articles dealing with the Roosevelt family; his Mutual broadcasts then ended temporarily. The *Post* publicly denounced the commentator in an editorial for his "reckless irresponsibility" and hailed as "America's gain" the fact that his Mutual broadcasts had terminated.

That same month—July 1945—Close initiated a semi-monthly newsletter, *Closer-Ups*, a new medium through which to attack Jews. Early issues contained numerous hostile remarks about Jewish personalities prominent on the Washington scene. "Rosenman, Frankfurter, Niles and his new friend, Victor Emmanuel," were labeled "Truman . . . sycophants." Bernard Baruch was reported as having given "F.D.R. two gifts in cash totaling one million dollars." Justice Frankfurter was labeled "little Frankfurter, friend of dark little Laski." The "White House little cabineteers" were accused of having "lost . . . wide sympathies and close contacts with the Jewish community generally . . . their feelings for fellow racialists and Democratic Party alike are on a purely opportunistic basis of self-interest."

Close's attitude toward the so-called "Jewish problem" was also made a matter of record in 1945—in a letter he sent to Nathan L. Ohrbach, the department store owner:

I wonder, if four million or forty million [dollars] . . . can buy or wheedle the love of people? I wonder if there is any solution at all to the problem of keeping the majority from regarding with some reservations a minority which makes its basic principle that of maintaining its own peculiar identity.

In October of that same year a Cleveland University Club audience heard Close say:

The greatest sorrow in my career and which may become America's greatest tragedy is the Communist control of the Jewish minority. . . . Only in a few cases do the better minds among the Jews do anything about this menace to America. . . .

In a Michigan speech in the fall of 1945 Close told his listeners:

Marxists are trying to smear all persons who are against them by labeling them anti-Semitic. . . . Those Jews who have been here in this country only a few years . . . and who don't read anything but the Communist papers have been taken in by the Communists.

Close confided to a Cleveland, Ohio, audience in March 1946 that the "Communists and certain races" hated him more than they hated Gerald Smith. "The majority has to be tolerant of the minority," warned Close. "It is about time the minority finds out it has to be tolerant of the majority."

In 1946 and 1947 Close's radio utterances earned him further public repudiation. An attack on Chicago's Bishop Bernard J. Sheil —in September 1946—prompted the cleric to blast Close's "untruthful statements . . . unjust implications . . . despicable insinuations and utter intellectual dishonesty." Francis E. McMahon, then writing for the New York *Post*, commented that "the record of the fellow is long and nauseating . . . Close is out to discredit every type of genuinely progressive thought in the country."

Close climaxed his checkered career as a network commentator by appearing over the Mutual Network under the sponsorship of Merwin Hart's National Economic Council, beginning in February 1946. These broadcasts ended abruptly and without explanation on February 7, 1947. The behind-the-scenes controversy that followed is interesting and revelatory.

Nearly a year before, Close, who had been drawing more than $500 a week for his radio program, was looking for a sponsor. Merwin Hart, the pro-Franco propagandist, was seeking to publicize his National Economic Council. The two men—whose political philosophies are in complete harmony—decided to join forces. The commentator agreed to turn the radio show over to the Hart organization, which would sponsor and pay him. Hart, in turn, would concentrate the efforts of his Council upon the task of raising funds for the program, and, in return, he would get national publicity for his organization.

(Close's personal fund-raiser, Leo F. Reardon, once Father Coughlin's right-hand man, was taken care of. In addition to commissions from his own fund-raising for Upton Close, he was to get 10 per cent of everything Hart raised for the radio operation.)

Money caused the trouble between Hart and Close. More than $235,000 was raised by the combination, but the commentator disagreed with his new partner's decisions regarding disbursement. Close did not like the size of the cut Hart had taken for his own organization's "expenses."

The resulting dispute, which almost concluded in litigation, was the subject of widespread gossip in nationalist circles everywhere. The reader will recall Elizabeth Dilling's inquiry of Joe Kamp, and how Kamp furnished her a reply provided him by Hart. The essence of the reply was that Close should not complain in view of the fact that he had received more than $30,000 as his share of the bargain.

The radio commentator, however, had a different view of the transaction. He analyzed the bookkeeping audit in a memorandum to Hart, in which he pointed out that the National Economic Council had deducted more than $7,000 for incidental expenses while he, Close, had not even thought of charging this kind of expense. Close pointed out, too, that Hart's organization had retained an additional $7,000 for expenses in connection with the broadcasts. Complaining that "there is no listing of those expenses," the commentator made a point of the fact that he had no agreement with Hart for the latter "to deduct administrative expenses of any kind." He commented, too, that Hart asked for the understanding to this effect *after* he had availed himself of the money.

In denying that "by any possible stretch of the imagination" Hart's contribution was worth $7,000, Close offered to produce "testimony" regarding the actual work of "administration" and who did it. Close did not think it was relevant to the issue that he had received "commentator's fees of $550 per week, totaling $28,600 for the year. . . ." In view of the fact that the amount of compensation was set long before Hart ever appeared in the picture, Close wrote he did not think that the amount of his annual payment for the broadcasts was "an excuse for the self-appropriation" of administrator's fees.

But by April 1949 the two men were again friends. So cordial is the re-established friendship that Hart recently placed *Closer-Ups* on

Washington, D.C.
July 23, 1949

Dear Personal Friend:

This is one of the most difficult letters I have ever had to write. Only a sense of responsibility to you and our other friends over the country could cause me to write with such urgency. I solicit your patience.

I am worried. Members of the House and Senate with whom I talk almost daily are worried. Despite the low ebb of American statesmanship produced by disintegration forces difficult to understand, there are still leaders of strength and character on Capitol Hill. I regard some of these men as among my closest friends.

As your observer, I sit this morning almost under the shadow of the Capitol building - our office being only five minutes' walking distance. Some of the most momentous decisions in the history of our country are being made almost a stone's throw away. And I am haunted with the knowledge that honest, straight-thinking Americans like you are NOT properly represented.

The very destiny of the world is being shaped by the Eighty-first Congress now in session - if, considering that control of the atom has been placed in the wrong kind of hands, there is to be a world! There is no doubt in my mind, and the present investigation proves that David Lilienthal is one of the most dangerous men ever to appear on the American scene.

Many of you have heard Senators and Representatives speaking with me, of late, on our weekly programs. These even have joined us in sounding a needed warning. They are helping us give the American people the message of enlightenment so much needed in the present crisis.

When one of them learned the other day about the hard financial problem we are now facing, he said: "Upton, you simply must somehow keep going. If you and others of similar vision fail, all will be lost."

In turning over in my mind the NECESSITY of appealing to our friends for the sake of survival, I resolved to write in a spirit of utter self-abandonment. Pride must be sacrificed in the interest of truth.

I could write a book on how the opposition is trying to wipe us out. We have never so much needed the moral and tangible support of our friends. Enemies are gloating over our financial plight. Leftist outfits who would supplant Americanism with Communism have plenty of funds. We who stand for the right are suffering the pangs of privation.

The next seven or eight days will determine the future of our radio, publishing and other labors. This is an S.O.S. call. Do not be offended at my urgency.

Letter from Upton Close referred to on page 58.

I have never before written such a letter and hope it will never be necessary to do so again! Your sympathy and quick cooperation are urgently needed.

And yet, the obligations that weight us down today and threaten to silence both our voice and pen, are just under eight thousand dollars.

This amount seems large as a lump sum. But let's break it down. Only 80 contributions of $100 each would be required to see us through this crisis.

Or 160 in amounts of $50 would accomplish the same purpose...or 800 gifts to this cause of $10 each would lift the load. Smaller or larger sums will be received with heartfelt thanks. Every dollar is precious. Your help will be highly esteemed at this crucial hour. A letter of encouragement will help. An old adage says: "In union there is strength".

There are reasons why hours are important with us. Please use air mail service in answering. I will report back to you the response received from this effort. Let me emphasize that everything hinges upon the quick replies received from friends like you.

* * * * * *

A friendly publishing house is bringing out a neat little book for us, entitled: WASHINGTON WATCHTOWER, WITH UPTON CLOSE AT THE MICROPHONE.

May I autograph one for you in acknowledgment of your gift.

I have confidence that the America we love will somehow weather this storm. We can look back with pride and thankfulness to the chain of providences that have operated in our behalf — from the day that George Washington was seen kneeling in the snow praying at Valley Forge, down to the present hour.

May the God of all grace come once again to our rescue! This is the thought I would leave with you, in anticipation of an early answer to this heart-to-heart talk.

I shall be watching for your letter. Kindly use the blank below.

Devotedly yours,

Upton Close

- -

Dear Upton Close: I feel as you do, that America is worth saving. Enclosed find a contribution of the amount marked X at the right. Yes, you may send me an autographed copy of your new book.

NAME_____STREET_____

CITY_____STATE_____

$500 ☐
$100 ☐
$ 50 ☐
$ 25 ☐
$ 10 ☐
$ 5 ☐
$ __ ☐

his "recommended list" of reading. Meanwhile, Close found a new collaborator, a reserve officer named Robert H. Williams, who qualified himself as an expert on communism and patriotism by virtue of his World War II experience in "Military Intelligence." Williams' record shows that during much of the war he was a major assigned to Air Intelligence duties—the weather.

The first big product of the new team—Williams was now a "staff member" of *Closer-Ups*—was a pamphlet, *"The Anti-Defamation League and its Use in the World Communist Offensive.* Issued in 1947 as a "supplement" to Close's newsletter, the scurrilous booklet, which credited Williams with authorship, showed a marked resemblance to Close's "line."

The essence of the booklet is that the majority of Jews are Communists, that the Anti-Defamation League was largely instrumental in the rise and continued growth of communism in this country and that Jews participated prominently in the Russian Revolution.

Twenty thousand copies were printed in the first two editions. The booklet received widespread distribution, it was circulated to all members of Congress. Professional anti-Semites throughout the nation helped to disseminate it. The hate press almost unanimously endorsed the Close-Williams effort. Leon D'Aryan's *The Broom,* Eugene Flitcraft's *The Gentile News,* Gerald Winrod's *Prayer Circle Letter,* Court Asher's *X-Ray,* and Charles B. Hudson's *America in Danger* approved the pamphlet wholeheartedly. Gerald Smith used it as a "give-away" for one of his fund-raising schemes.

The struggle in 1948 for the establishment of Israel furnished Close a fresh opportunity to express his anti-Semitic views. His wildest comments appeared in *Closer-Ups* and in his syndicated newspaper column, "Close Ups." The February 16, 1948, issue of *Closer-Ups* characterized the Israeli Zionists as a "loud-mouthed, intolerant, persecuting, violence-loving, dual-citizenship seeking group."

President Truman's de facto recognition of Israel was repeatedly described as a political bid for the Jewish vote. In his column of May 26, 1948, Close observed:

. . . Mr. Truman clearly has made up his mind not to offend the pro-Israel vote . . . at least not before the elections. . . . The minority vote of which the Jewish vote is a part . . . has exercised the balance of power . . . in recent national elections. . . .

Apparently unable any longer to secure radio network sponsorship, Close turned in 1948 to Mexican stations. He moved his offices from Hollywood to Washington, D. C., transcribed his programs there and shipped them below the border for broadcast.

Gradually, the commentator acquired supplementary, independent stations in the United States, and by the beginning of 1949 his transcribed voice was being beamed by twenty-five smaller outlets scattered throughout the country. Close used his broadcasts to build his personal mailing lists. However, there was no real income from this source, and the propagandist was hard put to make ends meet.

It appeared that Upton Close was finally reaching the end of the road. His popularity, steadily declining since 1945, had struck a new low. Subscriptions to *Closer-Ups* dwindled to such a degree that the price was cut from $10 to $5 a year. His syndicated news column was reduced to four outlets with a total weekday circulation of 54,000. (In 1947, Close's circulation was 1,921,000.) His lecture appearances, too, were fewer and farther between. And in radio, he was barely managing to maintain the status quo; the Mexican border station, XERF, and the twenty-five independent stations in the United States were the only ones carrying his divisive propaganda.

A desperate note began to creep into Close's mailings. A February 5 letter to his followers urged: "We still must get at least *twice* as many subscriptions as before. Otherwise—well I dare not think about that."

Unfortunately, his own fears proved premature. By September 1949 it became evident that the self-styled patriot was staging a comeback—at least insofar as his financial condition was concerned. His number of independent radio outlets had jumped to forty-eight as a consequence of his ability to pay for more radio time. By November Close reported to his subscribers that his transcribed propaganda was being carried by more than 100 stations.

Close's sudden comeback was made possible by a last-minute alliance he made in July 1949 with Allen Zoll, one-time Coughlin supporter and founder of the National Council for American Education. Close engaged Zoll to help launch a fund-raising drive.

The first effort of the new alliance was an appeal written over Close's signature in July 1949. The letter, cleverly contrived, marked a novel approach for Close. It frankly admitted that he was "broke" and "reluctantly" advised his followers that he would be forced to retire from the field unless substantial financial support was immediately forthcoming. The letter which was sent to a select list of his "Dear Personal Friends" appears facing page 56.

The response to this "begging" letter was apparently highly favorable. Enough funds came in to enable Close to stage a comeback and to enlarge the number of radio outlets carrying his propaganda.

Close maintains, with mounting fervor, that he is neither anti-democratic nor anti-Semitic. He has made "a standing offer of $1,000 in cash . . . to anyone or any organization which can prove that I am guilty of spreading religious prejudice."

But the record of Close's attitude toward Jews belies his dramatic denial. Whenever possible he incorporates thinly veiled attacks against Jews, seldom missing an opportunity to inject a defamatory innuendo or a phrase calculated to reflect unfavorably upon "minority groups." His January 6 column in the *Bucyrus* (Ohio) *Telegraph Forum* is typical:

The Georgia "crackers" who voted for Truman because of the checks they got from their County Farm Agents do not want his "Civil Rights Program" any more than the New York Jewish voters wanted his farm subsidies.

Close also uses the much favored device of professional anti-Semites—giving an individual's "real" name to inform readers that the person is Jewish. In his February 2, 1949, column in the *Telegraph Forum*, discussing two Canadian Communists apprehended by the FBI, the propagandist refers to them "as the Carrs (actual name, Cohens)" and again as "Chief Spy Sam (Cohen) Carr."

On May 7, speaking in Oklahoma before the Tulsa Women's Republican Club, Close told his listeners:

America today is made up of minorities all of which have special axes to grind. They are Polish, Lithuanian, Farmer, CIO, AFofL and a certain minority in New York City.

Close repeatedly attacks "Tolerance Machines" which he does not always identify. The Atomic Energy Commission investigation called forth this comment on June 20, 1949:

The opening hearings were poorly reported—"Liberal" and Tolerance Machine influences worked to create a fad of contempt among news men. This Tolerance Machine is the most powerful apparatus in the United States for moves behind the scenes. It is the best financed, has the largest sentimental hold, the greatest intimidation value.

Prominent Jews active in government are among Close's favorite targets. In July 1949 he reported that "Justice Felix Frankfurter had cut in on the older and more astute Bernard Baruch for domination of the mind of Truman. Both belong to the same general group, with the multi-million-dollar-financed Tolerance Machine to back them."

Recent press accounts of anti-Semitism in Soviet Russia provided the commentator with a springboard for his special brand of bigotry. Writing in the October 1949 issue of *Closer-Ups,* he subtly implied that the majority of Jews are Communists:

The small anti-Communist segment of *our* Jewish community is actively trying to publicize the Soviet anti-Semitism, but so influential are Jewish Communists in the Jewish community and press that the truth . . . is being suppressed. . . .

In the last months of 1949 Close barraged his followers with increasingly venomous attacks against responsible organizations which are spokesmen for large sections of American Jewry. The commentator's animus continued to be especially directed against the Anti-Defamation League. His almost pathological hatred of ADL—never far beneath the surface—erupted with full force in the October 29 speech before the Steuben Society at Milwaukee.

Frequently during 1949 congressmen who agree with Close's political views were invited to appear on his transcribed radio programs. Most of them confined their talks to politics. However, in at least one instance—the May 29 guest appearance of Representative Alvin E. O'Konski of Wisconsin—the broadcast was slanted with comments of a questionable nature. Among the subjects discussed was David Lilienthal's record as chairman of the Atomic Energy Commission. An excerpt from the dialogue between Close and Representative O'Konski:

CLOSE: Well, I remember, Congressman, at the time the Lilienthal nomination was up, one of the Senators on the Committee was telling me, and asking me not to use his name, that he didn't believe Lilienthal's was a proper appointment, but he (the Senator) would be called anti-something or other.

O'KONSKI: That's right—he would be called reactionary—he would be called fascist, he'd be called everything under the sun.

CLOSE: They would accuse him of religious intolerance?

O'KONSKI: That's right—and no more perfected smearing technique and organization has ever been evolved in the history of this country than that organization which exists today, and it's because the Administration is afraid of incurring the wrath of this group that it has no policy toward communism in this country.

Close's fundamental distrust of democracy was made evident in his March 20, 1949, radio broadcast. "The government of our nation is a representative republic," said the commentator. "All the wise men who won independence and founded it agreed that it should be a representative republic, not a democracy."

This political reasoning has kept Close, for two decades, an implacable foe of all progressive legislation. Bitterly anti-Roosevelt and anti-New Deal, he has transferred his antagonism to President Truman's civil rights program, characterizing it as "conceived in politics rather than any passion for the downtrodden." Close insisted in a March 1949 broadcast that the civil rights controversy "was introduced into present American politics by the foreign brains of the Communist Party."

Although shorn of much of his power and prestige, Upton Close cannot be ignored. His kind of bigotry is dangerous because he sells himself as an informed political observer sincerely concerned with preserving the American way of life. He is able to attract support from individuals who, through carelessness or callousness, overlook his attacks on minority groups. Responsible businessmen throughout the country invite him to speak before local chapters of such reputable civic and fraternal organizations as the Rotarians. Congressmen who appear on his radio programs give him added prestige. Unfortunately for democracy, Upton Close is still a widely accepted political expert.

MERWIN K. HART: Anti-Semitism such as Merwin K. Hart exhibits is never a sudden acquisition. It takes time, frequently years, to develop the peculiar narrowness of the professional Jew-hater. Hart is no exception; his anti-democratic roots lie deep. But as president of the National Economic Council, the Harvard-bred Franco sympathizer likes to pose as a high-minded patriot whose organization is "dedicated to the preservation of human liberty, including maintenance and invigorating private enterprise, rights of property and American independence." His record over the last ten years hardly fits this high-sounding description.

Hart is a clever bigot; he never reveals his anti-Semitism in a vulgar way. His attacks upon Jews are cloaked in opposition to opinions held by different groups of Jews. If the group does not exist, he creates it.

In the last ten years this clever propagandist has used at least three different issues to attack Jews—New Dealism (and more recently, Fair Dealism), communism and Zionism. An opponent of these different movements, he premeditatedly injects the Jew into each controversy and in hammering the issue defames the entire Jewish population. To be sure, Hart repeatedly disavows anti-Jewish prejudice; his day-by-day activity makes the repudiation necessary.

In an interview on January 5, 1941, in the face of charges that he and his Council were anti-Semitic, Hart declared: "Most of the people with whom we do business are Jews. . . . Why we have Jewish members on our Board of Directors. . . . All men are my friends—in a sense."

Hart's record belies his disclaimer. When Franklin Roosevelt died suddenly in April 1945, Hart immediately issued one of his Council letters on America's destiny—and used the opportunity to attack Jews in American life. He captioned his piece: "Shall Alien Minds Determine America's Future?" and he led his readers down the paths this country might possibly take. Said he:

It is hard to base a prediction for the future on past history, because a new factor has entered in. The art of modern propaganda has been developed. It has been clever, thorough, ruthless and often untruthful. Relatively few Americans understand either its source or its extent and potency. . . .

They do not realize that many of the very views they express have been formulated by cunning men and women, and that through New Deal control of radio and New Deal influence among most of the country's writers, these ideas have been implanted in their minds. . . .

This propaganda is alien in origin and conception. It stems directly from Eastern and Central Europe. . . .

In passing, it is worth noting some of those alien-minded persons who, whether in public office or outside, have been among the leading molders of public opinion in the United States in recent years. Some of them, for reasons best known to themselves, have changed their names. Some are Communists or fellow-travelers; and nearly all are more or less tolerant of Communism. Many are artists in the technique of 'smear.' Few, if any, give more than lip service to traditional American principles. . . .

Hart then listed 81 men and women in American life, most of them well-known personalities whose loyalty is beyond reproach and whose distinguished service to the United States is universally esteemed. Of the 81, no less than 72 are Jewish. Included were the late Stephen S. Wise, Henry Morgenthau, James P. Warburg, Paul M. Warburg, Albert Einstein, Nathan Straus, Abba Hillel Silver, Albert D. Lasker, Felix Frankfurter, Benjamin Cohen, Walter Winchell, Leonard Lyons, Adolph Sabath, David E. Lilienthal, Bennett Cerf and Ben Hecht.

Hart concluded with his customary disclaimer:

We question at this time neither the ability nor sincerity of any of the above. *But they are not believers in the American way of life.* They, and others like-minded, dominate our public opinion. The independent American Republic will be destroyed if their domination continues. [Italics ours.]

Of a piece with this "clever" anti-Semitism, is an article he wrote four years later, this time using Zionism as the springboard. Dated December 15, 1949, and timed for distribution during the Christmas season, it was a violent attack upon pro-Israeli Jews. Despite the insertion of a parenthetical disclaimer, the total impact was a malicious reflection upon all Jews. Among other things, he wrote:

Clearly a minority of a minority (for multitudes of Jews are loyal Americans and they thank God they live here) who have received privileges in this great Christian Republic such as they never enjoyed elsewhere, now seek to destroy the very religion and culture that have given them refuge. This audacious attempt to suppress American consciousness of Christianity has come only with the rise of the Zionists to power in the Jewish community, and the blame must be laid squarely on Zionist shoulders. . . .
For because of their overbearing greed and their recent and present willingness to involve this country in every kind of evil, they (Zionist Jews) are the number one enemy of American liberty and the Christian Church. They are the outstanding cause of most of the dire troubles facing America today. . . . The Zionists are chiefly responsible for our subsidizing British Socialism. They have been at the bottom of the scheme for the U.N. and most other international alphabetical agencies. . . .
From this, it is clear that the controlling influence in the world is not the United States nor U.N. . . . but the Zionists. The Zionists are willing to turn against both the U.S. and U.N.—if necessary to attain their aims.
A wealth of evidence can be adduced to show that the Zionists have Mr. Truman's Administration in the hollow of their hand. The Socialist program is their program, as it is in Britain. . . . When the American people awaken to what they have already done and what they seek to do, their wrath will be truly terrible. . . .

Rarely does Hart miss an opportunity to inject his prejudice into a public controversy that touches on one of his three favorite issues. When the U.S. Government refused to approve the visit of Walter Gieseking, the German pianist, to this country in January 1949, the *Economic Council Letter* of February 15 reported:

Jewish-communist influence dictated this high handed procedure. It is clear this influence overruled agencies of the Government of the United States.

Of course anti-Semitism is not Merwin Hart's sole activity. Garbed as a political economist, his principal interests include lobbying against social reform and in favor of native and Spanish fascism. He devotes most of his attention to pro-Spanish propaganda work.

In January 1948 Hart wrote to one of his attorneys asking whether he was violating federal law in failing to register as an agent of a foreign principal—the government of Franco Spain.

Hart had good reason for concern. His record of many years as a consistent Franco apologist shows clearly that if he is not under a legal compulsion to register as a foreign agent, he certainly is morally obligated to confess it.

Hart has pleaded the cause of the Spanish dictator with every means at his command. He has sung the praises of Hitler's former ally in pamphlets, books, newspaper articles, over the air, in testimony before Congressional Committees and in numerous issues of his *Economic Council Letter*. Typical of his attitude toward Franco is a 1947 article in the New York *Journal American,* following an interview with the dictator:

It seemed to me that here was one of the strongest characters in the world today. The very vehemence of his enemies testifies to the mark he has made in history. In the next few years he may rise to even greater stature.

According to Hart, El Caudillo has never done and can do no wrong. He is apparently unconcerned—even sympathetic—with the undemocratic way of life which exists in Fascist Spain: the lack of real freedom of assembly, or freedom of the press, or freedom of religion. He rationalizes his support of Dictator Franco's regime on the transparent theory that Spain is the sole remaining bastion against Communist domination of Europe. In February 1939 Merwin Hart attacked communism and declared that Hitler had driven it out of Germany.

Hart fell in love with Franco Spain on his first visit to that country at a time when the dictator was an active partner of Mussolini and the Fuehrer. The professional Franco apologist has gone back to Spain many times since then, always keeping his supporters in this country advised of the "true" state of affairs in that land. On the other hand, his antagonists in this country, opponents of the Axis powers, have constantly sought to keep Americans informed of *his* strange activities. Walter Winchell, for example, on October 13, 1944, exposed a particularly unsavory aspect of Hart's pro-Franco operations after Hart was discovered co-operating with Jane Anderson. Readers will recall this woman as an active Spanish agent who later went to Nazi Germany to begin regular broadcasts of Axis propaganda over the Berlin shortwave radio. Her consequent indictment for treason was quashed after the war.

Hart is today on intimate terms with high Spanish officials in this country and in Spain. A particular crony is Señor Pablo Merry del Val, chief of the Spanish press service in Washington, D.C. When "Dear Pablo" was invited in May 1949 to speak before a Hart-sponsored dinner at Utica's Fort Schuyler Club, train reservations for him were bought and paid for out of National Economic Council funds.

As in the past, Hart, in 1949, served as a transmission belt for "inside information" which he thought would be of value to the Franco Government. Robert S. Allen, writing in the New York *Post* on December 21, revealed an interesting sidelight on this aspect of the propagandist's subservience to Spain. The columnist reported that when members of the House Foreign Affairs Subcommittee were in Spain in the summer of 1949, they saw "a letter to the Minister of Justice from Merwin K. Hart, head of the ultra-conservative National Economic Council, urging action against charges that Protestants are being persecuted in Spain." (By "action," Hart meant counter propaganda.)

Columnist Allen quoted a portion of the Hart letter covering the latter's report to the Spanish minister, Don Raimundo Fernandez-Guesta y Merelo:

> The other day, I noticed that a certain alleged Protestant minister was to speak at a meeting held in New York and I arranged for one of our staff to attend this meeting and give me a report on what this man said.
> I am enclosing a copy of this report thinking that you . . . might wish to study this. . . . Here are some concrete statements which, if answered adequately, would serve to a large extent to offset impressions made in the United States by such speakers as this man.

Hart's Franco sympathies, like his anti-Semitic attitude, stem from an anti-democratic bias which has characterized him since the middle thirties. In 1938, for example, Hart recommended for "ready reference" two books from the hysterical pen of Jew-baiter Elizabeth Dilling. That same year, he addressed the members of Allen Zoll's American Patriots. On December 8, 1939, Hart presided at an Economic Council luncheon attended by two stalwarts of the German-American Bund, Fritz Kuhn and his lieutenant, James Wheeler-Hill. A month later, January 26, Hart participated in a meeting of the

American Coalition of Patriotic Societies, an organization which was later named in the so-called mass sedition case as a tool used by the defendants in furtherance of their charged misdeeds.

In 1940 Hart, while busily extolling the virtues of Franco's Spain, found time to proclaim publicly his fundamental distrust of American democracy. Speaking before the Nassau Club in Princeton, New Jersey, in February 1940, Hart declared: "Democracy is the rallying cry under which the American system of government is being prepared for despotism." The same year, a distinguished New York Union League Club gathering heard Hart speak on "The Alien Influence in Our Midst." Hart warned: "It is time to brush aside this word 'democracy.' . . . ."

During the war years, the Economic Council's mentor intensified his anti-democratic activities. Evidence of his fundamental attitude appeared in the May 15, 1941, issue of *Economic Council Letter*: "The Frankfurters seek control," warned Hart. "The nameless cabal that shapes our policies, despite its cries of 'democracy,' is trying to change America."

Between caustic remarks about Jews and selling the "glories" of Fascist Spain, Hart also managed to make frequent appearances before federal and state legislative committees. In 1941 he loudly opposed the British aid bill. A few months before Pearl Harbor, he white-washed the Japanese war lords before the Senate Military Affairs Committee, declaring that: "An unfriendly attitude on the part of the United States drove Japan into the arms of the Axis."

The war's end found Hart embarked upon a nation-wide campaign against fair employment practices laws. On December 6, 1944, he warned the New York State Temporary Commission Against Discrimination that proposed legislation for a state fair employment practices act was a "totalitarian measure" and "Communist-inspired." Said Hart:

It is Hitler's best style. This bill, if enacted, would try to force the races together. The proposal is fantastic. . . . It would create discord where none now exists. Where some exists, it would be made worse.

It was at about this time—February 1946—that the Franco apologist turned to the radio networks and Upton Close in an effort to publicize his own organization and increase its income. Characteristically, he announced the choice of Upton Close "to keep alive in this country the spirit of private enterprise as distinct from the curse of totalitarianism."

In 1947 Hart continued to add to his record of hostility toward Jews. Twice in that year he lent the pages of his *Economic Council Letter* to anti-Zionist, anti-Jewish diatribes by the peculiar Benjamin Freedman. Born a Jew, Freedman, writing in the December 15, 1947, issue, maligned a large section of the Jewish population by asserting that "American-Jewish supporters of political Zionism are guilty of un-American activity."

Freedman's charges against American Jews gave Hart an opportunity to level an attack upon those he called "political Jews." Saying that "the Truman Administration is in the hands of this group," Hart scored their "aggressive efforts to force through the Communist-inspired FEPC law [and] the so-called anti-discrimination laws." The pro-Franco propagandist also attacked "the violent efforts to force a modification of our immigration laws to permit the bringing in indiscriminately of more Jews from Europe."

Charging that "this and the preceding administration of Mr. Roosevelt were *infested* [emphasis ours] on almost all levels with Jewish appointees, many of them communistic," Hart warned:

> If anti-Jewism is stronger in the United States than at any time in the past, the Zionist Jews have brought it about. . . . This aggressive Jewish group can wreck the United States. . . . If their attitude continues . . . there will surely be a repetition here of all the outbursts and violence against Jews that have taken place in so many other countries. . . .

In the May 1, 1949, issue of Hart's publication he reverted to his attack upon aliens. He reiterated his assertion that "we Americans have passed under the control, still temporary but well defined, of an alien-minded force" and demanded a Congressional investigation "on the methods and the identity of this American Politburo":

> The alien element now ruling, commands huge public funds and the presence in vital Government positions of members of its group. . . . It was alien influence that involved us in World War II. . . . It was alien influence that dominated much of our war policy. Practically every major decision made with respect both to our domestic policy and practically all our foreign policy has been through the influence of men like Harold Laski and Felix Frankfurter and many others, either aliens today or alien born or of recent alien descent.

In his August 1, 1949, *Economic Council Letter,* Hart attacked many prominent Americans Jews on the Washington scene. Justice Felix Frankfurter, a particular target of Hart's wrath, is characterized as the leader of this "movement to destroy the American Republic." Also singled out for special attack is presidential as-

sistant David Niles. Following the usual pattern set by professional
anti-Semites, Hart provided his readers with Niles' "real" name:

> Who is Niles? David Niehaus. Where did he come from, and what has
> been his past record? He is not mentioned in Who's Who. Why did he
> change his name? Do any men in the Congress really know about him?
> Why is he there?

In the same *Economic Council Letter* the pro-Fascist publicist
reached new heights of bigotry by attempting—inferentially but
unmistakably—to prove the existence of an international Jewish-
inspired Communist plot. Discussing Niles, Justice Frankfurter,
Herbert Lehman and other Jewish leaders, Hart wrote:

> These men . . . have their contacts with men of similar minds in other
> countries. For instance, Harold Laski of London, one of the greatest props
> of the Communist Party in Europe. . . . Unquestionably he and his
> fellow-Zionist, Frankfurter, have collaborated.

Hart's relationship to important figures pays off. For instance,
during 1949 he made numerous trips to Washington to confer with
senators and congressmen on pending political issues. On June 15
and 16 he conferred with such congressmen as Roy Woodruff of
Michigan and Lawrence Smith of Wisconsin and then spent time in
the office of Senator James P. Kem, of Missouri. Hart helped the
Senator draft the so-called Kem Amendment to the ECA, which
would have attached as a condition of appropriation of ECA funds,
that no money be paid to any government persisting after a given
date in nationalizing its industry. Obviously, this was aimed directly
at Great Britain. Hart, while in Kem's office, actually dictated the
text of a special *Economic Council Letter* supporting the Kem
Amendment. In a letter dated July 1, 1949, Senator Kem wrote Hart,
in part: "I am returning herewith the copies of letters which you
were kind enough to send me, regarding our amendment to the ECA
Appropriation Bill."

Note the designation "our amendment."

While Hart now resorts to overt defamation with increasing frequency, he is still cautious in his dealings with less "respectable"
anti-Semites. He corresponds with such notorious persons as George
Armstrong, George Deatherage, Allen Zoll, Conde McGinley, Joseph
Kamp and Robert Williams. However, Hart is fearful of co-operation with any anti-Semite whom he believes capable of double-
crossing him or whose indiscretions might prove embarrassing. Open

identification with less cautious anti-Semites might well jeopardize some of the big money contributions to his National Economic Council.

Hart is a shrewd fund-raiser. In recent years, less able bigots have found the going difficult, but the National Economic Council has prospered. During 1949 the NEC's "take" was at least $140,000—a considerable increase, according to Hart himself, over the previous year. Hart recently announced that the Council's goal for 1950 is $300,000.

The bulk of the NEC's financial support comes from a small group of prominent industrial leaders who see Hart as an ardent champion of their narrow concept of the American way of life. A current list of contributors reads like a section of "Who's Who" in American industry. To identify a few: American Car and Foundry Company; American Rolling Mill; Armstrong Cork; Acheson, Topeka and Santa Fe Railway; Sears Roebuck; Union Carbide and Carbon Company; Remington Rand. One wonders whether the officials of these great businesses who make funds available to Hart know or understand his professional hate-mongering. One also wonders how much stockholders know about the use of their monies.

On December 7, 1949, columnist Robert S. Allen, writing in the New York *Post*, revealed that well-known American businessmen were also among Hart's largest individual contributors. The newspaperman also named some of Hart's political supporters: Lammot and Irénée du Pont, Sun Oil Company head J. Howard Pew and Wall Street broker E. F. Hutton.

"According to the evidence," Allen reported, "the two du Ponts contributed more than $90,000 to Hart over a period of years." Allen published excerpts from a letter written to Hart by Irénée du Pont:

IRÉNÉE DU PONT
WILMINGTON
DELAWARE

July 12, 1949

Mr. Merwin K. Hart
National Economic Council, Inc.
Empire State Building
New York City 1

Dear Sir:
A few weeks ago, I received from you a good, fighting letter pointing out what the real, basic underlying trouble is in Washington—an alli-

ance of "pinks" with some undesirable Jewish people who seem to have seized control of the Government. I would like to have you send me twenty copies of that letter, which unfortunately I passed along to somebody else and consequently do not find it when I need it.

Yours very truly
/s/Irénée du Pont

d/s

In addition to persuading the du Ponts to contribute money, the promoter has used the prominence of the du Pont name to secure other contributions. In December 1948 Hart induced Lammot du Pont to write an NEC fund-raising appeal letter which was mailed to approximately 3,000 prominent industrialists. (The contributions resulting from this du Pont letter were reportedly over $25,000.)

On November 25, 1949, another appeal for funds went out over the same du Pont signature. "I feel sure that you will conclude that the Council is doing a good job," wrote du Pont. . . . "Will you not stretch a point and make a contribution or make a larger contribution and promptly?"

In the summer of 1949 Hart conceived the idea of calling a political action conference at New York City's exclusive University Club to discuss ways and means "of preserving American liberty." Invitations were sent to thirty-six influential individuals throughout the country urging the need to combat the "Socialism which has infiltrated not only much of the Democratic Party, but important elements in the Republican Party." Hart's letter, marked personal and confidential, requested "that all those receiving this information [about the conference] keep the matter in confidence."

This meeting of Hart's most important business friends was originally scheduled for June 28 and 29. His desire for secrecy, however, was blasted when Walter Winchell, in his June 20 column, reported that Hart and the others would be meeting and "secretly working to create another America First outfit."

Hart hastily telegraphed his invitees advising them that the meeting had been "postponed." On June 26, Winchell, reporting over the air that Hart "was forced to cancel this planned meeting to start another America First outfit," added that "many of Hitler's old friends are among these people—some congressmen, too. I recommend the startling story to the first editor who has the guts to name their names. I have the whole list."

The list was subsequently published in the New York *Post* on June 30. It revealed that among the meeting's sponsors were: Robert B.

Dresser, "a GOP lawyer . . . whose political record . . . includes . . . sponsoring a dinner for Upton Close . . . and maintaining a friendship with Joseph Kamp"; and ex-Representative Fred A. Hartley, Jr., president of the Tool Owners Union which in February 1947 was refused the right to operate in New York State because the Board of Standards and Appeals had found it "undemocratic" and "fascistic."

The newspaper story also identified the following invitees: Harry W. Jung, organizer of the American Vigilant Intelligence Federation of Chicago; Kern Dodge of Philadelphia, former America First leader and currently active in Allen Zoll's National Council for American Education; Samuel B. Pettengill, who, in the early forties worked with America First; Charles S. Payson who helped finance the isolationist *Scribner's Commentator* in its last years of existence and John B. Trevor, head of the American Coalition of Patriotic Societies.

The "June" meeting of Hart's top clique was finally held at the University Club on October 4 and 5. Again Hart and his group tried their utmost to keep it a secret, but again Winchell—this time in his column of October 24—reported the story. Eighteen "big names" were present, he said. The list included: William Buckley of Pantepec Oil (Caracas, Venezuela); George Montgomery of Coudert Brothers (a Wall Street law firm); E. A. Kracke, accountant; former Senator Hawkes of New Jersey; John T. Flynn and others.

Early this year, Hart announced the formation of a speakers' bureau. His first "lecturer" was one Cecil Palmer, an obscure, ex-publisher who is unpopular even with British conservatives because he is a rabid and impossible reactionary. He arrived from England in February 1949 to attack the British government before American audiences. Palmer, whom Hart publicized as an expert economist, rapidly developed into a first class speaker who provided his lecture audience with dramatic, and often implausible, statistics about "what socialism is doing to British freedom."

Palmer's speaking tour proved an unexpected success, both from his and Hart's points of view. Palmer received $100 a week, living and traveling expenses, plus one-half of the "gate receipts" from his lectures. Hart got the remaining 50 per cent of the receipts—a welcome windfall. In addition, Hart found that the distinguished-looking Britisher's lectures dovetailed nicely with the NEC's campaign against the so-called Welfare State.

Palmer's lecture tour got off to an auspicious start in February.

Hart had arranged for Palmer to speak before a large dinner meeting in Washington, D. C., at which many congressmen were present. The high point of Palmer's Washington visit was his conference with President Truman—engineered by Hart's admirer, former New Jersey Republican senator, Albert Hawkes.

The Truman-Palmer meeting caused Robert S. Allen, broadcasting from Washington, D. C., on July 3, 1949, to speculate as to "just how Hawkes and Palmer got in to see the President." In an effort to "throw some light on this mystery," Allen read over the air a letter that Merwin K. Hart wrote to an associate in Washington:

> Palmer is coming to this country not as just one more British lecturer to tell America how much the British and Americans have in common. Palmer will devote himself to telling what a miserable failure Socialism is in Britain. That will be a very wholesome thing for the people of the United States to hear when Truman is pushing his Socialistic schemes very far—very hard.

Palmer's itinerary took him from Washington, D. C., to the West coast where he spoke before chambers of commerce, merchants' and manufacturers' associations, advertising and political clubs and a few special, smaller, "intimate" groups.

Palmer returned to England in July 1949 and came back to the United States in the middle of October for the second leg of his National Economic Council lecture tour. Hart arranged for a ten-dollar-a-plate dinner in his honor at New York City's Waldorf-Astoria Hotel. A strange aggregation of guests assembled on October 26 to applaud Hart's star performer. Big business was represented by J. Howard Pew and Lammot du Pont. Representative Ralph W. Gwinn of New York, Senator James P. Kem and ex-Senator Albert W. Hawkes were also on hand. *Reader's Digest* publisher DeWitt Wallace, a supporter of Hart, was unable to attend, but sent apologies and several lesser lights of his editorial staff. Rubbing shoulders with Hart's distinguished guests were such characters as Allen Zoll; the notorious Benjamin Freedman; Conde McGinley, publisher of the violently anti-Semitic *Common Sense*, and the convicted Joseph Kamp.

Palmer's December 1949 tour gave indications of being even more successful than his first. On December 6 he was a featured speaker at the National Association of Manufacturers' convention at the Waldorf-Astoria. Palmer was scheduled to talk for twenty minutes; instead, he spoke for over forty minutes. His anti-socialism speech—by now polished to a high sheen—drew a standing ovation.

At this writing, there are plans for Palmer to speak at a luncheon meeting of *Reader's Digest* officials and at a Washington, D. C., gathering of the National Association of Real Estate Boards.

Merwin Hart rang the bell, indeed, with his Palmer find.

In the middle of 1949, Yusif el Bandak, an Arab, arrived in the United States and called on Hart at the suggestion of Sir Frederick Morgan, a retired British Lieutenant-General. (In January 1946 General Morgan was ousted as UNRRA chief in Germany after a public indulgence in anti-Semitism.) Before the end of the year Hart was infected with the Arab's special anti-Israeli ideology. (Bandak's background is of some interest: In the middle 1930s, he propounded the Grand Mufti's political philosophy as publisher and editor of *Saud el Chaab*. In 1948 Bandak moved from Bethlehem to Cairo, where he renewed his association with Hitler's former Arab ally. Strangely enough, for a time during World War II, the man worked for the British as an Arabic translator.)

Two *Economic Council Letters* contained the evidence that its director had swallowed Bandak's "line." In the December 1, 1949, issue, Hart presented his readers with Bandak's "inside story" of alleged Zionist attacks in Palestine. He quoted Bandak as warning: "If this community fails, Christianity will be blotted out in the Holy Land."

To this Hart offered an anti-Semitic postscript of his own:

Meanwhile the United Jewish Appeal, which has financed much of the Zionist invasion, announces it will seek 250 millions in the United States in 1950. There is little doubt some of this would be used to help wipe out what remains of Christianity in Palestine.

American Christians, who are solicited to contribute, may well remember this.

Let them remember, too, that many prominent Communists and communist sympathizers, are also Zionists.

In the last months of 1949 Hart devised another of his endless little schemes to ensure a continuing income while catering to some of his wealthier followers. He ordered the columns of the *Daily Worker* checked closely for items supporting pending bills in Congress, in order to reprint these "kisses-of-death" on leaflets bearing the names of congressmen and other government officials who support such bills. His calculated intention was to associate such officials with communism—and to use the device for his own fund-raising purposes. He even planned an appeal to monied supporters to finance this 1950 project.

The year 1949 was good to Merwin Hart. His organization received munificent contributions to carry on its "patriotic" work; he lived well and traveled abroad. There came into his orbit, by force of his salesmanship and subtlety, important men and little ones. He seemed to have exerted influence over at least one great public figure, upon the owner of one of the world's largest publishing enterprises and upon other prominent men.

Despite his proximity to internationally renowned personalities, Hart continues to disseminate his mean, narrow, bigoted and ultra-chauvinistic propaganda. How he keeps his dirty secret from them —if he does—is difficult to understand. But until they know of it, and abandon him for what he is, Merwin Hart will continue to be one of the nation's key bigots.

A. ALDERSON ZOLL: In November 1949 a new periodical calling itself *American Intelligence Agency* appeared in New York City. Quite in character with its cloak-and-dagger name was the cryptic headline it bore: REPORT K-1-9.

Report K-1-9 purported to tell the "inside story" of the Lehman-Dulles senatorial campaign which had just come to a close with a victory for Mr. Lehman. In character, too, was the fact that the publication did not indicate ownership, management or editorship, but its contents, nevertheless, were most revealing. It emphasized the role allegedly played in the New York election by the "Jewish population." It charged that Jews "almost without exception" voted for Lehman.

Allen Zoll, after two years of trying, was back on the old pretentious scale at 1 Maiden Lane in Manhattan—back after an ignominious withdrawal from the public scene in 1942.

Zoll was a fascist propagandist and supporter of Father Coughlin. Coughlin's New York radio outlet, Station WMCA, had dropped the priest's broadcasts because he refused to submit copy of his script in advance. In reprisal, his followers threw a picket line around the station. After months of picketing, Christian Front insiders sensed defeat and knew that their demoralized followers would soon abandon their daily protest march. At this point Zoll allegedly went to Donald Flamm, owner of the radio station, and offered to withdraw the pickets for $7,500. Flamm went to the police and Zoll was indicted for attempted extortion.

In the ensuing months, while the publicity over the indictment (later nolle prossed) was spending itself, Zoll quietly retired from propaganda work.

Now he is back, and his record in 1948 and 1949 has been such that he fits naturally into this account of the activities of native, professional, nationalist propagandists. For during the past twenty-four months Allen Zoll has privately worked with them all—Gerald Smith, Joe Kamp, Upton Close and Merwin Hart.

Zoll sought to boost his income by hiring himself out, separately, to three of these professional anti-Semites as salesman, public relations counselor, and promotion adviser. On December 15, 1947, Zoll entered into a signed agreement with Merwin Hart to "solicit persons whose names we are handing you" for a period of thirty days at a 10 per cent commission.

On January 6, 1948, the two men signed a new memorandum continuing the arrangement with some slight modifications. Agreeing to reimburse him for "reasonable incidental expenses" for a trip to Philadelphia, Hart assigned Zoll to visit J. Howard Pew. The National Economic Council official also agreed to pay Zoll a bonus of 20 per cent "on any subscriptions from persons known to you and not known to us." To insure against any slip up or dispute, Zoll agreed that he would not call on anyone whom Hart did not in advance "authorize" as a prospective contributor.

Despite the care the two men exercised in reducing each term of their agreement to writing, Zoll found it necessary to remind Hart of several things when in September 1948 they decided to part company. Zoll did it by way of a memorandum in which he recapitulated what had occurred. He reminded Hart that the latter had "more than broke even on the money that I got in"; that the National Economic Council had gotten off to a good start in Boston with "some very influential people" only because of Zoll's help; that he had done the same thing for Hart in Detroit among important people "most of whom had never even heard of the Council." Always the fund-raising expert, Zoll argued that these contacts "properly followed up by mail and personal solicitation" would result in substantial contributions. He explained that some of these people should have been "called on a second and third time as it is necessary to gain their confidence. . . ." Pointing out that he had never had an opportunity to make more than a second call on most of the people, he advised Hart that it gave "an air of stability" to have the same solicitor calling on the same people at all times.

Despite the agreement to part, Zoll was apparently not anxious to break completely with Hart. He concluded his memorandum with the hope that the two would "never throw bricks one at the other or damn with faint praise."

The men continued as friends. By February 1949 Zoll was again recommending Hart as a public speaker, describing him as "an outstanding American."

While Zoll had been soliciting for Merwin Hart, he was also helping to raise funds—again, on a commission basis—for Joe Kamp's Constitutional Educational League. However, somewhere during 1948 this relationship, too, came to an end. Constant haggling over ownership of contributor lists did it.

It was about this time that Zoll began planning his own new agency. He announced it in July. The organization would be called the "National Council for American Education." Its purpose was "to eradicate from our schools Marxism, Socialism, Communism, and all other forces that seek to destroy the liberty of the American people."

Zoll still had no regular office, but he succeeded nevertheless in getting his new "educational" agency off to an impressive start. He managed to persuade a number of responsible Americans to endorse his venture, including such prominent persons as General Jonathan M. Wainwright, Senators McKellar and Vandenberg and Representatives Mundt, A. L. Miller of Nebraska, and Stanley High, a *Reader's Digest* editor.

Other members of Zoll's new advisory committee were cut from a different cloth: General George Van Horn Moseley, Verne P. Kaub, Midwest propagandist and Christian Fronter Reverend Edward Lodge Curran. Zoll, in an apparent effort at anonymity, listed himself among the trustees as "A. Alderson Zoll."

The venture was struck a body blow on August 25, 1948. The New York *World-Telegram* published a detailed report of Zoll's activities. The newspaper revealed that the promoter ten years before had been labeled a "very strong anti-Semite" by a U. S. representative; that in 1939 he had publicly opposed the appointment of Felix Frankfurter to the Supreme Court because the latter was Jewish; that in 1939 he had been indicted for attempted extortion.

Most of the propagandist's reputable sponsors promptly resigned. Withdrawals were announced by General Wainwright, Senators Vandenberg and Mundt, Congressman Miller and Stanley High. Senator Kenneth McKellar decided to remain in the organization.

The National Council for American Education did not go out of existence. Zoll managed to promote considerable sums of money despite the Scripps-Howard exposé. In the early months of 1949 he initiated a monthly newsletter, *The Educational Guardian,* and published a series of dossiers "exposing" alleged Communist influence at three large American universities—Yale, Harvard and Chicago. For this pamphlet he obtained the collaborative and research assistance of J. B. Matthews, former research director of the Dies Committee.

The controversy over federal aid to education provided Zoll's Council with material for endless propaganda. In the spring of 1949, the propagandist wrote *They Want Your Child!* a twenty-three-page booklet which attempted to discredit, as Communist inspired, the federal aid to education bill. In it he said that Communist domination of our educational system was the brainchild of "powers that have worked in darkness [who] . . . plan to control education . . . for the destruction of our Republican liberties [as] AN ESSENTIAL INGREDIENT OF THE MASTER PLAN." *They Want Your Child!* was Zoll's most successful publication venture in 1949. At this writing it is in its fourth printing, and its circulation is said to have approached 80,000 copies.

To support himself while building the organization, Zoll continued to hire himself out to fellow propagandists. In the summer of 1949 he closed a deal with Upton Close, who, the reader will recall, was in desperate need of funds at the time. Close engaged Zoll as a public-relations counselor for a specific fund-raising campaign.

The joint venture was brief but successful, resulting in a "take" which was reported to have exceeded $30,000. Zoll received his agreed-upon commission. From this arrangement, there grew an organizational working relationship between the two men. The new Zoll publication, *Educational Guardian* was inserted in Upton Close mailings of his monthly bulletin, *Closer-Ups.* In turn, Zoll gave favorable mention to Close in his own general mailings.

Another Zoll project in the summer of 1949 was a behind-the-scenes propaganda venture with Verne P. Kaub. In the early forties, Kaub, who lives in Madison, Wisconsin, was active in the outrageously un-American Chicago organization, Citizens U.S.A. Committee. In 1943 he was Western representative for Joe Kamp's Constitutional Educational League. He was a frequent contributor to the bitterly anti-Jewish hate sheet, *The Individualist.* Zoll hired

Kaub to work on an hourly basis; the July 15 issue of *Educational Guardian* listed Kaub as vice-president in Charge of Research of the National Council for American Education.

One result of the Kaub-Zoll alliance was the appearance in the fall of 1949 of a pamphlet entitled, *How Red Is the Federal Council of Churches?* published by the American Council of Christian Laymen at Madison, Wisconsin. Inquiry at Madison revealed that Kaub was the guiding hand behind the American Council and that orders for the pamphlet were automatically relayed from that city to Zoll's New York office. The author of the pamphlet in question is anonymous. Actually, it was compiled by Zoll—again with the assistance of his "research associate," J. B. Matthews.

At this writing, *How Red Is the Federal Council of Churches?* is in its third printing. Thirty thousand copies have been distributed, and further printings are planned. Gerald Smith's Christian Nationalist Party has begun a campaign to achieve mass distribution of the Zoll booklet.

In the closing months of 1949 Zoll frequented the offices of Khalil Totah, executive director of the Institute of Arab-American Affairs. Totah, a prolific letter-to-the-editor writer, is also an expert platform orator who consistently attempted to discredit Jewish aspirations during the 1948 Arab-Jewish conflict in the Holy Land. On May 29, 1949, Totah, speaking over station WICC, Bridgeport, Connecticut, observed: "If American Jews don't feel at home in America, their dual allegiance would, by logic, require all the Jews in America and Europe to go to Palestine." There may be a connection between Zoll's visits and Totah's recent attempt to raise additional, much-needed funds for the Institute's propaganda activities.

Recently Zoll revived a fund-raising technique which he used effectively a decade ago to promote his now defunct American Patriots, listed as subversive by the U. S. Attorney General. In those days the propagandist sponsored a series of luncheon meetings at which known anti-Semites participated in the presentation of "patriotic" discussions.

In the years since then, Zoll has become more cautious. Anti-Semitism is no longer a part of his luncheon meeting technique. He still concentrates on middle-aged, wealthy women who are potential contributors to his various patriotic projects—but now he remains properly vague.

In a short space of time, Allen Zoll has successfully re-established himself on the propaganda scene. For the first time in many years, he is again prosperous. His National Council for American Education is expanding its activities. His pamphlets have been receiving widespread distribution. The smooth-talking promoter is again on intimate terms with a wide circle of professional patrons of "patriotism" with whom he is working both in the open and behind the scenes.

Gerald Smith, Joseph Kamp, Upton Close, Merwin Hart, Allen Zoll—each operates in his own orbit, yet all are inextricably bound together in parallel drives for a way of life grounded in narrow bigotry and bounded by a malevolent nationalism. Undoubtedly, each is aware that he is helping to mold the thought and the action of a neurotic group of anti-democratic followers. These leaders who feed the fires of religious and racial hatred—while reaping large sums of money—are ever weakening the democratic fabric. Together, they must bear a full share of responsibility for the evil committed in the name of organized prejudice.

Chapter 4. Organized for Hatred

ORGANIZED anti-Semitism is any planned activity deliberately designed to undermine the security and welfare of the Jewish community. It is the subtle propaganda of a polished Merwin K. Hart and, again, the hysterical rantings of twisted Agnes Waters. It is the "white supremacy" of brute Klan groups and the distorted theology preached by hypocrite "Reverends." Organized anti-Semitism forms the backbone of Gerald Smith's blustering bigotry. It propels the street corner claptrap of petty fuehrers such as Yorkville's rowdy Kurt Mertig. It displays its venom in the torrent of anti-Jewish publications which circulate throughout the nation.

Money is the mainspring of organized anti-Semitism. More than any other single factor, financial support, or lack of it, determines the destiny of a professional bigot. As detailed in preceding chapters, a handful of promoters who make Jew-hating a business enjoyed a comfortable affluence in 1949. Gerald Smith, for one, high-pressured $150,000 from his supporters. Merwin K. Hart increased his income by 15 per cent over the preceding year, his "take" at least $140,000. Gerald Winrod, the Fundamentalist from Wichita, Kansas, garnered a gross income of better than $100,000. Upton Close earned $50,000 —twice his 1948 earnings—and Joseph Kamp's Constitutional Educational League did as well. Allen Zoll, back in business after an inactive 1948, raised $40,000, a sum matched by Wesley Swift, the "Anglo-Saxon" preacher of Los Angeles.

But for the bulk of the hate merchants, the pickings were slim, a fact which explains the disappearance during 1949 of at least thirty-five once-active groups.

In 1949, fifty-seven organizations, twenty-three of them newcomers or reactivated groups, were engaged in spreading anti-Semitism in the United States. Nine other outfits, while not directly involved in anti-Semitic activity, were controlled by known anti-Semites and therefore suspect. Geographic breakdown of the sixty-six: Northeast, 18; Midwest, 24; South, 16; Far West, 8. They used an assortment of façades in search of respectability: thirty-six disguised themselves as politico-economic groups; sixteen others used religion as a front; two posed as educational organizations. But twelve boldly publicized themselves as out-and-out racist groups. All are described fully in the Appendix, Chart I, page 222.

There were fewer organized anti-Semitic meetings in 1949 and, except for the West Coast, public attendance at these sessions was poor. The distribution of anti-Semitic publications, always a significant index, likewise showed a slight diminution. Circulation of regularly published periodicals remained fairly constant, but there were fewer miscellaneous books and pamphlets.

During the past decade, the number of organizations has fluctuated considerably as is evident from the ten-year chart reproduced below. From 1940 to 1943 the total remained fairly constant—60 to 75 each year. Beginning with 1944, however, there was a sharp increase, and by 1946 the total had reached 130—more than double the 1940 count. Then the tide began to recede. In 1947 the total had shrunk to 115, by 1948 it was down to prewar level.

Anti-Semitic Organizations in the United States, 1940 to 1949[1]

	"RELIGIOUS"	"POLITICO-ECONOMIC"	"EDUCATIONAL"	RACIST	TOTAL
1949	16	36	2	12	66
1948	15	46	5	12	78
1947	15	73	1	26	115
1946	11	95	0	24	130
1945	10	89	0	13	112
1944	10	66	0	15	91
1943	8	57	0	8	73
1942	8	54	0	7	69
1941	6	61	0	6	73
1940	6	45	1	8	60

The total of 73 anti-Semitic organizations for the year 1941, varies from the 121 organizations reported for the same year in the Anti-Defamation League's Survey published last year. The figure of 121 was based upon the estimate of Donald Strong, published in his book, *Organized Anti-Semitism in America* (1941, American Council on Public Affairs). Strong's total included all organized hate groups, both active and moribund. The current figure of 73 hate groups for the year 1941 excludes some 48 then inactive anti-Semitic organizations.

The total of 78 anti-Semitic organizations listed for 1948 is not inconsistent with the figure of 45 organizations listed for 1948 in last year's survey. The 78 figure reported in the comparison includes organizations which were of concern because of their anti-Semitic leadership. These were not included in the total of 45. In addition, the Klan groups are listed separately in the total of 78. In last year's computation they were counted as one. Finally, there are some individual anti-Semites who are listed as "organizations" after re-evaluation of their full-time activity; they were not so designated in last year's total.

The ranks of professional anti-Semites include a handful of dissident preachers whose religion is dosed with a heavy mixture of prejudice. Gerald Winrod, the glib, gray-haired minister from Wichita, is the most successful operator in this branch of the trade, if one is to judge by his $100,000 income for 1949. (He got an $8,000 rebate last year on his 1946 income tax payments.) Winrod owns considerable property, including a $50,000 printing plant, and for years he has maintained a smooth-functioning organization. One of his important assets is a 100,000-name mailing list; it supports his two sanctimonious publications, *The Defender Magazine* and *The Prayer Circle Letter,* as well as thousands of "less spiritual" pieces supplied him by Joe Kamp, Lawrence Reilly, Robert Williams and other propagandists.

1949 was also a profitable year for Wesley Swift, the smooth-talking missionary for the "Anglo-Saxon" brand of theology. The Reverend Mr. Swift contends that Anglo-Saxons are the true descendents of the Ten Lost Tribes of Israel and, therefore, entitled to be known as Israelites; the Jews, he says, are "impostors." This nonsense was worth $40,000 through such West Coast outfits as the Great Pyramid Club, the Anglo-Saxon Christian Congregation and the Anglo-American Bible Study Group, all of them served by Swift as spiritual and financial leader. His meetings were well attended. He is also active as a publisher—he purchased $6,000 worth of printing equipment during the year—and in addition to publishing his own fantastic sermons, Swift was responsible for running off 10,000 copies of Myron Fagan's *Moscow Over Hollywood.*

The Anglo-Saxon line is also evangelized by organizations in Chicago, Portland, Oregon, and other cities. They maintain a loose affiliation based on ideological ties, but operate independently in such pertinent matters as leadership and finances. (Swift denied that his congregation was part of it.) Headquarters for the movement is maintained in Haverhill, Massachusetts, by Howard B. Rand. His Anglo-Saxon Federation, which has intensified its anti-Semitic program, publishes *Destiny Magazine,* house organ for all "new-born Israelites."

Dean of the Dayton (Ohio) Theological Seminary is Millard Flenner, for many years an outspoken anti-Semite. Flenner staffed his faculty with "Anglo-Saxon" theologists, sent his students, many of whom were enrolled in the seminary under G.I. educational benefits, to different meetings in all parts of the country. They were particularly prominent at one of Wesley Swift's sessions.

William Blessing of Denver, C. O. Stadsklev of Minneapolis, and Lawrence Reilly of Detroit also are prominent among preachers of anti-Semitic gospel. And in Minneapolis, the father-and-son team of Paul and Luke Rader, having delivered prayerful sermons to their congregation on Sundays, spend the rest of the week penning bigoted messages for their church bulletin.

Mordecai F. Ham, a Louisville revivalist and proselytizer, preaches the anti-Semitic word in the pulpit, through *The Old Kentucky Home Revivalist* and over a 32-station radio network. For his April 17, 1949, radio sermon Preacher Ham included the reference, "not all Jews are Israelites, many are still Jacobs. Jacob was the name of the trickster bargain-driver, the trafficker." Such interpretations are not uncommon for Ham, whose anti-Semitism is recorded since 1924, and they have earned the enthusiastic endorsement of brother bigot Gerald Winrod. However, there are many ministers who decry the un-Christian diatribes of the radio preacher. At this writing the Federal Communications Commission has under advisement a petition aimed at preventing Ham from abusing radio facilities "by stirring up religious hatred of citizens and residents of the United States."

In addition to gospel preachers of anti-Semitism, there are the laymen, wealthy Americans, not directly affiliated with any particular organization, but responsive to the financial needs of the organized hate movement. Their dollars, and often their names, are contributed to the criss-crossing web of anti-Semitic activity. Typical is Benjamin Harrison Freedman, an apostate Jew, who until 1948 headed the League for Peace with Justice in Palestine, a pro-Arab propaganda machine. Freedman was also a supporter of the Institute of Arab-American Affairs and Conde McGinley's anti-Semitic *Common Sense*. During 1949, he busied himself co-operating with Merwin Hart in the preparation of anti-Jewish propaganda.

Another wealthy supporter of organized bigotry is Robert Donner, a retired Colorado steel tycoon. Donner, who has circulated such anti-Semitic diatribes as the Benjamin Franklin forgery and the Close-Williams libel[1] of ADL, contributed funds in 1949 to Joe Kamp, Fred Kister, former Gerald Smith lieutenant, and others. He also supported Allen Zoll's National Council for American Education and worked with Hart and the violent Jew-hater, Agnes Waters.

Only a handful of the several score anti-Semitic organizations have an effective influence among wide audiences; most of the others guide only local followers. In Chicago, the German-American Citizens League, a Bund-like outfit, was one of the few German nationalist groups active in 1949. Arthur Koegel, a former Bundist, now serves as editor of the League's German language weekly, *Deutsch-Amerikanische Buergerzeitung*, which consistently inveighs against Jews.

On the West Coast, Myron Fagan, a self-styled anti-Communist crusader, operates his Cinema Educational Guild. Fagan, born a Jew, does not resort to public defamation of Jews, but has been identified with Gerald Smith and other professional anti-Semites. Smith has urged support of the Cinema Educational Guild and his Patriotic Tract Society distributes Fagan's ostensibly anti-Communist leaflets.

There was also a concerted drive in 1949 to rally sentiment for the release from prison of William Dudley Pelley, founder of the defunct Silver Shirts, an anti-Semitic movement that was organized along fascist lines in the early thirties. Pelley was jailed in 1942 for sedition. Purpose of the Justice for Pelley Committee, led by Melford Pearson, Pelley's son-in-law, was to exert political pressure for a pardon. In February 1950 Pelley was paroled from Federal prison after serving approximately seven years of his fifteen-year sentence.

Many of the less talented professional anti-Semites find it difficult to compete with the Smiths, Winrods, and Kamps for bigotry's dollars. Lack of finances forced Mrs. Jessie Welch Jenkins of Columbus, Georgia, and her National Patrick Henry Organization to remain inactive. Conde McGinley found it difficult to publish his *Common Sense* except when he could collect enough money for printing costs. Elizabeth Dilling's Patriotic Research Bureau suspended its publishing activities, ostensibly because she was "writing a book." Stephen Nenoff's *American Commentator*, which got a big send-off in 1948 as a national weekly newspaper, struggled through five issues for the whole of 1949. And Charles Hudson's *America in Danger* didn't get to press once during the year.

Isolated incidents of anti-Semitic hoodlumism reported to ADL offices during 1949 were fewer than in previous years. The decline in assaults upon individuals, desecrations of houses of worship and cemeteries, and vandalism on homes and shops corresponded with the decline in organized anti-Semitism.

Some incidents, though ugly and malicious, received no publicity —such as the tragedy of a little boy in Boston who twice was viciously beaten because he is Jewish. His was the only Jewish family residing in a city housing project, living there in terror and under constant threat of bodily harm. The family was forced to move to another neighborhood.

On the other hand, the outrageous assault in November 1949 on eleven-year-old Laurence Goldstein of Lynn, Massachusetts, won national attention. The son of a soldier killed in action while on a voluntary mission in the Battle of the Bulge, young Laurence was beaten by anti-Semitic hoodlums as he made his way home from a boy scout meeting.

Public condemnation of the assault revealed more accurately the temper of the American people than did the original attack on the boy. Among the numerous statements from political and civic leaders were these cogent words by former UN mediator Ralph Bunche:

. . . Our society suffers from the malignant social disease of prejudice, with its attendant exclusions and rejections. Our educational process has barely begun to meet this ominous threat to our national unity, if not, indeed, to our very existence and survival as a free democratic nation. I say in deep earnestness that I do not believe that our schools, from kindergarten to graduate level, are even mildly discharging their social responsibility in this regard. Through effective inter-group education, we in this great nation can have the means of building a fully matured democracy so strong in the hearts and minds of the people that it will be forever invulnerable.

There were forty-nine anti-Semitic periodicals which repeatedly appeared in 1949. These were supplemented by pamphlets, leaflets and books. (See Appendix, Charts II and III, pages 230 and 234.) The format of the nation's hate press varied from crudely mimeographed "throwaways" to expensively printed magazines. The styles of writing are equally diversified, running the gamut from the extreme illiteracy and vulgarity of Court Asher's *X-Ray* to the polished prose of Merwin Hart's *Economic Council Letter*. Whatever the format and style, the impact of each piece is the same—to defame and malign Jews.

The basic anti-Jewish themes embraced by the hate press are monotonously repetitious. Much dirty ink is spilled attempting to "expose" an international Jewish "conspiracy to gain control of the world." A consistent proponent of this line is the bellicose Gerald Smith who, in the June 1949 issue of *The Cross and the Flag*, told his readers: "The Jews have organized on an international basis, as well as a national basis a campaign for world power."

Equating communism with Judaism is still a favorite device

of anti-Semitic editors. Typical of those who spread the lie that the Russian Revolution was led and financed by Jews, and that Jews today constitute the majority of the Communist Party, is ex-Army officer Robert H. Williams. He wrote in his *Williams Intelligence Summary* (December 1949):

We see . . . the combination of Marxist, Jewish banker and Zionist working together like the blood brothers that they are. It was Mr. Jacob Schiff and the Warburgs of Kuhn, Loeb and Co. who financed Lenin and Trotsky and who helped arrange for their passage through Germany (then at war with the liberal Kerensky government) and into Russia so that they might set up Bolshevik power. . . .

Williams' sentiments were paraphrased in true Goebbels' style by the May 26 issue of *Women's Voice,* official publication of the Chicago chapter of We the Mothers Mobilize for America, Inc.:

If you will study the Protocols and the Communist platform, you will, if you have an open mind, find that they are one and the same. Communism is the front for Judaism.

The subject of aid to European countries is also used to attack Jews. Among those who see a sinister "plot" behind the Economic Cooperation Administration is Conde McGinley. To quote from the August 15 issue of *Common Sense:*

Paul Hoffman, President of Studebaker Corp. and head of the Marshall Plan (E.C.A.), is travelling over Europe, giving orders as to how governments must be run if they are to receive American taxpayers' money. Lehman Brothers Corp. controls the Studebaker Corp. and one of the Lehmans is Vice-President. Hence, we see that Zionists behind a machine of international bankers have taken over Europe after our military forces and taxpayers' money rendered it helpless. . . .
It is also interesting to know that the Marshall Plan was written by a Zionist born in Russia, Lewis LEVITSKI (LEVINE). . . .

There is also a steady growth of pro-German sentiment in the super-patriotic press. "American people must defeat the Morgenthauists," warned McGinley in the February 1, 1949, issue of *Common Sense.* "They must so overwhelm Acheson with demands that the dismantling will be stopped, that the whole group of Morgenthauists cannot bribe or brow-beat him into continuing them. . . ."

Merwin Hart, too, sheds sympathetic tears for dismantled Germany. "I have noted the effect on German minds of Nuremberg and Dachau trials and the other persecutions," he wrote in his *Economic Council Letter* of September 15, ". . . all apparently the work of a group of Americans and 'adopted Americans' steeped in their narrow racism. . . ."

Israel and Zionism continue to be favorite subjects in the press of the professional anti-Semites. Seldom is an opportunity missed to link communism with Zionism and Israel to Russia; to allege that Zionism is an "international plot" for world control, or to question the "loyalty" of American Jews to the United States. Gerald Smith, writing in *The Cross and the Flag,* charged:

> The powerful Jewish cabal, if it has its way directed and controlled by Zionists, will enforce a policy in Washington to read: "England must submit to the Palestine Jews or be broken and bankrupted by Washington and New York financial manipulators."

Destiny, the official publication of the Anglo-Saxon Federation, which frequently attacks Jews as part of its pseudo-religious program, posed this rhetorical question in its February 1949 issue:

> If unbelieving Palestinian Jews are to have no part in the kingdom, on what grounds can Christ-hating, Zionist pseudo-Jews lay claim to Jerusalem? . . .

The creation of the United Nations and the participation in it by the United States also calls forth a steady stream of anti-Semitic invective from various anti-Jewish publicists. Lyrl Clark Van Hyning, in the February 24, 1949 issue of her *Women's Voice* charged:

> The U.N. Charter was written by a Jew and is the successor of The League of Nations, which was written by the Grand Orient of France. A persistent question of mine, since I know that Free-masonry is Judaism, is, *how* could the Catholics sponsor U.N.? (Leaving out the fact that God has never been named in any U.N. meeting.)

Another favorite target of the "hate pamphleteers" is civil rights legislation. They denounce the civil rights program as a scheme imported from Moscow and/or a plan blueprinted by Jews. *Moscow's Master Plan,* by Lawrence Reilly, an expensively printed booklet and widely distributed, goes to great lengths to "document" this false charge. Gerald Smith's "explanation" of the national civil rights campaign, charged that the proposed legislation is a "plot of the mongrelizers." He warned his readers that "a highly-financed campaign promoted by Jewish extremists, left-wing politicians and demagogues, is now in force which if successful, would mix the black with the white and mongrelize the American race."

In addition to propounding their stock libels, all of the professional hate publishers make it a practice to defame respectable and responsible Jewish organizations engaged in combating totalitarian and un-American influences and in promoting American democracy. More often than not, the intensity with which such attacks are leveled is an accurate gauge of the effectiveness of the civil rights organizations singled out for abuse.

Not all of the hate publications openly attack Jews. Some periodicals, listed in Chart II, are identified because of the known prejudices of their editors and because many of them have long histories of expressed hostility toward Jews. Some campaign against other minority groups.

No survey of hate literature is complete without reference to such hackneyed stand-bys as the forged *Protocols of the Learned Elders of Zion* and the bogus *Benjamin Franklin Prophecy* which are still circulated by anti-Semites. These are the classics of the trade, although their dissemination, together with all other anti-Semitic material of this type, had little impact or influence on public opinion in 1949.

Chapter 5. Slightly Poisoned

A CAREFUL LOOK at ordinary life in America reveals little evidence of deliberate anti-Semitism in responsible quarters. But on occasion community tensions and controversial public issues bring latent hatreds to the surface, producing biased comment in a newspaper editorial, a syndicated column, a radio program, a sermon or a statement on the floor of Congress.

Public issues which touch on fundamental fears are most likely to draw forth expressions of racial and religious bias from men who might otherwise be most guarded in their public utterances. The threat of communism, for example, arouses such deep-seated fears. So do the new relationships with Israel, the efforts to liberalize DP immigration, and the demands for new and stronger civil rights legislation.

These are some of the controversial problems which afford men in responsible positions the opportunity to vent their bigotry in what they believe to be an acceptable framework. Opposition to communism can be used as a cloak for an attack upon Jews; anti-Semitic clauses can be incorporated into DP legislation under the camouflage of protecting jobs of American workingmen; racial and religious arguments can be employed in opposition to civil rights legislation under the pretext of protecting free enterprise.

This kind of anti-Semitism emanating from apparently respected sources has a far greater impact on the public mind than that which issues from a professional rabble-rouser. When it comes from a congressman, an industrialist, a radio commentator, or other comparable public figure, it may seriously influence the American people.

The "Peekskill incidents" and the November "Chicago riots" meaningfully reflected the tensions which existed in 1949. Large numbers of Americans were involved; police agencies were present during the occurrences; American opinion was divided as to whether the effect was good or bad.

In a Westchester picnic grove near Peekskill, about 35 miles north of New York City, a concert was scheduled for August 27 by a left-wing group. Paul Robeson, the Negro singer, was to be the star attraction on the Sunday summer afternoon.

The concert never took place. Local veterans organizations, knowing that the United States Attorney General had listed the sponsoring agency, the Civil Rights Congress, as subversive, organized protest parades. The veterans appeared at the picnic grounds at the time when the concert-goers were gathering; soon there was a bloody clash. Local police were apparently unable to prevent the disturbance—during which anti-Semitic and anti-Negro epithets were heard above the din.

On the following Sunday a second attempt was made by the same group to hold a Robeson concert. This time it scheduled the affair on the grounds of an old country club, four miles north of Peekskill.

Fifteen thousand people came in cars and chartered busses. Hundreds of police were detailed to keep order. Again protest parades were organized; again a riot occurred. Cars were overturned, rocks were thrown, bus windows were broken, and 145 persons were injured.

The anti-Semitic note which had been present in the first riot was even more evident this time. Busses were plastered with anti-Semitic stickers, hoodlums roaming the area attacked groups they came upon, shouting anti-Semitic imprecations. In the aftermath, local Jewish residents who had no part in the affair were the targets for anti-Jewish vilification and whispering campaigns.

Reaction to both riots was mixed. Some believed that the attempts to prevent the concerts were a healthy sign of Americanism; others believed the "protests" to be a menace to democracy. The Anti-Defamation League recognized in these incidents an invasion of civil liberties destructive of the democratic fabric.

Two months after the Peekskill occurrences, a four-day racial and religious riot shook the city of Chicago. A meeting of eighteen people, including a number of Negroes in the South Side home of Aaron Bindman, a Jew, was the spark that touched off this mob demonstration. The tinder for the fire was the false rumor that the Jewish home owner was negotiating the sale of his property to a Negro.

On the first night of the incident some fifty people congregated in front of the Bindman house to object vociferously to the Negro "invasion" of the all-white neighborhood. The second night the situation was worse. By evening a crowd of some 200 people were milling around the trouble area; stones flew and anti-Semitic cries were heard.

On the third night approximately 400 people congregated in the vicinity of the Bindman property and there was more trouble. The next night the crowd had swelled to 2,000. Tempers ran high. Anti-Jewish, anti-Negro and anti-Communist epithets came from all sides—"lynch them" . . . "drive them out!" As the evening wore on, the crowd's threats became predominantly anti-Semitic. Fist fights broke out on all sides. Anyone who looked like a "stranger" or "appeared Jewish" was beaten.

The essential factors involved in Peekskill were present in the Chicago riots; Jews and Negroes were scapegoated and lumped together with the controversial Communist issue.

Hoodlums on the streets of America are not the only ones who seek to equate Judaism and communism. The halls of Congress resound with similar efforts. Anti-Jewish attacks, however, have come from less than a handful of congressmen. And those who talked loudest surprised no one; for their records of hatred were long and well known.

The ineffable John Rankin of Mississippi is typical. Despite the presentation of documentary proof to the contrary, he persists in proclaiming that "atheistic communism is largely composed of a racial minority . . . more akin to Pharaoh than they are to Moses."

Rankin notwithstanding, there were fewer anti-Semitic remarks in Congress in 1949. By actual count in 1947-48 at least four representatives and one senator were recorded in frequent use of anti-Semitism; the first session of the Eighty-first Congress recorded only Rankin as a consistent bigot.

It is true that on occasion damaging anti-Semitic innuendo and ambiguity have crept into debates. Also, congressmen who express no open anti-Semitism on the floor of either house—in contrast to previous years—demonstrate on the lecture platform and in private conversations that their attitudes have not changed.

Representative Ed Gossett of Texas uses the displaced persons problem as the lever for his expression of anti-Jewish bias. In April, speaking before the Washington, D. C. Chapter of the American Association of University Women, the congressman attacked the admission of Jewish DPs into the United States. He said that such immigration was "an injection of virus into our bloodstream which is already becoming polluted." He singled out Russian Jews as being especially undesirable. Most of the Jews in DP camps are not those who have been persecuted, he charged, but are "Communistic Russian and Polish Jews," who, says Gossett, are planning to destroy the United States from within.

Gossett apparently understood the implications of his own remarks for he preceded them with:

Now there is a Jewish angle to this question, too. You can't discuss the Jewish angle without being called anti-Semitic. I don't care what I am called, I am going to give you the facts.

When Rep. Emanuel Celler of New York demanded Gossett meet him in a public debate on the charges, the Texas congressman denied that his speech had been anti-Semitic:

I did say that the proposed Displaced Persons Bill would reward the least deserving, least desirable and most dangerous groups among the many million people who would like to come to this country. I also said that the present bill does not discriminate against Jewish folks, as they have charged. If there has been any discrimination it has been by Jewish folks against others, because they have gotten the lion's share of immigration into this country.[1]

Rep. Gossett's prejudice extends even to such an issue as the Electoral College. Addressing the House Judiciary Committee, he said he favored a proposed constitutional amendment abolishing the College because it would reduce what he regarded as the undue political influence of minorities. Gossett made it clear that the minority groups whose influence he fears were the Negroes and "our fine Jewish citizens."

On June 15 the Texan told the delegates to the annual Rural Women's Short Course at Maryland University:

By and large the people in the displaced persons camps in Europe are the refuse of Europe. The camps are filled with bums, criminals, black marketeers, subversives, revolutionaries and crack-pots.

In connection with the same DP issue, Pat McCarran of Nevada, in much politer fashion on the Senate side, demonstrates his essential hostility toward Jews. McCarran was in a strategic position, as Chairman of the Judiciary Committee, to make his antipathy effective. By a series of maneuvers and outright obstructionism he prevented reform of the Displaced Persons Act which President Truman and others had branded as anti-Semitic. This act, which had become law in 1948, was the work of ex-Senator Chapman Revercomb and Senator McCarran. In 1949 he was leader of the group which plotted the handling of the DP bill in such a way as to keep displaced Jews out of the country.

Early in the hearings on a House-approved bill to amend the DP Act of 1948, he refused to permit any testimony concerning the plight of European Jews. Ironically, he agreed to schedule hearings on displaced Pakistanians, Arabs and Germans.

Senator McCarran's public statements are replete with careful cir-

cumlocutions to avoid anti-Semitic pitfalls. But these very circum-
locutions (ambiguous references to "certain groups" and "certain
organizations," innuendoes in his emphasis upon "mass migration
of certain select groups which would discriminate against others")
demonstrate his bias.

The federal legislative halls are the backdrop for other anti-
Semitic expressions. The fair employment practices issue provides
Representatives Rankin and Hoffman with an opportunity to show
their hostility to the Jewish people. In May, testifying before a
special sub-committee of the House Committee on Education and
Labor on a proposed fair employment practices bill, Hoffman said:

> There is no such thing as discrimination against the Jews. In this
> country, if I understand the situation clearly, the Jews have the world by
> the tail. They are on top. So I don't think it [FEPC] applies to them.

The issue over the creation and recognition of Israel was the basis
for greater expression of prejudice than any domestic issue, not only
in the houses of Congress, but from other high places in the nation.
In the House of Representatives, Rankin is in the forefront of the
anti-Israel forces. Despite generally favorable congressional sentiment toward the young nation, he uses Israel to further emphasize
his false communism-Judaism equation:

> This Palestine proposition has developed into a satellite state of Soviet
> Russia. I am not willing for the Congress of the United States to join in
> making war on Great Britain or aiding Russia by financing or feeding or
> supplying her satellite state."

In the fight over the internationalization of Jerusalem and the protection of holy places in Israel, some anti-Israeli groups indulged
in irresponsible propaganda and arguments which had an unfortunate secondary impact—anti-Semitism.

Some responsible Christian leadership, recognizing the harmful
effect, attempted to offset it by public statements. In early 1949 the
National Catholic Welfare Conference released a statement by the
Ministry of Religious Affairs of the Israeli Government:

"Despite the chaos of war, the overwhelming majority of religious
establishments have been safeguarded from destruction and interference due to the special precautions taken by the Israeli authorities." The Israeli Government rejected the "irresponsible charge
that the Government of Israel seeks to expropriate church property."

Msgr. Thomas J. McMahon, national secretary of the Catholic
Near East Welfare Association, after personal investigation of con-

ditions in Israel made public his letter to Trygve Lie, Secretary General of the United Nations. In it he declared that he could "testify to the genuine desire of the Government of Israel to repair the damage done and to maintain proper relations with the religious institutes within its boundaries."

In the summer, however, the allegation was revived that holy places were desecrated. It was accompanied by charges of mistreatment of Christians and Arabs. Vatican circles released a report charging the government of Israel with being inimical toward the Roman Catholic Church. The magazine *The Sign* was typical of Catholic publications in the United States, when it wrote:

The really big question and the mystery is: how does a minority group here in America manage to get all this consideration from Government policy-makers? . . . A great block of American foreign policy is being built around the whim of a minority.

Stemming from the Israeli problem, too, was a clash which was a source for anti-Semitism. A sector of the American public, encouraged by the anti-Zionist American Council for Judaism, alleged that the establishment of the State of Israel created for American Jews a choice between loyalty to the United States and their sympathy for Israel. This produced the base charge of divided allegiance which, repeated by some respected spiritual and intellectual leaders, created a harmful public opinion.

The statements ignored the fact that American Jewry is "America-centered"; and that while American Jews have a sympathetic heart for the success of the new state, their national allegiance to the United States is not impaired by one whit.

The unhealthy climate created by the deliberate and provocative anti-Israel propaganda manifests itself in strange ways. For example, the tragic death of James Forrestal was the occasion for a number of misleading and harmful remarks by radio commentators. In one broadcast from Washington, D.C., a commentator recalled that the former Secretary of Defense had possessed a "dynamic mentality that distinguishes leaders and thinkers from the mob on the sidewalk." He went on to say, "that mob on the sidewalk has hounded Jimmy to death. The demagogues, by typewriter and microphone, made themselves famous with the mob, but it was the mob that killed Jimmy, largely for his views which ran counter to strong interests connected with the Middle East and Israel."

The fact is that radio and television broadcasting in the United States is virtually free of religious prejudice. Rarely do radio stations knowingly permit the dissemination of anti-Semitism over their facilities.

But there is a small number of commentators and prominent radio personalities broadcasting over the networks who, through carelessness or failure to understand the full implications of their statements, sometimes have overstepped the bounds of good taste and propriety. The issue of German pianist Walter Gieseking's entry into the United States, the *Oliver Twist* motion picture controversy, and other similar civil liberties disputes, were among the public arguments that engendered thoughtless prejudicial comments.

Walter Gieseking, the internationally renowned pianist, was a collaborator of the Nazis and one of Adolf Hitler's most important cultural assets. At the end of the war he wanted to tour the American concert stage, but the United States Military Government in Germany blacklisted him. Gieseking did not surrender hope, and finally, in January 1949, entered the United States on a visitor's visa.

When the news broke that he was booked for a nation-wide tour a groundswell of protest quickly developed, resulting in picket parades and protest marches before his first scheduled appearance at Carnegie Hall in New York City. The United States Department of Justice, aware of the outraged public opinion, re-examined the evidence against Gieseking and ordered him held for further investigation. Gieseking turned on his heels and went back to Europe.

One newscaster who reported on the abortive Gieseking concert used improper innuendo: "On the basis of the screamings of a news columnist who shouts his views over the radio once a week plus the screams of pressure groups which seem more and more to influence our way of life, on such basis the Gieseking concert is called off."

Two days later he again referred to the incident and thanked his listeners who ". . . like this corner preferred the American way of handling such a case instead of heeding the hysterical howls of a columnist and a minority pressure group he appears to lead."

Two weeks later the same commentator took another misstep. Referring to the controversial selection of eighty Germans (by the American Military Government) to work in the United States on religious projects, in his February 5 broadcast he stated, ". . . which leads this corner to hope that Sunday's radio screamer will do his screaming now and not try to pull the plug on these German clergymen or have them picketed by minority groups two hours before they appear in their first pulpits."

The American press, older and wiser than radio, more experienced in recognizing racial and religious pitfalls, was even freer of prejudicial error than radio and television. Indeed, many important publications made notable contributions, as did radio, to the cause of better human relations.

Of course there are exceptions to the rule. A number of newspapers used the Walter Gieseking controversy to stir up bitterness. They gave the impression that the complex issue could be handily reduced to the formula of "Jews" against everybody else. One of them falsely declared that "the decision to arrest Mr. Gieseking was made in Washington, in response to pressure from various Jewish organizations." The presence of Jewish war veterans among peaceful pickets in front of Carnegie Hall was sufficient for a midwestern newspaper to accuse summarily a number of Jewish organizations of having "very nearly provoked a riot." It implied that "race hatred" motivated those who protested Gieseking's appearance, and hinted at a possible conspiracy among Jewish groups to intimidate the government in the Gieseking affair.

A scurrilous piece captioned "The Wheel of Hate" appeared in the March 1949 issue of the monthly magazine *Progressive*. In it Milton Mayer, who is himself Jewish, libelled Jewish organizations as "blood-drinkers" for their alleged stand on the Gieseking matter. Unfortunately one big city newspaper saw fit to repeat the defamation by reprinting Mayer's outpourings in condensed form.

The foreign language press, responsive to old-world schisms and hates, showed less bias in 1949 than in past years. Improvement was especially evident in periodicals printed in the Eastern European, Spanish, and Italian languages. Flights of Jews from Iron Curtain countries, and anti-Israel statements by nations within the Soviet orbit, helped dispel harmful notions. Spanish papers showed concern over prejudice against Puerto Ricans; Italian papers fought discrimination against Jews, Negroes, and Italians. Only the German-American periodicals revealed more intense nationalism and anti-Jewish hostility. In their columns, Jewish DPs, Israeli citizens, Bernard Baruch and responsible private Jewish agencies were libelled, while Gerald Smith and Upton Close were praised and defended. Papers such as the *Deutsche Wochenschrift* of St. Louis, Missouri, and *Der Wanderer* of St. Paul, Minnesota, led the attack.

Only a handful of men associated with American journalism stepped over the line that distinguishes honest opinion from hate mongering. It is doubtful that they made any serious impression upon America.

Chapter 6. Calipers Against Prejudice

READERS of this book obviously seek the answer to at least one question: "Is anti-Jewish prejudice greater or less today than last year, the year before, or the year before that?" While the query seems simple enough, it is actually most complex.

The question can be approached in one of two ways *or* both. The first is rule of thumb: comparing the number of anti-Semitic organizations, individuals, and incidents evident in one year as against previous years. The second approach is to test the extent of anti-Semitism by scientific methods and to compare the results with examinations made in previous years.

In foregoing chapters, we obviously employed rule-of-thumb methods in evaluating the impact of professional anti-Semites upon the American community. In 1949 the Anti-Defamation League attempted, on the basis of existing scientific data, to determine whether there had been any trends in anti-Jewish feeling during the last decade, and if so what those trends were. Perhaps such an examination could reveal not only how much anti-Semitism there had been but where and in whom.

It was quickly recognized that to evaluate such findings properly for the reader, a careful statement would have to be presented indicating the precise limitations of the available poll information and the social science methods used to accumulate it. The word "anti Semite" would have to be clearly defined.

Elmo Roper, one of America's authorities on public opinion polling, was called in for consultation. He was asked to undertake the examination of all poll data available on the specific subject of anti-Semitic sentiment for the past ten years. Mr. Roper agreed to do the study and confer about the meaning of his findings. The results follow: it is an attempt to describe what has been learned in the last ten years about the nature, extent and distribution of anti-Semitic attitudes in the American population, through the use of the sampling survey of opinion, known popularly as the public opinion poll.

The techniques of public opinion surveying have been developed over the past twenty years and have been extensively and successfully employed on a large scale in marketing research for business. They have also been used effectively in studying such community and national problems as education, social security, unemployment, race relations, and housing.

Any discussion of what the public opinion surveys reveal about anti-Semitism in America must begin with a definition of the thing to be measured, namely, the "anti-Semitic attitude." Anti-Semitism is, of course, a matter of degree, and some people are more anti-Semitic than others. In general, however, we can describe a person as having anti-Semitic attitudes when he does three things. First, he habitually distinguishes between Jews and Gentiles, noting whether the people he comes in contact with are one or the other. Second, he tends to behave differently in situations involving Jews than in situations not involving them; the difference being that he is more unfavorable in his judgment of Jews, more concerned with defending himself against them, more likely to take advantage of them when opportunity to take advantage is offered, and less willing to admit them to close personal relationships. Finally, the anti-Semitic person has a picture in his mind of "what Jews are like" that "explains" and "justifies," to himself, the actions he takes toward them. One may summarize these three aspects or conditions of anti-Semitism in a sentence: The anti-Semite picks out Jews as objects for less favorable treatment than he would accord Gentiles and has a rationalized set of beliefs about the nature of Jews that gives him what he regards as a personal rationalization for doing so.

In attempting to measure the anti-Semitic attitudes of people the public opinion survey has certain definite advantages and certain limitations. Probably the major advantage of the survey is its use of modern sampling techniques, whereby the population under investigation can be described accurately. Far too much research on anti-Semitism has been done with "twenty-six students in elementary psychology at Jerkwater University," or "fifty-two people who lived in the neighborhood of the researcher and were willing to be interviewed." It is easy to draw conclusions that are completely unwarranted from samples of this sort. On such a subject as anti-Semitism any sample that is in any sense self-selecting is particularly dangerous if there is any desire to report the attitudes of any sort of representative group.

A second advantage of the public opinion survey is the possibility it offers of measuring trends, of finding out whether the situation is getting worse or better. A third advantage is the information that a survey may yield about the attitudes of all sorts of sub-groups in the general population. Is anti-Semitism more prevalent among the well-to-do or among the workers? Does it increase or decrease with age? Questions like these can be answered by survey methods. And decisions on strategy in dealing with anti-Semitism should be influenced by facts on its distribution. Where are the hotbeds of prejudice that need especially to be attacked?

But the survey technique has also some definite limitations when it is used to investigate anti-Semitism. In the first place, the information collected through interviews on doorsteps (and that is the way most survey information *is* collected) is confined almost entirely to those attitudes the respondent is (1) conscious of having, and (2) able to verbalize. This leaves out of account those unconscious biases and prejudices which frequently motivate the behavior of individuals without their knowing it.

A second important limitation has to do with the resistances of people to admit attitudes that they are secretly ashamed of, or that they think will lower their status in the eyes of the interviewer. Anti-Semitic attitudes do not comport well with the love-thy-neighbor injunction in the Christian ethic, consequently there is sometimes a temptation to give "respectable" answers to interviewers rather than completely honest ones or, still better, to evade answering at all by claiming one does not know how one feels on the issue presented. All this hesitancy about admitting anti-Semitism does not, however, invalidate the findings from surveys, for there is evidence that many people go ahead and answer the questions truthfully anyway. The survey results undoubtedly underestimate anti-Semitism somewhat, but they still yield a picture that is more complete in many respects than that provided by other methods of research.

There is a third limitation of the public opinion survey of anti-Semitism, one that is slowly being overcome but is still important in most of the research that has so far been published. An individual may have reported a conscious bias against the admission of more Jewish immigrants, but the bias may be little more than a conventional gesture, for he may not care very much what is done. Another person may give the same response to the interviewer's question, but for him the issue may be a burning one. Public opinion surveys frequently fail to distinguish between these two individuals—they neglect to include some measure of the attitude's importance in the scheme of things of the individual who holds it. They thus fail to make the important distinction between the active and the passive anti-Semite. Public opinion surveys are beginning to include measures of attitude intensity on the one hand, and of attitude importance in the individual's scheme of things on the other. But the development is fairly recent, and in much of the material to be reported in this chapter this information is lacking.

So much, then, for the advantages and disadvantages of the sampling survey technique as a means of studying the phenomenon of anti-Semitism. What it yields is a standardized measure of the prevalence in specifically defined groups of various anti-Semitic attitudes, attitudes that people are conscious of having and are able to put in words. With this understanding of what we may hope to get from survey results we are now ready to examine the work of the public opinion researchers in the period from 1940 to 1950. What insights do these studies provide into the problem of anti-Semitism in America?

THE NATIONAL PATTERN OF ANTI-SEMITISM: Let us first take an over-all look at what might be termed the national pattern of anti-Semitic attitudes. Neglecting for the time being any differences between the attitudes of sub-groups, let us ask, "How do the American people as a whole react to the Jew in their midst?" What is the attitude of the "majority American" toward Jewish citizens? Although most anti-Semitic actions are the work of individuals, or of small groups, there is a value in trying to get a preliminary description of the total Gentile response to the totality of Jews in the nation. What do Gentiles in general think Jews in general are like? What is it they fear the Jews will do that they must protect themselves against? What kinds of protective action do they individually and collectively lean toward? To answer these questions is to describe the American cultural pattern of anti-Semitism. It is impossible to fill out this pattern description from public opinion survey materials alone, but the surveys have made a contribution to the description, and this contribution will now be summarized.

THE STEREOTYPE OF THE JEWISH PERSONALITY The picture the Gentile has in his mind of the "typical Jew" (not of the few Jews he knows who are "different") is a very important element in the whole anti-Jewish complex. The stereotype acts as a justification for past discriminatory behavior and at the same time it provides a set of distorted spectacles through which one looks at the world of Jewish-

Gentile relations and finds the Jews continuing to behave in accordance with stereotyped expectations. Also, the stereotype probably tends itself to create prejudice and discrimination. As Walter Lippman long ago pointed out, once a "picture in the head" has been formed about the nature of Jews, one tends thereafter to find in the Jew one comes in contact with only those traits that conform with the picture; the other characteristics tend to be rejected as minor and unimportant, if noticed, and indeed there is a tendency not to see them at all.

What are the traits that go to make up the conventional picture of the Jewish American? There is distressingly little in the way of actual research findings that bear on this point. A small study by Katz and Braly[1] in which 100 college students were asked to pick from a long list of adjectives those that best described the Jews, a question in an Opinion Research Corporation study in Denver in which respondents were asked how they thought Jews differed from other people,[2] a *Fortune* Survey question inquiring what people thought were the reasons for hostility toward Jewish people,[3] and an Office of War Information study which asked, "Do you think that in general there is any feeling against the Jews?" and "Why do people feel that way?"[4]—these constitute the sum total of the material available. Out of them comes a familiar list of alleged Jewish characteristics, which can be placed only in rough order of frequency of mention because the studies do not yield results that are 100 per cent consistent. At the top of the list are traits like clannishness (refusal to intermarry, setting up of barriers to assimilation); a love of money coupled with shrewdness and possible shady ethics in relation to the accumulation of it; pushy, aggressive, uncouth social behavior; and a combination of intelligence and ambition which, taken with the characteristics aforementioned, leads to rapid "getting ahead."

One would like to know how widely held is this stereotype and what proportion of Americans hold a different, and more favorable, picture in their minds. Direct evidence on this point is lacking, except for the single fact that four out of ten of the Denver citizens answered "No" to the question, "Do you think of most Jews as being different from other people in some ways other than their religion?" In all probability this 40 per cent who gave the reasonable answer and declined to set Jews off as different is too low a figure even for Denver, and lower still for some other parts of the country. But we can only speculate, and draw inferences on what people think of

Jews from the more adequate data on how people behave toward them. The study of people's conceptions of what the Jew is like is one of the presently most neglected areas of research on anti-Semitism.

FEAR OF JEWS   It is hard to tell whether people's expressed fears of what Jews might do to the country in general, or to them personally, are fictions created to justify their own prejudices, or whether the prejudices are actually the result of the fears. The question is probably one of the chicken-or-the-egg variety, with cause and effect so mixed up in the individual's unconscious as to defy analysis.

But whether or not the fears of Jewish domination, interference, or encroachment are the *actual* reasons for anti-Semitic behavior, or only rationalizations, there is no doubt but what people express them. While apparently no survey organization has asked a question of the form "What are the things you are afraid the Jews might do if they got too numerous?" there have been repeated testings of public reactions on such questions as "Do you think the Jews have too much power and influence in this country?" or, "Do you think any of these groups (Jews, Protestants, Swedes, Negroes, etc.) are getting too much political (or economic) power for the good of the country?" Depending on how the questions are asked, one gets percentages of from 35 to 60 of the population who testify to a feeling that the Jews have more power and influence in some phases of our national life than they should have.

When, however, the question is asked, "Are there any organizations or groups of people in this country which you feel might be harmful to the future of the country unless they are curbed?" the answer "Jews" turns up in only about 5 per cent of the national sample. These 5 per cent are the "self-igniting anti-Semites," the people who single out the Jews among all the possibly dangerous groups in this country as one of those most worth mentioning. When the question was asked in 1948, 52 per cent mentioned the much more popular menace, the Communists, but in 1945 Communism got only 14 per cent of mentions while the Jews had the same 5 per cent they had in 1948.[5]

A similar question, "Are there any groups of people trying to get ahead at the expense of people like you?" brought forth the answer "Jews" from 6 per cent of the respondents when it was asked in 1945, and when the question was asked again in 1948 the results were the same. Here again the stigmatizers of Jews are probably of the "self-igniting type." These people are sufficiently obsessed with the idea that the Jews are dangerous competitors to seize an opportunity to name them as the group that is most to be feared in the competition to get ahead in life.

Fragmentary survey data indicate some fear of Jewish encroachments on Gentile neighborhoods, where they may possibly be thought undesirable because of the stereotype of their uncouth social behavior and the fear that they will bring in their friends. There are probably other things that some people think the Jews might do unless defensive measures are taken against them, but the basic fear seems to be that Jews will somehow get themselves into a position of influence, and then use that influence to discriminate in favor of their co-religionists. This may be a projection of the anti-Semite's own guilt feeling for discriminating in favor of non-Jews, a sort of unconscious "they do it so we have to" justification, but the surveys cannot prove or disprove the existence of this unconscious mechanism. They can only report that a considerable minority of Americans will agree with propositions implying a possibility of Jewish monopolies in politics and business, when these propositions are presented to them in doorstep interviews.

DEFENSE ACTIONS AGAINST JEWS   When anti-Semitism goes beyond the mere expression of unfavorable sentiments about Jews it usually takes the form either of an effort to keep Jews at a distance or an attempt to deny them equal opportunities. Of course in the process of keeping Jews at arm's length there tends to grow up a set of discrimination patterns that deny Jews equal access to educational or recreational facilities and to jobs. The maintenance of social distance thus gets tied up with the denial of opportunity, but it will be convenient to keep them separate for the purposes of this discussion. They have been tackled separately in most of the survey research that has been done so far.

The idea of trying to express minority group prejudice in terms of the relative degree of "social distance" the majority group wants to maintain with respect to the minority is one that goes back to Professor Emory S. Bogardus, of the University of Southern California, and some research he did in 1926.[6] The essence of the Bogardus technique was to inquire whether people would admit other people of a named race or nationality to varying degrees of relationship. For instance, a question series might be: Would you be willing to admit Jews to the United States as immigrants? Would you be willing to work alongside them in an office or factory? Would you be willing to have them move into your neighborhood to live? Would you be willing to entertain them as guests in your home? Would you be willing to have one of them marry a near relative? When similar questions are asked about Jews and about other nationality groups and races a picture of the whole minority group social distance pattern emerges. It is discovered that white Gentile Americans are willing to admit the other racial, religious, and nationality groups to different degrees of association, and that in fact those groups can be arranged in a hierarchy of rank with respect to the closeness of the relationship which will be tolerated by the average majority American. A typical ranking of this sort, derived from a 1946 Bogardus study[7] is shown in Table I, along with a similar one taken from Roper 1948 research,[8] and a third taken from a study by J. P. Guilford.[9] The Bogardus list actually contained thirty-six different minority groups, but has here been simplified. It was based on what Bogardus describes as a "roughly defined stratified sampling," but the sample was admittedly somewhat loaded for the younger age groups. The Guilford study was made with a sample of one thousand students from a number of different colleges. The Roper study used a national cross section.

TABLE I: Social Distance Rankings of Different Groups
(*The higher the rank the less social distance insisted on by majority group members*)

BOGARDUS STUDY	ROPER STUDY	GUILFORD STUDY
1. Italians	1. Italians	1. Italians
2. *Jews*	2. *Jews*	2. *Jews*
3. Chinese	3. Chinese	3. Mexicans
4. Mexicans	4. Filipinos	4. Negroes
5. Filipinos	5. Mexicans	5. Chinese
6. Negroes	6. Negroes	

Jews appear second to Italians in social-distance rating in all three studies, and it seems safe to assume that they also rank lower than most North European nationalities as well. In the Bogardus study they are also below Central and South European nationalities such as Poles, Czechs, Rumanians, and Bulgarians. The fact that the three studies agree as well as they do is not an absolute guaranty of the truthfulness of these findings, since all may have a similar constant bias. Nevertheless there is a presumption of validity established. The table of social-distance ratings does seem to be a convenient way of summarizing a lot of data on group prejudice. It is worth noting that Jews in general are less acceptable than Italians in general, and more acceptable than Chinese and Negroes. By providing a sort of general frame of reference the social-distance comparisons help to define the nature and extent of the Jewish discrimination problem in graphic terms.

When it comes to the specific details of the social-distance pattern between Jews and Gentiles in America the studies are quite revealing. In Table II are shown the percentages of the national non-Jewish adult population in the 1948 Roper study who would prefer *not* to admit Jews to the different degrees of social relationship. The Negro figures are also given for contrast.

TABLE II: Social Distance Attitudes of Non-Jewish Adults
Toward Jews and Negroes

	JEWS	NEGROES
Prefer not to work with Jews (Negroes) if they had an equal position to mine and worked side by side with me	14%	42%
Prefer not to have them as guests in my home	14	56
Prefer not to have them move into my neighborhood to live	22	64
Prefer not to have them marry a near relative of mine	48	80

Resistance to intermarriage may be based on religious grounds but objections to living in the same neighborhood are clear reflections of anti-minority group prejudice. It must always be remembered that any such question-answer percentages as those given in the table are almost certainly underestimates of the actual amount of resistance to close social contact that people would initially exhibit if a Jew did start to move into their neighborhood or propose marriage to their wife's sister. What the study does reveal by and large is the amount of social distance it is still thought respectable to insist on, but this is itself an important social indicator. When 22 per cent of American adults *say* they would object *if* a Jew *did* move into their neighborhood, this is a fact worth noting, and if the percentage should go down to 10 per cent in five years, an important social gain will have been achieved.

Turning now to the more active measures that might be taken to enforce social distance or maintain an advantage in the struggle for status, the question of job discrimination immediately comes up. A number of studies have been made that show employment opportunities are often not made equally available to Jews and Gentiles, but the concern here is more with the attitude that people have toward such discriminatory practices. Do they approve of and justify a segregation pattern of Jews and Gentiles in their work situations or do they not?

There is surprisingly little survey data that bears on this question. The Psychological Corporation in its 1946 *Barometer of Public Attitudes* asked the somewhat platitudinous question, "Jews and Gentiles, Negroes and whites, all should have an equal chance at any job: is this good Americanism or not?" and about 85 per cent of the people not surprisingly said that it was.[10] The question served, however, to identify the 12 per cent who were clearly either anti-Negro or anti-Semitic.

A Roper question asked in 1948 put the matter somewhat differently: "Which of these things do you think people who employ large numbers of workers should do—hire the most capable people whether they are Jewish or not, hire Jews in proportion to the number there are in the community, hire Jews only when they are so outstanding that no one else could do the job as well, or hire no Jews at all?"[11] The answer on a national non-Jewish cross section was 65 per cent for the first alternative (hire the best no matter whether Jew or Gentile). Eleven per cent would hire no Jews at all —again the outspoken anti-Semitic bitter-enders, but this time maybe a more accurate measurement of them because it deals with a more specific situation.

Several surveys have dealt in passing with the question of what to do to stop job discrimination. A Roper *Fortune* survey in 1948[12] asked the following question:

"What would you like to see done about legislation that prohibits employers—when they are hiring people—from turning them down solely because of their race or religion?"

1. Would like to see laws passed by Congress to do this	25%
2. Would like it left up to each state to pass their own laws if they want them	29%
3. Think it would be better not to have any laws at all of this kind and work the problems out some other way	37%
Don't know	9%

A 1946 question by the American Institute of Public Opinion approached the matter in a different way: "Do you favor or oppose a law in this state which would require employers to hire a person if he is qualified for the job, regardless of race or color?" The answers on a national sample were 43 per cent in favor of such a law, 44 per cent opposed, and 13 per cent undecided.[13] During the period between 1945 and 1949 the Institute repeatedly put variants of this question to a national sample and got percentages from 35 to 70 who favored state or federal legislation to stop job discrimination. It must be remembered that all the questions applied to job discrimination against Negroes as well as against Jews, but it does appear, even from the somewhat varying results of all the question asking, that there is a considerable public in favor of some legislative measures to control discrimination in employment of Jews.

There are obviously many other kinds of discrimination than job discrimination. Equal opportunities may be denied Jews to hold political office, acquire citizenship, use public facilities (including schools and hotels), or participate in all sorts of recreational or civic activities in the community. In 1937 the American Institute of Public Opinion asked, "Would you vote for a Jew for President who was well qualified for the position?" and got practically an even split on the issue. In 1943, 33 per cent answered "Too many" to the Gallup question, "Do you think Roosevelt has appointed about the right number of Jews to jobs in Washington, too many, or not enough?" This is about all that has been done on the important issue of discrimination in office holding.

On the issue of Jewish immigration to the United States the data is also meager. The most direct question was asked in 1944 by the National Opinion Research Corporation: "Do you think the Jews of other countries should have the same chance as non-Jews of other countries to settle in America after the war?" Those who were opposed to equal treatment for Jews constituted 30 per cent of the national sample.

In the last few years the problem of the European refugee has come to the fore. In 1948 about 40 per cent of Americans were opposed to admitting any of these refugees to the United States at all, and more than half of this 40 per cent were in favor of putting a special limit on Jewish refugee immigration "if most of the refugees turn out to be Jews."[14] These facts must be interpreted against a backdrop of general disinclination on the part of Americans to open the doors to any new and large influx of immigrants of any race, religion, or nationality.[15] There is also some apparent tendency to feel that the place for Jewish refugees is in Israel, as indicated by answers given to several Gallup questions.

There is little evidence from surveys to prove discrimination against Jews in the primary and secondary schools but the pattern of discrimination at the college level is now well described and documented.[16] However, a considerable proportion of Americans are apparently not aware of the extra barriers the Jewish student faces in his effort to go to college. In the *Fortune* Higher Education Study of 1949, Roper found that 33 per cent of a national sample thought the statement that "A Jewish student has a harder time getting into most colleges than a non-Jewish student with the same high school marks" was false. Another 37 per cent didn't know whether it was false or not, and only 27 per cent thought it true.[17] In still another study Roper found 63 per cent of non-Jews who would prefer "to send a child of theirs to a college which admits the best students who apply whether they are Jewish or not."[18] The rest were either uncertain or wanted to compromise the principle to some degree or other. Fifteen per cent preferred to send their child to a school that admitted no Jews at all.

SCALES FOR MEASURING "GENERAL ANTI-SEMITISM"   So far this chapter has been dealing with specific attitudes concerning the role of Jews in various different situations. The over-all picture that emerges is one indicating many inconsistencies in the public mind, with considerable support for discriminatory practices of some types and relatively little support for others. Such a finding gives rise to questions about the nature of the thing we call anti-Semitism in the individual. Is the individual himself as inconsistent in his attitudes toward Jews as the public taken as a whole seems to be? Is there really such a thing as an anti-Semitic personality—an individual who is rabid on the subject of Jews in any context? And if there is, how many such persons are there, and how many people are simply anti-Semitic in one or two situations, and not in others?

One of the obvious methods for getting answers to these queries is to take a group of anti-Semitic attitude revealing questions, submit them to a sample and see how many people give anti-Semitic answers to all of them, how many to all but one, how many all but two, and so on. Two things come out of this sort of research. First, one gets an idea of what types of anti-Semitism cluster together in given individuals, and an answer to the question, "Is there any such thing as general anti-Semitism?" Second, if the question on the existence of a general anti-Semitism is answered affirmatively, the procedure yields the necessary information for constructing a device to measure this general anti-Semitic attitude. The device is an "anti-Semitic scale," a group of questions to be asked an individual whose answers are scored in such a way as to yield a single anti-Semitism rating for him. If he gets a high score rating, he is a person consistently anti-Semitic in all the hypothetical situations presented to him in the questions; if he gets a low score, it is because he rarely gives anti-Semitic answers, or gives no anti-Semitic answers at all.

Probably the best-known attempt to construct a scale for anti-Semitism has been made by Raymond Franzen at the instance of the Anti-Defamation League. In Table III are given the eleven items in the Form 2 Franzen scale that were finally selected from an original list of thirty-four questions.[19] The items are listed in the order of frequency with which people gave the indicated response in the initial cities studied (Roanoke and Bridgeport). More people think "marriage between Christians and Jews should be discouraged" than think "Jews are less fair in their business relations"; more people think "Jews are less fair in business relations" than think "Jews have too much control over the radio," and so on. The items at the bottom of the list are those where the expression of prejudice is least frequent and is only made by those who have expressed prejudice on all other items. These items at the bottom of the list therefore represent maximum prejudice.

TABLE III: Items on the Franzen Scale for Measuring General Anti-Semitism (Form 2) With percentages obtained from the studies in Roanoke and Bridgeport (combined) and in Denver

ITEM	ROANOKE AND BRIDGEPORT (COMBINED)	DENVER
1. Think marriage between Christians and Jews should be discouraged	86%	49%
2. Think Jews are less fair in their business relations	65	40
3. Think Jews have a larger share of control over radio than they should have	*	27
4. Do not like to do business as well with a Jew	55	45
5. Would object to working for a Jewish employer	50	16
6. Would object to living in the same neighborhood with Jews	44	13
7. Think better class neighborhoods should be restricted against Jews	33	*
8. Think Jews are worse at athletic sports	28	23
9. Think Jews have never established their own nation because they don't trust one another well enough	25	20
10. Think Jews' contributions to arts and sciences are less than those of other groups	17	14
11. Think Jews are all alike	*	10

*Asked in Denver differently from the way it was asked in Bridgeport and Roanoke

While there may be an argument over some of the individual items in the Franzen scale, the research on which the scale was based does establish the fact that people do differ in the consistency with which they apply an anti-Semitic bias in varying situations. It indicates also that a useful measure of this consistency, in other words an index of the degree of a person's anti-Semitism, can be developed. The Franzen index has been employed in small-scale studies of four cities (Roanoke, Dayton, Worcester, and Bridgeport)[20] and in a somewhat larger-scale study in Denver.[21] The rankings for the individual items vary some from city to city, as might be expected because of differences in the community culture. However, average scores for the cities differ significantly, indicating a possible utility for the device in locating local centers or hotbeds of anti-Semitism in different parts of the country. The Franzen scale might also be used to measure trends of change, both locally and nationally, but so far its use has been confined to single studies in the communities named above.

Franzen is not the only research man who has experimented with measures of general anti-Semitism. Levinson and Sanford[22] (sponsored by the Department of Scientific Research of the American Jewish Committee), at the University of California, have developed a scale which in some respects may be an improvement on the Franzen index, but there are no published reports of the use of the Levinson-Sanford scale with any population other than college students. Samuel Flowerman, of the American Jewish Committee, has experimented with modifications of the California scale, but his results are also unpublished. All in all, one can say that the use of scales for research on anti-Semitism is a promising field that has so far been little cultivated.

TRENDS IN NATIONAL ANTI-SEMITISM: In spite of the fact that survey techniques are probably more reliable for measuring trends over a time period than they are for getting an absolutely accurate picture at any given instant, there has been remarkably little anti-Semitism research that can be plotted to show a trend line. One reason for this has been the fact that survey techniques are improving, and a research organization in 1949 is seldom satisfied with the wording of a question used in 1947, much less one that was employed in 1940. Yet the questions must be worded identically and

TABLE IV: Trends in Anti-Semitism as Revealed by the A.J.C. Eight-Year Study

	MAR. 1938	FEB. 1939	APR. 1940	AUG. 1940	FEB. 1941	OCT. 1941	JAN. 1942	DEC. 1942	JUNE 1944	MAR. 1945	FEB. 1946
% who believe the "Jews have too much power in the United States"	38	41	43	42	46	48	47	51	56	56	55
% who believe a widespread campaign against the Jews is likely	23	22	30	25	25	24	18	29	—	30	—
% who would support such a campaign against Jews	17	16	12	12	13	14	11	14	—	17	—
% who would sympathize with but not support such a campaign	—	—	9	10	12	11	11	11	—	14	—
% who would actively oppose such a campaign			29	31	28	31	33	34	—	27	—
% who believe Jews are a threat to America								12	21	19	22
% who would vote for a Congressional candidate who came out against Jews								—	21	23	23

placed in the same position and context in the questionnaire if comparisons are to be defensible. The public opinion survey can be extremely useful as a running audit of the state of anti-Semitism in this country, but it is necessary to have a carefully designed and regularly repeated study (preferably including a general anti-Semitism scale) to make it so. Such a study requires the continued support of an organization.

The longest continued trend study of anti-Semitism is the one made by the American Jewish Committee for the period March 1938 through February 1946 (Table IV).[23]

There were eleven successive samplings between March 1938 and March 1946, and while there were some question additions and subtractions and some wording changes during this period there were also a few questions that continued unchanged from 1938 to 1946.[24] One would conclude from the Table that anti-Semitism, so far as it can be measured by the belief that the Jews have too much power, has been definitely on the increase. But this is only a single question, and the results on the other questions shown in the Table do not support this conclusion. The need for measurement with a generalized index that includes a number of dimensions of anti-Semitism is evident.

Beyond the American Jewish Committee data there is very little of a trend nature to report. Roper has repeated one or two questions in recent years and plans to repeat more in the future, but the intervals of time covered are still too short to expect any important changes. The Bogardus social distance study previously referred to was done first in 1926 and then repeated in 1946 with the Jewish ranking among the thirty-six nationalities remaining almost exactly the same in 1946 as it was twenty years previous.

Public statements to the effect that anti-Semitism is on the increase, or on the decrease, have not been lacking over the years—and it seems an obvious and useful function of public opinion research to put these statements to the test and find out to what extent they are factually supportable, at least so far as verbalizable anti-Semitism is concerned. It is regrettable to have to report that little of this sort of testing has been done to date.

ANTI-SEMITISM IN SUB-GROUPS OF THE POPULATION: The question of where in the population—in what race, class, place of residence, or other sub-group—is most anti-Semitism to be found is one that recurs constantly. Because public opinion surveys deal usually with samples of the total population, and consequently represent the different sub-groups without distortion, they should be good instruments in providing a picture of how anti-Semitism is distributed. Does the survey material that is available yield any clear-cut generalizations on where the anti-Semites are located in the American body politic?

SEX DIFFERENCES IN ANTI-SEMITISM   Examination of the Franzen index anti-Semitic scores for the five cities, and also the available individual question material from other sources, points to the conclusion that there is about the same average amount of anti-Semitism among women and men. Women seem to be somewhat less extreme in their attitudes toward Jews—there are less strong "pros" and strong "antis" among them than among men. Women are also slightly more likely to be opposed to marrying a Jew themselves and also to having a near relative marry a Jew than are their menfolk. But apart from these small differences, men's and women's answers to the question concerning their attitudes toward Jews tend to parallel each other.

GEOGRAPHIC DIFFERENCES   When people residing in the four major geographic regions (Northeast, Middle West, South, Far West) are compared in regard to the prevalence of anti-Semitic attitudes no clear-cut pattern emerges which would indicate that people in any one section of the country are *consistently* more hostile to Jews than those in another section. We can create a rough sort of index of general anti-Jewish prejudice by averaging the percentages of people giving anti-Semitic answers on eleven different Roper questions, and when this is done it is found that the Midwest average is well above those for the other regions, even though the Midwest leads in anti-Semitism on only two of the questions. When a similar averaging procedure is applied to five Opinion Research Corporation questions asked repeatedly between 1938 and 1946, the East tops the Midwest in average anti-Semitism, but the O.R.C. and Roper series agree in assigning the least average anti-Semitism to the Far West. It all seems to depend pretty much on what questions are included in the averaging process, which is another way of saying that different regions have their own favorite forms of anti-Jewish prejudice. For instance, Southerners show a little more desire than people in other regions to keep Jews out of colleges they want their children to attend, and show definitely more opposition to the idea of having their close relatives marry Jews. All this is a possible reflection of a clannish Southern tradition. On the other hand Southerners are the least worried of people in any region concerning the growth of the economic and political power of the Jew.

SIZE OF PLACE IN RELATION TO ANTI-SEMITISM   The evidence on the relation between anti-Semitism and urbanization that comes from public opinion surveying is still too limited to be conclusive. Rural people seem to be more anti-Semitic than city folk on some counts, less anti-Semitic on others. The hypothesis that anti-Semitism should always be greater in the cities, where there are more Jews, and less in rural areas, where Jews are rare, does not seem to be substantiated by the data—nor does the reverse hypothesis.

SOCIO-ECONOMIC LEVEL   There seems to be no conclusive evidence to indicate that over-all average anti-Semitism either increases or decreases with economic level. The Franzen data show no significant differences between the average index scores for the different economic groups in four of the five cities studied. In Denver there is less prejudice in the upper economic group, but the differences are small.

Survey results seem to indicate that on the question of discrimination in employment, which is of more vital interest to the lower economic levels than to the upper, the former are more antagonistic to Jews. On the question of vacation hotel guest policy, which is of comparatively minor interest to the poorer respondents, they are less anti-Jewish. All of this fits well with the theory of prejudice that says one can afford to be liberal about other people's contacts!

When it comes to the "self-igniting anti-Semites," the ones who seize an opportunity to name the Jews both as people who are trying to get ahead at the expense of the respondent and who might "be dangerous to the country unless curbed," Roper found in 1946[25] that the upper-economic levels provided a disproportionately large share of the total. It is, of course, perfectly possible for the strong anti-Semites for whom the Jews are a burning issue to be distributed through the economic levels one way, and the common lip-service anti-Semites to be distributed in another. It was pointed out earlier that one of the major problems of research in this field is to segregate the active and passive anti-Semite, the Jew-hater from the person who merely gives verbal assent to common prejudices.

RACIAL DIFFERENCES IN ANTI-SEMITISM   What little evidence there is indicates that Negroes have less anti-Semitic prejudice than whites. This is a not unexpected finding, in view of the fact that Negroes are fellow victims of discrimination.

AGE IN RELATION TO ANTI-SEMITISM   There seems to be a fairly definite, if not completely universal, tendency for anti-Semitism to increase with age. In two out of five of the Franzen cities, and with almost no exception among the questions asked by Roper, Gallup, and the Opinion Research Corporation, there is a greater incidence of anti-Semitic replies among the older age group, and less among the younger. Such a finding is explainable in terms of two different hypotheses. Since anti-Semitism is something that is learned by individuals as they grow up in a society, and since anti-Semitic attitudes are frequently useful in protecting vested interests, it is perhaps not surprising to find that the people who have had more time to learn from others, and have acquired more vested interests to protect, are the more anti-Semitic. On the other hand it is quite possible that the lesser degree of anti-Semitism among the young is a presage of declining prejudice among the population as a whole. The inter-cultural education program in the schools may be making enough headway to be reflected in the age distribution of anti-Semitism that has just been cited. Some additional evidence that this is actually the case is presented in the next two chapters.

This ends the story of the public opinion research contribution to the measurement of anti-Semitism, except for some special information on college students that is set forth in Chapter 8. The chronicle so far has largely been one indicating great promise in the survey approach, but only limited accomplishment. That the tool is capable of providing much valuable information on anti-Semitism in America must now be apparent, but it must be equally apparent to the reader that the gaps in the survey data are at present wider than the areas filled in with solid facts. In the next few years the Anti-Defamation League proposes to see that at least some of the needed survey research on anti-Semitism is carried forward, and especially the measurement of trends and the study of program impacts. Such research is, in a sense, the auditing phase of the organization's activities.

Chapter 7. Cracking the Quota

1. THE "CASE" FOR THE QUOTA: Until November 1949 George W. Armstrong of Fort Worth, Texas, was little known outside the borders of the Lone Star State. Some Texans and agencies such as the Anti-Defamation League were, of course, familiar with the activities of the octogenarian millionaire. They had watched him for years create and finance anti-Semitic and anti-Negro propaganda. But neither Armstrong nor his Judge Armstrong Foundation had made any significant impact upon the general American community.

In November the whole nation suddenly became very much aware of Armstrong: he announced a grant of oil-bearing land allegedly worth $50,000,000 to Jefferson Military College, a tiny and little-known institution located near Natchez, Mississippi, on condition that the college pledge to exclude non-Caucasians and to include in its curriculum the teaching of white racist supremacy. From all parts of the country came ringing condemnation of the Armstrong plan, and within a matter of days the Board of Trustees of the Jefferson Military College rejected the proffered grant.

The revulsion of the American people was a healthy sign. They reacted as if education in America was truly consecrated to the democratic ideal of equality of opportunity. The truth is that American education at the college level is stained with discrimination. Armstrong had merely asked an unimportant school (which, incidentally, had long since lost its collegiate status) to do overtly what too many American colleges and professional schools have been doing covertly for many years—to discriminate against students belonging to racial and religious minority groups.

Theoretically, the doors of American colleges and professional schools are open to all students who have the necessary financial resources and scholastic ability. In practice, however, many institutions exclude or limit Jews, Negroes, Italians, and in some cases Catholics and others. Of course, some of the best colleges in the United States live up fully to the American tradition of equality of educational opportunity. Great institutions—Harvard, New York University, the University of Chicago, the University of Pennsylvania, to name a few—place no racial or religious barriers upon admission.

The discrimination suffered by Negroes who seek higher education differs from that of members of other minority groups. Segregation is established by law in seventeen states and the District of Columbia. Negroes cannot share the same classrooms with white students in these jurisdictions; while the law requires "separate-but-equal" facilities for Negro students, such "equality" is a myth in theory and fact. Organized separation presupposes inferior and superior groups. Negro institutions are inferior in financial resources, facilities, and teaching staffs. According to the President's Commission on Higher Education, ". . . the ratio of expenditures of institutions for whites to those of institutions for Negroes ranged from 3:1 in the District of Columbia, to 42:1 in Kentucky." "Equality" and "segregation" are a contradiction in terms.

If the Negro is at a disadvantage in obtaining a college education, he is even worse off with respect to entering a professional or graduate school. Here the greatest toll is taken by a quota system under which the number of students from selected minority groups is kept down to a pre-established percentage. Medical schools discriminate against Negroes to a greater extent than against any other minority group. A Public Affairs pamphlet entitled, *Religion and Race: Barriers to College?*, published in 1949, reports that of the seventy-seven (including non-accredited) medical schools in the United States, there are twenty in the South which accept no Negroes. While the remainder do not admit to an exclusion policy, actually only one-third of them accepts Negro students.

Segregation and exclusion of Negroes in the South is, of course, a publicly avowed policy. Jews are discriminated against in schools in every section of the United States. No college or professional school, however, publicly admits using a "quota system." There are a number of arguments which have been offered to justify discrimination through the use of the quota system, and they deserve careful examination:

1. The schools must conform to the prejudices of the students and faculty; otherwise the morale of the campus community will be damaged irreparably.

This argument assumes a degree of student prejudice which will be shown by scientific test, in the ensuing chapter, to be greatly exaggerated. There may be some ground for charging that when students maintain a caste system based upon race and religion in their fraternities (here the tests show much greater prejudice), they thereby give tacit endorsement and encouragement to the practice of discrimination by the colleges. However, during the past year, there has been an intensification of the struggle by some fraternity members themselves to abolish fraternity discrimination. More and more, too, student bodies have taken an active role against discrimination in education.

In November 1949 a dramatic, precedent-shattering step was taken by the National Inter-Fraternity Conference when it recommended that college Greek letter societies wipe out existing barriers to membership on grounds of race, religion, or nationality. The action was the culmination of long effort on the part of undergraduates who had no vote in the conference but who prevailed upon the delegates to revive the issue of prejudice after it had been excluded from the program.

Students on other campuses were active in 1949, not only on the fraternity question, but on the question of discrimination in admissions to the colleges themselves. For example, in November, at the University of Michigan Medical School, twenty-two student organizations united in a campaign to eliminate all discriminatory questions from application forms as a first step in a struggle to wipe out racial and religious discrimination from all aspects of campus life.

Youth leaders at the 1949 Methodist Conference on Christian Education, held in Grand Rapids, Michigan, initiated a move to abolish racial discrimination by Methodist educational institutions. These leaders revealed that more than half of fifty-five Methodist colleges that they had surveyed excluded Negro applicants. Interestingly enough, none of these institutions practiced overt discrimination against Jewish students, but some did attempt to maintain a "balanced" enrollment.

Some college teachers, too, have evidenced interest in the subject of discrimination. In July Dr. Harold S. Diehl, Dean of the University of Minnesota Medical School, issued a statement *urging* Negroes to apply for admission.

In October 1949 the faculty of the University of Wisconsin, rejecting the recommendations of its leadership, took the position that the fight against discrimination on the campus called for deeds not words. A faculty committee had filed a report, deploring racial and religious discrimination in admissions and campus housing, but indicating that no specific action was required. However, the faculty itself directed its university committee to draft a program for action against any traces of discrimination found on the University of Wisconsin campus.

In November more than 3,000 college teachers and officials,

replying to a poll conducted by the Southern Conference Educational Fund, Inc., declared their overwhelming support for the admission, without segregation, of Negro students to professional and graduate schools. Only 25 per cent of the respondents expressed approval of the "Regional Compact," a South-wide segregation plan which went into effect in the South in September. (This "Compact" will be discussed in the last section of this chapter.)

It is clear, then, that the main prejudice which precipitates racial and religious discrimination stems neither from the students nor the faculties. They are merely the excuses behind which the policy-makers hide. If, perchance, the students and faculties were the culprits, the responsibility would be to eradicate the prejudice by education, not encourage it by conformance.

2. *If quota systems were not maintained, the colleges would be swamped with students from minority groups.*

It is true that if the quota system were abolished by only a small number of colleges, these institutions might then find their enrollment of minority group students disproportionate to the minority in the nation's population. However, if all or even most of the colleges dropped discriminatory barriers, minority group students would disappear into the national collegiate body; no school would have to contend with a disproportionate number.

3. *It is just and logical to have quotas equaling the percentage of racial and religious divisions in the general population.*

This is an undemocratic argument which violates the American tradition that the individual stands on his own merits. Under it, a student's rights are governed and limited by the faith of his fathers and not by his talents. The quota system arbitrarily renders educational opportunity the privilege of the majority, and denies it to the minority—though all have contributed historically to make this country great.

4. *Quotas reduce anti-minority prejudice.*

This argument is based on the notion that minorities can expect tolerance only so long as they present themselves in respectfully small numbers. The fact is that no noticeable prejudice has developed in those colleges where minority representatives make up a substantial segment of the student population.

5. *Although geographical quotas frequently cause hardships to minority groups, they may be necessary if a college desires to become a truly national institution.*

Proportionately more students from the Northeast than from other parts of the country desire to attend college, according to a survey[1] conducted in 1948 by the Elmo Roper organization for the American Council on Education. Most private colleges limit the number of Northeasterners accepted. This would appear unobjectionable provided all students, whether from minority or majority groups in the Northeast, were treated simply as Northeasterners. Too often, the announced objective of seeking a nationally representative student body is used as a subterfuge to discriminate against minority groups.

6. The colleges must cater to community prejudices lest they lose status and their students have difficulty obtaining jobs after graduation.

In the spring of 1949 a student committee in a great Far West university met with the Director of Admissions of that institution to discuss questions regarding race and descent on the school's admission application form. The Director of Admissions, who passes upon applications not only to the liberal arts college of the university, but to its medical, law and dental schools, argued for the continuance of the questions. He contended that it would be unfair to an applicant to admit him to a professional school if that student subsequently finds it impossible to perform his apprenticeship and to be placed within his chosen profession. He recalled that a representative of a professional accrediting agency had visited the university and remarked: "We trust that you are watching your intake of certain proportions of students."

This college official was admitting that his approval or disapproval of applications was affected by the prejudice of an outside agency. In discussing teacher training, he asserted that there had to be racial and religious limitations because the field could not absorb more than a given number of students from certain minority groups.

In short, the university in question practices discrimination in admissions because of pressures from without. Responsibility for throwing off this medieval yoke of bigotry is clearly in the hands of education's administrators. They follow community prejudice blindly at the penalty of equal guilt. If the university persistently sends forth graduates qualified without regard to race or creed to assume professional responsibilities, the community can have no choice but to accept them, or suffer the risk of shortage. Our institutions of higher learning must seek to elevate the community, rather than permit the bad customs of our society to degrade our academic leadership.

2. AMERICAN EDUCATION SELF-APPRAISED: The fact that American institutions of higher learning condone the use of racial and religious standards makes it pertinent to examine what impact, if any, recent reports and recommendations on educational discrimination have had upon the key men and women who run America's colleges and professional schools.

In the last two years, several authoritative studies have been made of the extent of discrimination against minorities in higher education. In 1947 the President's Commission on Higher Education charged that quota systems and policies of exclusion practiced by American institutions of higher learning had prevented young people of many religious and racial groups—but particularly Jews and Negroes—from obtaining higher education and professional training.[2]

A 1948 study, sponsored by the New York State Temporary Commission on The Need for a State University, concluded that Jewish applicants from high schools in New York State had significantly greater difficulty in obtaining admission to college than did their non-Jewish classmates of equal ability.[3]

An American Council on Education study, published in 1949, revealed that the average Jewish applicant for college admission had considerably less chance of acceptance than a Catholic or Protestant of comparable scholastic ability.[4]

Also in 1949 a study was sponsored by the Connecticut Interracial Commission. This was an acceptance and rejection study[5] designed to determine the degree of success or failure of Connecticut high school graduates of various racial, religious, and national origins in seeking admission to institutions of higher learning. It concluded with the now familiar finding—the Jewish applicant had a comparatively limited range of choice and succeeded in getting into college only after applying to a greater number of institutions.

The charge that American higher education is pervaded by un-American discrimination was for years met by a concerted silence on the part of colleges and professional schools. In November 1949 the wall was breached at a conference of educators. The meeting took place in Chicago under the auspices of the American Council on Education and the Anti-Defamation League. For the first time more than 100 of the country's leading educators, many of them university presidents, college deans, and admissions officers, met to assay the entire question of discrimination in higher education.

Dr. Floyd W. Reeves, chairman of the Committee on Discrimination of the American Council on Education and Professor of Administration at the University of Chicago, provided the Conference with the following findings of fact:

1. All available research agrees that racial, religious and economic barriers to higher education exist.

2. For many youths, restricted curricula and inadequate educational facilities present formidable obstacles to education.

3. Many institutions employ techniques in the admission of students which lend themselves to discriminatory practices and appear to serve no purpose other than that of discriminating against youths from certain minority groups.

Dr. Reeves' blunt charges were followed by an equally forthright statement from the Conference keynoter, Dr. A. C. Ivy, vice-president of the University of Illinois, who, in discussing the purposes and scope of the Conference, condemned selection of students on grounds other than ability and character as "the most anti-democratic aspect of higher education."

After three days of deliberation, members of the Conference concluded that discrimination in higher education on the basis of race, religion, or national origin, is completely incompatible with democratic principles. These American educators proposed that the colleges themselves should develop a program, the goal of which would be the elimination of such discrimination; the enactment of legislation, such as fair educational practices laws wherever necessary; government financial aid to improve the quality and quantity of higher educational facilities in order to remove economic barriers facing many students who seek college and professional education.

The Conference's Committee on Admissions Procedures in Undergraduate Institutions called for a long-range educational program to abolish the use of discriminatory criteria in the selection of students. It recommended that every college make public a clear and concrete statement of the procedures it employs in admitting students.

A second committee—on admissions procedures in professional schools—branded the quota system as obnoxious and un-American; declared that the doctrine of "separate-but-equal schools for Negroes and whites" was uneconomic and undemocratic; adopted the principle that discriminatory practices should be discontinued and that students selected for admission to graduate and professional schools in the United States be chosen only in terms of the common good and an evaluation of the applicant as an individual. This committee further urged the elimination of potentially discriminatory questions used on application forms by professional schools. It asked for the issuance of clear statements of admissions criteria. It expressed disapproval of over-emphasizing any single criterion, such as future placement possibilities.

The Committee on Regional Problems deplored the fact that an unfortunate combination of factors in some regions of the country worked a hardship upon certain groups of young Americans. Specifically citing the Northeast, the Committee found that a shortage of higher educational facilities and factors relating to religion, nationality, and place of residence adversely affects the ability of Jewish and other minority groups to gain admission to colleges of their preference. The report noted progress in some areas, citing the state of New York for having created a university in order to expand higher educational facilities.

A fourth committee of the Conference studied economic factors as a barrier to higher education. It recommended a system of grants-in-aid for tuition and subsistence to needy students of ability. The committee proposed that the federal government take the principal responsibility for financing grants-in-aid, and declared that the assistance allotted to a student should fully meet the difference between the complete cost of a higher education and the private resources available to meet these expenses.

Thus did some of America's leading educators acknowledge that some colleges and professional schools in the United States are guilty of practices which violate the pattern of democratic life. Thus, too, did some of America's leading educators do something about tearing down the barriers against the minorities' contribution to the arts, sciences, and professions.

3. COLLEGE ADMINISTRATORS SPEAK: The foregoing section reveals what is common knowledge, that religious and racial barriers are a serious impediment to the opportunity for higher education. Scientific research has fully confirmed the widespread nature of this educational discrimination. The Chicago Conference of Educators recognized and reported that some American colleges and professional schools permit bigotry to influence their selection of students. These facts, among others, prompted the Anti-Defamation League

to initiate a survey designed to elicit frank statements from American institutions of higher learning regarding the 1949 admissions policies of their schools. We hoped thereby to obtain an even more exact delineation of the discriminations picture in higher education in the United States.

In November and December 1949, interviews were sought with presidents, deans, admissions officers, and other administrative officials of institutions of higher learning throughout the nation. Four different kinds of schools were questioned in each of nineteen communities: liberal arts colleges, medical, dental, and law schools.

By means of a scientifically prepared interview, the League tried to determine: (a) whether these schools discriminate on the basis of race or religion, and if so the reasons for the practice, (b) the effects of the report of the President's Commission on Higher Education on their admission policies, (c) the institutions' opinion of fair educational practices laws, and (d) recommendations to reach the goals—the elimination of discriminatory barriers—set forth by the President's Commission.

All interviews were conducted with the understanding that while the results would be reported, names would be held in complete confidence.

To augment the data obtained in this interview project, a letter was sent to 140 liberal arts colleges and professional schools throughout the nation who, in responding to an earlier ADL request for application forms, had offered to furnish any other information which could conceivably be of value. The League's letter accepting the offer and making the further inquiry, assured anonymity to the respondents and asked the following four questions:

1. The Conference of Educators agreed that colleges should select students only on the basis of ability and character. Does your institution use any other criteria in student selection? If so, what are these other criteria and why are they used?

2. The Report of the President's Commission on Higher Education urged that American institutions of higher learning should abandon racial and religious quotas in the admission of students. What effect, if any, did this recommendation have on the admission policy of your institution?

3. What is your opinion of the value of fair educational practices laws in combatting discrimination in higher education?

4. What steps (other than legislation) should be taken to eliminate discrimination in higher education?

The results of the interviews and the responses to the letter are equally astonishing. Almost without exception, each college and professional school which responded reported that it has no quota system and uses no racial or religious criteria for the admission of students. (Southern institutions, of course, admitted that race was a criterion.)

We select only on the basis of ability and character. . . . In selection of students, we select only on the basis of ability and character, and residency in the state. . . . Our law school predicates its admissions on ability and character.

Again, with almost complete unanimity, those responding condemned the undemocratic nature of the quota system:

I think it would be a fine policy if all higher institutions would admit students irrespective of race or religious creed. . . . I am in hearty accord with your efforts to eliminate discriminatory practices in the field of college admissions. . . . I am pleased with the President's Commission on Higher Education urging that American institutes of higher learning abandon racial and religious quotas. . . . We do not tolerate "quota" ideas. . . . Our admissions policy is based purely on a student's school record. . . . I am not interested in whether a student is a Jew or a Negro.

Astonishing, indeed. If only the facts matched the words!

There was virtual unanimity, too, *against* fair educational practices legislation. Almost without exception, the respondents looked down their noses upon the wisdom of it:

I expect that discrimination is a result of deep-seated attitudes and it is doubtful to me, at least, if laws would do more than strengthen these attitudes. . . . I am not too enthusiastic about accomplishing greater tolerance through legislation. . . . I am opposed to any kind of "fair practices laws" that are based on an undemocratic principle. . . . I do not believe that such laws are in the long run the best manner of achieving the objective that you have in mind. . . . You cannot pass a law and say that everyone must be unselfish. . . . I don't believe that legislation is the answer. . . . In my opinion, administrators who wish to practice discrimination would be intelligent enough to evade the laws.

Finally, with respect to the report of the President's Commission on Higher Education, nearly all agreed that it had had no effect on their admission policies:

The Report has had no effect on our admission policy because the quota system has never been in use here. . . . There was no need to make any change. . . . The Report in no way changed our policy on admission. . . . It does not affect us at all. . . . Our policies were already in line with the Commission's recommendation.

Significantly, of the institutions which had offered co-operation, only *seventy-nine* responded. The silence of the others, in face of their previous gratuitous offer to be helpful, seems weighted with meaning. Of course, the statements which *were* received cannot be accepted as the national picture unless we are prepared to reject scientific research, the findings of the Chicago Conference of Educators, and common knowledge. Perhaps America's educational administrators are unaware of what has been happening on some university campuses. Perhaps not.

4. THE COLLEGE QUESTIONS THE APPLICANT: The difficulty in documenting discrimination practiced by institutions of higher learning is revealed in the preceding section. There are many excuses which a college or professional school can offer as a subterfuge to justify the rejection of an applicant; "balanced enrollment" or "true geographical representation" are but two. Detection of prejudice is rendered still more difficult by the reluctance of applicants to come forward with the evidence they possess; students are understandably fearful of jeopardizing their academic careers.

However, there is available a means of measuring the universities' *interest* in the face, faith, and color of its applicants for admission. The President's Commission on Higher Education pointed out that many such institutions are ". . . anxious to ascertain the racial origins, religion, and color of the various applicants for a purpose other than judging their qualification for admission." It concluded that ". . . the request for certain information on application forms constitutes an all but prima facie case that such information is likely to be used for discriminatory purposes."

In 1948 the Anti-Defamation League analyzed the potentially discriminatory questions found in the admission application forms used by 450 American liberal arts institutions.[6]

In 1949 ADL communicated with 565 accredited liberal arts colleges[7] and requested copies of their application forms. Excluded were colleges which are primarily divinity schools; institutions for Negroes; colleges that enroll fewer than 100 resident students in regular session, or which graduate less than ten students annually. The 565 colleges include co-educational institutions, schools for men, schools for women, public, private, denominational, and non-denominational institutions.

Five institutions responded that they are not liberal arts colleges, leaving a possible 560 applications to be analyzed. Forty-one others failed to respond (to two requests) or indicated that application blanks were being revised; two more refused co-operation. (Union College in Schenectady, New York, suggested that the inquiry be sent to the Administrator of the New York State Fair Educational Practices Act. Houghton College, Houghton, New York, advised, in a letter signed by President Stephen W. Paine: "It is our preference not to participate in this investigation which you are making of school and college procedures." It is noteworthy that Houghton College, whose admission application form was examined despite the refusal of co-operation, asks more potentially discriminatory questions than does any other liberal arts college in New York State.) The 1949 Anti-Defamation League analysis, therefore, is based, by actual count, on 518 application forms.

The New York State Department of Education has set forth the kinds of questions which, when they appear on application forms of colleges and professional schools, it terms "controversial." The Department divides the suspect questions into two groups for the non-denominational institutions and two different groups for denominational institutions:

Non-Denominational Institutions

DIRECT QUESTIONS	INDIRECT QUESTIONS
Race or Color	Photograph
Religion	Photograph made Optional
Religion made Optional	Place of Birth
Parents' Religion	Father's Place of Birth
Nationality	Mother's Place of Birth
Parents' Nationality	Grandparents' Place of Birth
	Mother's Maiden Name
	Church Organizations
	Clergymen Suggested as Reference
	Language Spoken at Home
	Change of Name

Denominational Institutions

DIRECT QUESTIONS	INDIRECT QUESTIONS
Race or Color	Photograph
Father's Race	Place of Birth
Mother's Race	Father's Place of Birth
Nationality	Mother's Place of Birth
Father's Nationality	Mother's Maiden Name
Mother's Nationality	Change of Name
	Language Spoken at Home

Using these same standards, the 518 applications were analyzed to determine the extent to which potentially discriminatory questions (direct and indirect) appeared on them. The results were then compared with the Anti-Defamation League analysis of the college applications used in 1948:

	TOTAL APPLICATIONS		APPLICATIONS WITH AT LEAST ONE POTENTIALLY DISCRIMINATORY QUESTION		AVERAGE NUMBER OF POTENTIALLY DISCRIMINATORY QUESTIONS PER APPLICATION	
	1948	1949	1948	1949	1948	1949
All Applications	450	518	91.11%	92.27%	4.38	4.68
Non-Denominational	199	244	92.46%	91.43%	5.44	5.57
a. Private	132	135	93.18%	92.50%	5.37	5.73
b. Public	67	109	91.04%	89.90%	5.57	5.37
Denominational	251	274	90.03%	93.06%	3.52	3.90
a. Protestant	163	177	88.34%	92.65%	3.42	3.98
b. Roman Catholic	88	97	93.18%	93.81%	3.70	3.76

From the above it appears that the admission application form problem was worse in 1949 than in 1948; the national percentage of questionnaires containing at least one discriminatory question was higher. In 1949 non-denominational colleges showed a somewhat better record than denominational schools. Within the non-denominational group a higher percentage of private colleges used discriminatory questions than did public institutions. Within the denominational group, the percentage for Roman Catholic institutions was a little higher than for Protestant schools. At the same time the 1949 figures reveal that the average number of discriminatory questions in the at-least-one group was substantially higher for private and public colleges than for Protestant and Roman Catholic institutions.

In 1948, for all colleges, the West produced the highest percentage of admission applications containing at least one discriminatory question; the South, the lowest. The 1949 results disclosed a noteworthy change in this picture: the Midwest had the highest percentage of discriminatory application forms; the South remained the lowest; the Northeast moved from second place in 1948 to third place in 1949.

An analysis was made of regional differences:

	TOTAL APPLICATIONS		APPLICATIONS WITH AT LEAST ONE POTENTIALLY DISCRIMINATORY QUESTION		AVERAGE NUMBER OF POTENTIALLY DISCRIMINATORY QUESTIONS PER APPLICATION	
	1948	1949	1948	1949	1948	1949
All Colleges						
Northeast	122	144	92.62%	89.58%	4.16	3.78
South	105	122	85.71%	86.88%	3.66	4.43
Midwest	170	186	91.17%	96.77%	4.80	5.04
West	53	66	98.11%	95.45%	4.86	5.93
Non-Denominational Colleges						
Northeast	66	77	87.87%	87.00%	4.50	4.25
South	46	60	91.30%	88.30%	4.80	5.54
Midwest	62	70	90.76%	98.70%	6.64	6.44
West	25	37	96.00%	91.90%	5.87	6.47
Denominational Colleges						
Northeast	56	67	96.42%	92.53%	3.79	3.27
South	59	62	81.35%	85.48%	2.66	3.32
Midwest	108	116	88.88%	95.68%	3.66	4.17
West	28	29	100.00%	100.00%	4.00	5.31

The potentially discriminatory question most frequently asked seeks information regarding the applicant's birthplace; it was found on almost 80 per cent of the applications reviewed. Least frequently asked is the inquiry about "Language Spoken at Home"; only 7.5 per cent of the applications contained this query.

The appreciable decrease from 1948 to 1949 in the number of discriminatory questions asked in the universities of the Northeast cannot be ignored. New York and New Jersey were the only states that had the benefit of fair educational practices legislation during 1949. Their forty-nine colleges were almost 35 per cent of the total number of colleges surveyed in the Northeast. An analysis was made in an attempt to determine to what degree these two states had affected the Northeast's totals. In addition, the necessary data was accumulated to prepare a comparative analysis of New York and Pennsylvania, and of New Jersey and Connecticut. The choice of Pennsylvania and Connecticut as comparable states that did not have fair educational practices acts was made on the basis of the approximate similar geographical and population characteristics and the numbers of colleges within each of the pairs of states:

	APPLICATIONS WITH AT LEAST ONE DISCRIMINATORY QUESTION		AVERAGE NUMBER OF DISCRIMINATORY QUESTIONS PER APPLICATION	
	1948	1949	1948	1949
Nation	91.11%	92.27%	4.38	4.68
Northeast	92.62%	89.58%	4.16	3.78
New York	82.75%	75.60%	4.25	1.75
Pennsylvania	97.05%	100.00%	5.12	4.74
New Jersey	100.00%	87.50%	2.83	2.71
Connecticut	100.00%	100.00%	4.50	4.14

The comparison discloses that while the national percentage of discriminatory application questions rose slightly from 1948 to 1949, the Northeast's percentage dropped three points—visibly accountable in good measure to considerable decreases in the New York and New Jersey percentages.

Vivid contrasts are supplied in the two-state comparisons. Pennsylvania's percentage of discriminatory applications rose to 100 per cent in 1949, while New York's dropped to 75.6 per cent. In New Jersey the percentage of colleges using discriminatory questions went from 100 per cent in 1948 down to 87.5 per cent in 1949. In Connecticut, on the other hand, the 1948 figure of 100 per cent remained unchanged in 1949.

As will be explained in detail in the ensuing section, the fair educational practices laws of New York and New Jersey outlaw discrimination in higher education but do not specifically (as in the case of the new Massachusetts law) enjoin schools from asking certain kinds of questions in admission application forms. Therefore, the distinct changes which have taken place in New York and New Jersey lend further support to the theory that the use of potentially discriminatory questions is almost prima facie evidence of intent to discriminate. Certainly ADL's survey demonstrates the desirability of legislation.

One additional research project deserves mention. In October 1949 two letters were sent to each accredited liberal arts college in New York, New Jersey, Pennsylvania, and Connecticut. One letter was signed with an apparently "Jewish" name and the other with an apparently "non-Jewish" name, both with New York addresses.

The letter signed with the Jewish name preceded the letter with the non-Jewish signature by one week. Neither letter indicated grades or rank in high school, and both simply requested application blanks for entrance in the fall term of 1950. The device was not employed to entrap, merely to ascertain whether the schools involved in the survey treat "Jewish" applicants for admission the same as "non-Jewish" applicants.

Of the total of 106, forty-one responded differently to the "non-Jewish" letter from the "Jewish" letter. This distinction in handling was revealed in any number of ways. In some instances the "Jewish" applicant received only an acknowledgment, while the "non-Jewish" applicant received an application form; or the "Jew" received no response whatever, while the "non-Jew" did; or the "Jew" received only a preliminary application form, while the "non-Jew" received a final application form.

To prevent any unfair conclusions from this survey, the forty-one institutions which responded differently were re-examined in November, using two further different names; again, one apparently "Jewish" and the other apparently "non-Jewish." The final codification of the two surveys discloses that in the four states, only *four* institutions in *both instances* gave apparently preferential treatment to the non-Jewish names.

Albright College of Reading, Pennsylvania, sent the two "non-Jewish" applicants formal application blanks, secondary-school record forms, and personality rating sheets; the two "Jewish" applicants received only preliminary application blanks and mimeographed forms giving information about entrance requirements and tuition fees. From Pennsylvania, too, Geneva College, of Beaver Falls, wrote the two "Jewish" applicants that enrollment had been closed, but the two "non-Jewish" applicants received admission application forms.

In New York State, Bard College, Annandale-on-Hudson, sent the two "non-Jewish" applicants letters with which were enclosed health examination blanks and admission application forms; the two "Jewish" applicants received envelopes containing merely "preliminary application blanks" with no accompanying letters or other documents. Manhattan College, Riverdale, New York sent application forms only to the "non-Jewish" applicants and ignored the letters signed by the "Jewish" names.

Of the four colleges, three—Albright, Geneva, and Manhattan—are denominational institutions. Bard College is not; it is privately controlled.

5. THE PROFESSIONAL SCHOOL QUESTIONS THE APPLICANT: In 1949 the Anti-Defamation League also conducted a content analysis of application forms in use by fully accredited schools of medicine, law, dentistry, engineering, architecture, business administration, veterinary medicine, education (including teachers' colleges), pharmacy, and optometry.[8] Request letters were sent to all these professional schools for copies of the admission application forms used by them; 609 out of a possible 696 were received:

	NUMBER OF FULLY ACCREDITED SCHOOLS	NUMBER OF APPLICATIONS RECEIVED
Medicine	69	65
Law	106	95
Dentistry	28	23
Engineering	125	111
Architecture	18	16
Business Administration	55	52
Veterinary Medicine	10	10
Education	225	183
Pharmacy	54	49
Optometry	6	5
TOTAL	696	609

The 609 applications were analyzed for potentially discriminatory questions and a particular breakdown was made for professional schools in the states of New York and New Jersey:

	APPLICATIONS WITH AT LEAST ONE POTENTIALLY DISCRIMINATORY QUESTION (Nationally)	APPLICATIONS WITH AT LEAST ONE POTENTIALLY DISCRIMINATORY QUESTION (N.Y. & N.J.)	AVERAGE NUMBER OF POTENTIALLY DISCRIMINATORY QUESTIONS PER APPLICATION (Nationally)	AVERAGE NUMBER OF POTENTIALLY DISCRIMINATORY QUESTIONS PER APPLICATION (N.Y. & N.J.)
Medicine	100.00%	100%	4.29	1.11
Law	91.57%	70%	3.25	2.28
Dentistry	100.00%	100%	5.17	1.00
Engineering	93.69%	75%	5.09	1.66
Architecture	87.12%	60%	2.92	1.00
Business Administration	90.38%	50%	4.76	2.50
Veterinary Medicine	100.00%	100%	4.90	1.00
Education	75.95%	40%	4.15	3.87
Pharmacy	95.91%	80%	4.36	1.75
Optometry	100.00%	no schools	3.20	no schools
TOTAL	88.83%	65.21%	4.29	2.02

The analysis discloses that every one of the 88 schools of medicine and dentistry, whose applications were received asks potentially discriminatory questions. This is significant in view of the special difficulties confronting Jewish students who attempt to obtain medical or dental educations.

It is interesting that the lowest figure in the use of discriminatory applications is attained by schools of education. Teaching holds the least financial attraction of all the professions. As a consequence, its schools frequently need more newcomers than they get, perhaps causing them to relax racial and religious barriers to a greater extent than other professional schools in the United States. Or perhaps those who administer schools of education are less interested in irrelevant information about applicants than are the others.

While 88.83 per cent of all the professional schools in the country used potentially discriminatory admission applications, the percentage for all the professional schools in New York and New Jersey was 65.21 per cent. Similarly, while the average number of discriminatory questions nationally was 4.29, the figure for New York and New Jersey was substantially lower—2.02.

The situation varies noticeably in the different regions of the nation:

NATION-WIDE 1949	TOTAL APPLICATIONS	APPLICATIONS WITH AT LEAST ONE POTENTIALLY DISCRIMINATORY QUESTION	AVERAGE NUMBER OF POTENTIALLY DISCRIMINATORY QUESTIONS PER APPLICATION
Northeast	181	83.42%	2.99
South	141	87.94%	4.77
Midwest	199	92.46%	4.78
West	88	93.18%	4.85

This comparison reveals that the Northeast has the lowest percentage of professional schools using discriminatory applications and the lowest average number of discriminatory questions per application, whereas the West is highest in both respects. That New York and New Jersey are largely responsible for the comparatively good showing made by the Northeast, is apparent when one considers that, of the 181 professional schools in the Northeast, 69 (or 38 per cent) are located in these two states; and that in 1949 only 65.21 per cent of the New York and New Jersey schools used discriminatory applications.

The dramatic decrease in 1949 in the use of discriminatory questions by colleges and professional schools in New York and New

Jersey, as contrasted with the rest of the nation, demonstrates in part the effectiveness of fair educational practices laws. Part of the credit for the advances made in these two states must also be given to those charged with administering the laws; the main credit, of course, goes to the people of New York and New Jersey for enacting the laws.

In December 1949 Frederick W. Hoeing, administrator of the New York State Fair Educational Practices Act, reporting to the New York State Board of Regents, showed the extent to which controversial questions had been removed from the application forms of colleges, universities, junior colleges, and state institutes in New York:

NON-DENOMINATIONAL

COLLEGES, UNIVERSITIES, JUNIOR COLLEGES, AND STATE INSTITUTES
Summary of controversial questions on application blanks and of elimination of such controversial questions for 193 administrative units of 75 colleges, universities, junior colleges, state institutes:

Direct Questions	REMOVED	STILL	REMAINING
Race or Color	5	0	–
Religion	32	2	1%
Religion Optional	2	0	–
Nationality	6	1	½%
Father's Nationality	3	0	–
Mother's Nationality	3	0	–

Indirect Questions	REMOVED	STILL	REMAINING
Photograph	24	68	36%
Place of Birth	68	53	28%
Father's Place of Birth	25	8	4%
Mother's Place of Birth	21	8	4%
Grandparents' Place of Birth	2	0	–
Mother's Maiden Name	25	3	1½%
Church Organization included in Extracurricular Activities	9	2	1%
Clergyman Suggested as Reference	6	3	1½%
Language Spoken in Home	4	3	1½%
Change of Name	7	2	1%

DENOMINATIONAL

RELIGIOUS OR DENOMINATIONAL COLLEGES, UNIVERSITIES, AND JUNIOR COLLEGES
Summary of elimination of controversial questions on application blanks for 70 administrative units of 47 colleges, universities, and junior colleges:

Direct Questions			
Race or Color	10	Nationality	9
Father's Race	1	Father's Nationality	2
Mother's Race	1	Mother's Nationality	1

Indirect Questions

Photograph	8	Change of Name	2
Place of Birth	19	Mother's Maiden Name	11
Father's Place of Birth	5	Mother's Place of Birth	5
		Language Spoken at Home	1

The following eliminations of questions on religion also have been made: Father's Religion—1; Mother's Religion—1; Religion Optional—1.

[At this writing, there are not available statistics on the number of controversial questions still remaining on the application blanks of denominational institutions. Ed. note.]

Elsewhere in the United States remedial work was undertaken by the Anti-Defamation League and other human relations agencies designed to terminate the practice by institutions of higher learning of asking potentially discriminatory questions. In some cases these efforts met with success. In the state of Oregon the effort resulted in the elimination by all colleges and universities of questions about race and religion. This success, however, is not typical. From many other states came reports of abortive attempts to induce college administrators to remove discriminatory questions. In college after college Anti-Defamation League representatives were met with stubborn and illogical refusals to modify the questionnaires. The most frequent reason advanced to justify the collection of racial and religious data was that the information was needed for "statistical" purposes and for the proper orientation of the students after admission. The obvious answer, of course, is that the data can be collected *after* the admission of the student rather than *before*.

The application form is by no means the only medium through which colleges and professional schools secure facts which can be the basis for racial or religious discrimination. Such information can be obtained at other stages of the application process. The applicant's letter requesting the admission form gives the name and address of the student; this knowledge is sometimes sufficient. A preliminary application questionnaire provides clues as to minority affiliation. Letters of recommendation and personal interviews are also direct means for learning about the applicant's creed or color.

The New York State Commission on the Need for a State University has wisely declared that no college or professional school can claim to have abandoned racial or religious criteria for admission simply because it has removed questions about race and religion from application forms.

These considerations point to the need for more affirmative investigation and action than the mere cleansing of application forms.

At the same time, it must be granted that the removal of objection-able questions *reduces* substantially the potentiality for discrimination. It is to be hoped that the recommendations of the Chicago Conference of Educators and continued remedial drives by human relations agencies will have salutary effects. Yet it must also be recognized that the greatest progress in the revision of application forms has been made as the result of legislation.

In 1949 attempts in several states failed to secure corrective legislation. In Missouri the state House of Representatives overwhelmingly passed a bill permitting Negroes to attend state-supported institutions of higher learning. The proposed legislation was supported by such organizations as the Missouri Association for Social Welfare, National Association for the Advancement of Colored People, Urban League, Catholic Interracial Council, St. Louis Civil Liberties Committee, labor unions, and others. After months of delay the Senate Education Committee finally reported out a watered-down substitute, but the Senate adjourned without taking action even on the amended proposal. In Connecticut a fair educational practices bill was introduced into the legislature, only to be defeated as a result of organized pressure by representatives of Connecticut colleges. In Illinois a fair educational practices law was offered for enactment; consideration was deferred in favor of a fair employment practices law. Similarly in Ohio a movement initiated for the enactment of a state law against discrimination in education later was discontinued in favor of a campaign for a fair employment practices law. In Pennsylvania the Committee on Fair Educational Opportunities of the Philadelphia Fellowship Commission drafted a Fair Educational Opportunities bill which was introduced in the General Assembly. The legislature, however, failed to act upon it. Indeed, with regard to fair educational practices bills, 1949 seemed to be the year of frustrated effort.

6. DISCRIMINATION IN EDUCATION AND THE LAW: What is the status of the law in respect to the problem of discrimination in education? Is it a help or a handicap to the advocates of equality of educational opportunity? Are there little known or rarely used statutes which can be called into play? Is there a body of statutory law permitting discrimination which should be repealed? These are vital questions to all who are interested in a democratic solution to

CRACKING THE QUOTA   137

the problem of unequal opportunity for education in the United States. Here are some of the answers as of 1949:

Under the Constitution of the United States the regulation of education is left to the forty-eight individual states. Each state has its own educational law, each one different. This does not mean that federal law can be ignored on matters of educational discrimination. On the contrary, the fundamental provision against discrimination on account of creed, race or color is contained in the 14th Amendment of the Constitution, adopted after the Civil War. It provides that no state shall "deny to any person within its jurisdiction the equal protection of the laws." This has been interpreted by the highest court in the land to mean that each state must grant to all its citizens equal opportunity for state-supported education. A measure adopted by a state, therefore, which restricts the admission of Jews or Catholics to state-supported schools on the basis of a quota system or other similar standard would be in clear violation of the 14th Amendment, and could not withstand legal attack.

The situation is different with regard to discrimination practiced by private schools. The equal protection clause of the 14th Amendment, as construed by the United States Supreme Court in the famous Civil Rights Cases[9] in 1883, binds each state and all state agencies, but not *private* persons or *private* agencies in the states.

Thus a private educational institution is not barred by the federal Constitution from discriminating against members of religious or racial minorities. Whether such discrimination is lawful or unlawful depends wholly on whether, and to what extent, it is prohibited by the law of the particular state.

Of course the federal government can help in the fight against discrimination in education. One effective way would be to provide that its grants of federal aid to education be limited to those facilities which admit students of all races and religions without discrimination. With the end of the educational aspects of the G.I. Bill of Rights in sight, American colleges are facing an ever increasing deficit and their need for federal assistance becomes concomitantly greater. Thus an anti-discrimination condition attached to a federal grant becomes that much more effective.

Since the federal government has no direct jurisdiction in the matter, let us turn to the laws of the forty-eight states:[10]

As stated above, public schools at all levels, including municipal and state colleges and universities, are prohibited by the equal protection clause of the 14th Amendment from discriminating, in any respect whatever, against persons because of their creed, race or color. (A discussion of the inconsistency of racial segregation with this constitutional provision is set forth in ensuing pages.) If, therefore, the state constitution or a state law expressly prohibits religious and racial discrimination in public schools, such a provision is only a declaration of the legal situation prevailing throughout the United States by virtue of the 14th Amendment. This does not mean that such statements contained in state jurisprudence are of no importance. They may have the practical advantage of providing special sanctions for violations of the law; for example, dismissal or other penalties for school officials. They may facilitate the effective prosecution of violations. They demonstrate also that public opinion within the particular state is in favor of prohibiting discrimination on account of race or creed.

It is really with respect to private educational institutions that we are confronted with fundamental differences in the laws of the various states. In the absence of state laws prohibiting discrimination on account of religion or race these institutions are free to discriminate, even though the law has long since recognized their quasi-public nature. There are no such prohibitory statutes in most of the states. If a private school or college in Minnesota, California or Texas, for example, should reject an applicant on the openly admitted ground that he is an Italian, a Negro, a Catholic or a Jew, no remedy would be available to the person thus aggrieved.

On the other hand, in a few states laws have been passed which are directed against discrimination by all or most private educational institutions. Idaho prohibits questions concerning religion in connection with applications for admission to any institution of learning incorporated under the law of that state. In Illinois, schools, colleges or universities which refuse admission to applicants solely on account of race, color or creed are subject to a state law which provides that they are not to be considered reputable institutions of learning; graduation from such schools would not qualify a person for admission to certain professions and occupations. The weakness of this type of law is that it can victimize innocent students who matriculate in ignorance of the school's disability. By far the most effective laws in this respect are the fair educational practices laws; it is here that some progress was made in 1949.

The first law of this kind was passed in April 1948 in the State of New York. It prohibits schools above the secondary level from excluding or limiting or otherwise discriminating against persons seeking admission as students because of race, religion, creed, color or national origin. Religious and denominational schools are left free to select students exclusively or primarily from members of their *religious* denomination; a Catholic, Protestant or Jewish denominational school would violate the law, however, by refusing a Negro student because of his *race*.

Enforcement of the law is divided between the Commissioner of Education and the Board of Regents, the members of which are elected by the legislature. The Commissioner of Education has authority to investigate charges of religious or racial discrimination and to bring about the elimination of such practice by the informal methods of persuasion, conciliation or mediation. If these methods fail, the Commissioner has power to refer the matter to the Board of Regents which must conduct a formal hearing, take evidence, and decide the case. The Board of Regents may order a dismissal of the complaint or direct the defendant to cease and desist from the unfair educational practice. Such an order is enforceable through court action.

In 1949 two states followed the lead of New York by adopting fair educational practices laws. The Freeman law of New Jersey[11] amends the fair employment practices laws of that state, officially called the Law Against Discrimination. It extends its application to discrimination in educational institutions and elsewhere, and assigns *one* agency the task of enforcement in all the fields covered by the law. Massachusetts, on the other hand, passed a fair educational practices law[12] which, like the law of New York, is in no way connected with the fair employment practices law; it delegates enforcement to the State Board of Education.

Despite the basic similarity of the three fair educational practices laws, a comparison reveals a number of important differences. The New York law covers only educational institutions beyond the high school level. The laws of New Jersey and Massachusetts are not so limited but apply to schools at all levels including kindergartens, elementary schools, high schools and trade schools. On the other hand, the laws of New Jersey and Massachusetts specifically exclude from their coverage schools which are in their nature distinctly private; the law of New York has no such clause, although the limitation of the New York law to institutions "subject to the visitation, examination or inspection" by the state educational authorities has a somewhat similar effect.

Whether an educational institution is distinctly private may not, in all cases, be easy to determine. The fact that an educational institution is not a public school in the sense of a school maintained and controlled by public authorities does not make it a school "in its nature distinctly private." To fall within the description "distinctly private" such institutions must limit themselves to a very narrow group of persons. An ultra-exclusive private finishing school for girls would be an example. A private institution that accepts applications from the public generally would certainly remain outside the definition, as would an institution appealing to the public for funds.

With regard to religious and denominational schools, the law of Massachusetts follows closely the law of New York; it permits the school to give its own denominational adherents a complete priority. The law of New Jersey exempts such schools from its coverage altogether; it is not unlawful in that state for a denominational school to discriminate against persons on account of their race or national origin. There seems no valid reason to exempt such schools from the fair educational practices laws in any respect except to give them the right to choose students of their own denomination, as in the law in New York and Massachusetts.

On the other hand, the Massachusetts law does not appear to be free from objectionable features either. It declares it to be an unfair educational practice for an educational institution to discriminate "against any United States citizen," thus leaving aliens without protection. There seems to be no good reason why an alien who is a lawful resident of this country should not enjoy the same protection against discrimination granted to citizens; it is ironic that a law directed against discrimination by reason of race, creed, color, *and national origin*, actually discriminates against persons on the ground of alienage, which is closely connected with national origin.

Thus in some respects the fair educational laws of New Jersey and Massachusetts fall short of the standard set by New York; in other respects these laws represent a definite improvement over the New York law. New York, while prohibiting discrimination against persons seeking admission to educational institutions, does not cover discrimination against students once they have been admitted, i.e., in the use of recreational, social, and other similar campus facilities. The New Jersey law affords this additional protection, but the law in Massachusetts does not.

One major defect of the New York fair educational practices law is the failure to outlaw discriminatory questions in application forms. The information obtained by questions about race, religion or national origin makes easier discriminatory practices in the admission of students. Such questions should, therefore, be barred. If a school wants personal data about its students for statistical or other non-discriminatory purposes, it can be gotten after the student has been admitted. The law enacted in Massachusetts expressly declares that it is an unfair educational practice "to cause to be made any written or oral inquiry concerning the race, religion, color or national origin of a person seeking admission." In conforming to its policy with regard to religious and denominational schools, the law in Massachusetts does not prohibit inquiries by such schools about the religious affiliations of applicants.

A consideration of the shortcomings and advantages of the various laws already enacted has led the Anti-Defamation League to prepare a model bill embodying what it believes to be the most desirable and most potentially effective form of suggested state legislation directed against discrimination in education. The text of that model bill is set forth in the Appendix page 217.

There is reason to rejoice that one year after the enactment of the New York fair educational practices law—which represents a completely new approach to the problem of combating discrimination in educational institutions—two more states, in which some of the most important private educational institutions in this nation are located, adopted similar laws. It is, of course, too early to assess the practical results of the operation of these laws; whether they will achieve elimination of educational discrimination will largely depend on the efficiency and devotion of those charged with enforcing them. It will also depend on the degree to which individuals affected by unfair educational practices avail themselves of the protection given them by the new enactments. And, in the final analysis, of course, it will depend upon the spirit in which educational institutions accept the fact of the existence of such laws.

The foregoing is a general view of state laws on discrimination in education based essentially on religion. The picture is the same with respect to discrimination based on color or race, with one very important reservation. Throughout the South, individual states make mandatory the segregation of Negroes—and in some cases, Indians—in education as well as in other spheres (public accommodation, housing, etc.).

Soon after the adoption of the 14th Amendment prohibiting the states from denying a person the equal protection of the laws, the question arose as to whether the segregation laws could be reconciled with this constitutional mandate. In 1896 the Supreme Court of the United States held, in the case of Plessy v. Ferguson,[13] that a state law requiring segregation of Negroes in railways does not deny them the equal protection of the laws.

Following this short-sighted decision, the separate-but-equal doctrine was developed. Under this doctrine it is held in effect that segregation of Negroes does not deny them equal protection provided that the facilities granted them are "substantially equal" to those available to members of the white race. Applied to the field of education, the principle means that state laws requiring or authorizing separate public or private schools for members of a minority race are not unconstitutional. Under this doctrine, as applied, a member of the Negro race in a state which has adopted segregation in educational institutions has no right to attend the public schools reserved for white persons; the state is simply under an obligation to provide him with educational facilities which are "substantially equal" to those which it offers white persons.

Of course, actual educational opportunity for the Negro in the South is far from being "substantially equal" to that offered persons of the dominant race (or in the North, for that matter, where the quota system is used in place of the segregation law.) This lack of equality where separation is mandatory applies to all aspects of education at all levels, including school building facilities, number of children attending a class, qualification of teachers, variety of subjects taught and so forth.

To achieve something like "substantial equality" between white and Negro education within the framework of segregation would mean the complete duplication of existing "white" educational facilities in the South—an economic impossibility for individual states. Some improvement of educational facilities for Negroes, however, can be found in many parts of the South. This is the result of a series of court decisions rendered in actions brought by Negroes on the ground that the educational opportunities offered in the public schools reserved for colored pupils are far inferior to those enjoyed by the whites.

A recent example is the decision[14] of the Federal District Court in Arkansas handed down on July 8, 1949. The school authorities of DeWitt Special School District No. 1 of Arkansas County were ordered, among other things, to improve a certain elementary school for Negroes by providing sanitary facilities, new desks, and a safe and comfortable vehicle for the transportation of pupils, and to bring the length of school terms of Negro schools into parity with the school terms of white schools.

The Court refused to restrain the school authorities from completing a new high school for white children at an estimated cost of $140,000; the corresponding Negro school had a valuation of $6,000. The Court added, however, that after its completion the authorities would be restrained from constructing any additional building or facilities for the white children or from making any capital improvement on existing buildings until such time as the plant of the Negro elementary school is improved and brought up to a status of "substantial equality" with the physical plant of the white elementary school.

In November 1949 the U.S. Circuit Court of Appeals in Baltimore held[15] that Pulaski County, Virginia, was discriminating against Negro high school students in compelling them to travel a longer distance in school busses than white students.

Another step forward within the undemocratic framework of the separate-but-equal theory was made in May 1949. Four school officials of Gloucester County in Virginia were fined $250 each by the Federal District Court in Richmond for disobeying a permanent injunction under which they were required to equalize Negro educational facilities in the county.

The separate-but-equal doctrine applies to state universities as well as to public primary and secondary schools. (Private schools, as said before, are not bound at all, of course.) However, the higher and more specialized the school, the more costly it becomes to maintain the semblance of equality in segregation. Few Southern states are in a financial position to establish and maintain, in addition to the graduate schools for whites, another group of similar schools which would give Negroes an equal graduate education in all fields offered white students.

A number of Southern states tried some years ago to circumvent this difficulty. They devised a scheme under which qualified Negro students would be given scholarships to attend courses in a school in another state chosen by the white educators. However, state laws providing for such schemes were held by the United States Supreme Court in 1938 to be in contravention of the equal protection clause in the 14th Amendment. The court said[16] that a state was obligated to provide substantially equal education facilities for Negroes *within* its own territory; it ordered the University of Missouri to admit a Negro to its law school in the absence of other and proper provisions for his legal training within the State of Missouri.

The Supreme Court reiterated this view in a 1948 decision[17] in which it declared that the State of Oklahoma must *simultaneously* provide law school facilities for a Negro girl if it does so for applicants of any other group.

On the authority of these Supreme Court decisions, a Federal District Court in Kentucky held, in a case[18] decided in 1949, that the Negro plaintiffs are entitled to be admitted to the graduate and professional schools of the University of Kentucky until such time as the Commonwealth of Kentucky provides substantially equal training in a separate institution of learning located within the state.

As a result of these and similar decisions, state universities in several Southern states—at least Kentucky, Oklahoma, Arkansas, Maryland—admitted qualified Negro students in 1949 to graduate courses; in Oklahoma, a law making such admission legal was passed in 1949.[19]

Actual classroom instruction in at least some of these universities is still technically segregated; different rooms, separate teaching times, etc. In a controversy now pending before the U.S. Supreme Court, the McLaurin *v.* Oklahoma State Regents case,[20] the petitioner, a graduate student of the University of Oklahoma, claims that his exclusion from the regular classroom (he is relegated to a different room from which he participates in class work through an open door) denies him equal protection of the laws.

Regardless of the outcome of this or similar suits, daily contact between white and colored students appears to have a tendency to overcome artificial barriers. Attempts are being made, however, to reverse this salutary trend in graduate education in the South. The "Regional Compact" entered into by fourteen Southern states on February 8, 1948, and ratified by the legislatures of seven states in 1949 is nothing more than an attempt to turn back the clock. The announced objective of the Regional Compact is to arrange for the pooling of educational facilities in various Southern states so as to insure that every student receives the best possible graduate education. While officially applying to all students regardless of race, the thinly-disguised purpose of the Compact is to concentrate colored graduate students into a few schools set aside for Negroes. The declaration by the Supreme Court that such an arrangement is unconstitutional is being met by the argument that under this regional plan white students as well as Negroes might be sent to other states if there are no adequate schools in their home states. Its opponents argue, of course, that virtually every Southern state has graduate and professional courses for its white students so that the regional plan will rarely be used for them.

The highest court of Maryland will soon have the opportunity to pass upon the constitutionality of the legislation implementing the Regional Compact. An action[21] has been brought by a Negro woman, who was rejected by the University of Maryland for admission to the Graduate School of Nursing. She was informed that, in view of the segregation policy of Maryland, she could not be accepted by that school but that financial provision (the Regional Compact) would be made to enable her to study at the nursing school of Meharry College in Tennessee, a Negro institution.

The separate-but-equal doctrine on which the segregation of Negroes in public educational institutions is based has been under constant attack by liberal circles from its very beginning. Again and again, the inherent invalidity of the theory has been expounded. It has been shown that, contrary to the opinion of the majority of the United States Supreme Court in Plessy v. Ferguson, segregation of Negroes is perforce based on the false principle that they are inferior. It has been amply demonstrated that as long as there exist two sets of educational institutions, one for whites and one for Negroes, actual inequalities in educational facilities will arise not only in graduate schools but in schools at all levels.

The requirement of the 14th Amendment can be met only by providing the *same* education for all, i.e., giving every person meeting the general educational requirement the same opportunity to attend any school regardless of color or race.

There are several cases now before the United States Supreme Court in which that tribunal will have the opportunity to consider these and other arguments for the elimination of the separate-but-equal doctrine in education as well as in other fields. One of these matters—Sweatt v. Painter case[22]—is concerned, in particular, with segregation in educational institutions. In a joint brief submitted as amicus curiae in May 1949 the Anti-Defamation League and two other organizations supported the Negro petitioner.

At present twenty-one states, in addition to the District of Columbia, authorize segregation of Negroes in some or all public schools. These states are: Alabama, Arizona, Arkansas, Delaware, Florida, Georgia, Kansas, Kentucky, Louisiana, Maryland, Mississippi, Missouri, New Mexico, North Carolina, Oklahoma, South Carolina, Tennessee, Texas, Virginia, West Virginia, and Wyoming.

In three of the twenty-one states—Kansas, New Mexico, Wyoming —segregation of Negroes is permitted but not required. In Kansas, such permission applies only to certain classes of public schools. Segregation of Negroes in Arizona is mandatory in elementary schools, permitted in high schools. In the other seventeen states, segregation of Negroes is mandatory in all public schools. Four of them, Florida, Kentucky, Oklahoma and Tennessee, have laws which expressly require segregation even in private schools.

In a number of states the law requiring segregation is coupled with a clause requiring that equal facilities be granted the schools set aside for Negroes. Such a provision based on the constitutional guarantee of equal protection must, of course, be read into the law even though a state may not have expressly spelled it out.

In the remaining twenty-seven states, segregation of races in public schools is prohibited. (In states with fair educational practices laws this prohibition extends to private schools.) These twenty-seven states include Indiana[23] and Wisconsin,[24] in which laws prohibiting discrimination and segregation based on race, creed or color were passed by state legislatures in 1949. In Indiana the law provides for a gradual process of elimination of separate schools, extending over several years, to be completed in 1954.

In most of these states prohibition of segregation is grounded in constitutional or statutory provisions expressly banning classifications in public education based on race or color. In a few states the same prohibition derives from laws providing for uniform systems of public schools open to *all* children, as in Iowa, Montana and Utah.

Two states, Ohio and California, passed laws in 1887 and 1947 respectively, repealing earlier legislation which had authorized segregation of races.

In the remaining states—Maine, Nebraska, Nevada, New Hampshire, North Dakota, Oregon, South Dakota and Vermont—the law is silent on the question of racial segregation. Fortunately, the courts have universally held that in the absence of constitutional or statutory authority separate public schools may not be established for different races.[25]

The fact that in twenty-seven states of the Union segregation of Negroes in public schools is forbidden by law does not mean that segregation is not practiced in the public schools of many of these states. Special circumstances frequently cause many public schools to be attended exclusively by members of one race. Where the main Negro population of a city is concentrated in certain residential districts, the schools in these districts actually are attended only by Negroes. Conversely, Negroes do not attend schools in those parts of the city where no Negroes reside. Unfortunately, too, in school districts containing large numbers of both races the parents of white children frequently withdraw them and send them to other schools.

In some instances public officials have themselves contributed to the segregation of races in public schools in the twenty-seven "prohibited" states. Subterfuges are evident, particularly in the Middle West. One method employed by authorities to circumvent laws prohibiting segregation of races is to draw boundaries of school districts in such a way that Negroes and whites reside in different school districts and, therefore, attend different schools (gerrymandering). This method, for example, was used by school authorities of Johnson County in Kansas with the result that colored pupils were segregated from white pupils despite a provision of the law of Kansas.

The Supreme Court of Kansas, in a decision handed down in 1949,[26] exposed the gerrymandering practices of the school authorities in question. The Court held that what the school authorities could not do directly, they could not do by subterfuge; it ordered the authorities to admit Negro pupils to the school previously reserved for white children.

In Illinois racial and religious segregation of children in public schools has been banned for years. Yet, significantly, the Illinois legislature found it necessary, in enacting its 1949 school appropriation law,[27] to deny funds to school districts in which any student is excluded or segregated because of his race, color or nationality.

The Illinois school appropriation law had at least one immediate effect. East St. Louis, a city in down-state Illinois, on December 20, 1949, voted unanimously to end an eighty-five-year-old policy of segregation in its public schools by January 30, 1950, "in a spirit of fair play and in accordance with true democracy." Incidentally, the city was faced with the loss of over half a million dollars in state school aid funds.

The decisions of the United States Supreme Court in 1950 in the segregation cases now pending will, it is hoped, finally eliminate the educational segregation which is written into state constitutions and state laws.

Chapter 8. Prejudice on the Campus

THE PREVIOUS chapter examined the instruments of potential discrimination maintained in 1949 against American Jewish youth who want a college education. Now it would be interesting to see how the prejudice of those who run some of the schools compares with that of the young Americans for whose benefit the educational institutions exist. The previous chapter shows convincingly that there are unrelenting efforts on the part of some educators to keep to a minimum the number of Jewish students on the campuses of the nation. Does the student for whose benefit presumably this discrimination is practiced want to be shielded from contact with Jews? Is he willing in his school life to associate with Jewish youth? Does he feel the same way as his would-be protectors?

It would be interesting to learn at the same time how the college student compares to the average American in his bias. When he enters the university, are his sentiments the same as those of the average American; better or worse? What does four years of college instruction do to him; make him less or more prejudiced? After four years of college how is he different from the average American—if he is—in his prejudices against Jews?

As will be shown in ensuing pages, the overwhelming majority of American college students prefer a college which admits the best students regardless of religion. They simply don't agree with their elders on the wisdom of barring Jews. The survey indicates, too, that college students are found to be much less prejudiced than the average American. This is not to say, however, that they are without anti-Jewish bias.

In order to ascertain what these student prejudices were in 1949, the ADL again called upon Elmo Roper, this time to poll and analyze anti-Semitic attitudes among college students. The Roper organization conducted the study during the early weeks of the 1949 fall term.

One thousand college freshmen and a thousand college seniors were personally interviewed by Roper interviewers. Interviews were distributed among fifty different campuses in the United States, with allocations so arranged as to make the total a representative cross-section sample of college freshmen and seniors in the four-year-degree granting institutions in the United States.[1]

Students were interviewed with a questionnaire, and the questions were for the most part of the fixed alternative type. The qualifications that must be made with respect to anti-Semitic attitude research of this type were outlined in detail in Chapter 6. The survey yields information on verbalizable attitudes that the respondents are willing to admit having. By inference, it yields also a limited amount of information about prejudices the respondent reveals without being aware he is doing so. College students are used to being "tested," however, and they are probably more alert to the implications of the questions asked them than are many adults interviewed on doorsteps or in their homes. College students may also be more aware of the stigma attached to the anti-Semite and less willing to confess to having feelings in that direction. These factors must be taken into account in interpreting the results of the study that follow. It may be that college anti-Semitism is actually somewhat greater than these results indicate. Nevertheless, the amount of prejudice that the study does reveal is enough of itself to cause concern. For these college students represent a large share of the "thought leaders" of the future.

THE PATTERN OF COLLEGE ANTI-SEMITISM: How much anti-Semitism *does* the study uncover? And in relation to what situations and issues? In reporting on what might be termed "the pattern of college anti-Semitism" attention will be concentrated on the senior group. The freshmen had been on the campus only for a brief period at the time the study was made, and at this early stage of their college careers they may be said to reflect more the attitudes of secondary school seniors than *bona fide* members of the college community.

That these college seniors share in some measure the popular fear of Jewish dominance over some areas of American life is indicated in Table I. Twenty-three per cent name the Jews as a group that is getting more economic power than is good for the country, and from one viewpoint this is a large percentage of educated people to share this old stereotype. On the other hand, however, two-thirds of the seniors think no one of the four groups (Protestants, Catholics, Jews, Negroes) is getting either too much economic power or too much political power for the country's good, and there is a considerable feeling that Jews (25 per cent) and Negroes (70 per cent) should be "getting a better break than they are now." There is, therefore, considerable awareness of minority group difficulties.

TABLE I: Attitudes of College Seniors Toward Minority Groups

	SHOULD BE GETTING A BETTER BREAK IN THIS COUNTRY THAN THEY ARE NOW	ARE GETTING MORE ECONOMIC POWER IN THE U.S. THAN IS GOOD FOR THE COUNTRY	ARE GETTING MORE POLITICAL POWER THAN IS GOOD FOR THE COUNTRY
Protestants	3%	3%	8%
Catholics	12	7	14
Jews	25	23	6
Negroes	70	3	5
None of them	21	64	66
Blank ballot* or refused	3	4	4

*The answers to the questions in this table were recorded by the respondents themselves on "ballots" provided for them, and then inserted in a "ballot box" carried by the interviewer.

TABLE II: Social Distance Attitudes of Non-Jewish College Seniors

	WOULD PREFER NOT TO WORK WITH IF THEY HAD AN EQUAL POSITION TO MINE AND WORKED BESIDE ME	WOULD PREFER NOT TO HAVE AS GUEST IN HOME	WOULD PREFER NOT TO HAVE MOVE INTO MY NEIGHBORHOOD TO LIVE	WOULD PREFER NOT TO HAVE MARRY A CLOSE RELATIVE OF MINE
Negroes	15%	26%	45%	75%
Mexicans	7	9	22	38
Chinese	2	6	12	43
Filipinos	4	7	15	39
Jews	5	3	10	25
Italians	2	2	5	10
Catholics	1	0	0	12
Protestants	0	0	0	3
No difference	78	68	47	19
Not answered	3	5	4	5

The general social distance pattern for college seniors is a more or less typical one, with Jews ranking after Negroes, Mexicans, Chinese, and Filipinos as a group to be held at arm's length. Five per cent of the non-Jewish seniors would not want to work alongside a Jew, only 3 per cent would not want to entertain a Jew in their home, 10 per cent would not want one to move into their neighborhoods, and 25 per cent would prefer not to see intermarriage between a Jew and one of their close relatives. By the same token 20 per cent of the *Jewish* seniors would not want one of their close relatives to marry a Catholic or a Protestant.

Actually, if the responses of the seniors can be trusted, there is an encouraging number who do not want to set any limits, short of actual intermarriage, to their association with any of the named "minorities." Almost 80 per cent of the non-Jewish seniors said it would make no difference to them if any member of the groups worked beside them, and almost 70 per cent would be willing to entertain any of them in their home. When it is proposed to move a minority group member into the neighborhood the shoe really begins to pinch, but even here 47 per cent say they would not object. As to marriage with a near relative, the frequent answers of students were, "That's up to the relative, if he doesn't mind, I don't," or "It's none of my business what a relative does." While only 20 per cent said it made no difference to them if a relative married a minority group member, a number of others qualified their statement that they preferred not to have a close relative marry a Negro, a Filipino, a Jew, etc. by adding, "But of course it's really up to him (or her) to decide whom to marry."

Another way Gentiles have of making Jews "keep their social distance" is to exclude them from colleges or apply some restrictive quota to them. As Table III indicates, college seniors are over-whelmingly outspoken against these practices. However, when it comes to the question of admitting Jews to a more exclusive group than the student body, the college fraternity, or sorority, more prejudiced attitudes come into play. But, as Table IV shows, there is still an over-all majority opposed to any discrimination even here;

TABLE III: Attitudes of Non-Jewish Seniors Toward the Admission of Jews to Colleges

I would prefer a child of mine to go to	TOTAL NON-JEWISH SENIORS
A college which admits the best students who apply whether they are Jewish or not	90%
A college which only admits Jewish students in the same proportion as there are Jews in that region	5
A college which only admits Jews if they are especially outstanding	3
A college which admits no Jews at all	2
Don't know and no answer	0*
	100%

(*) Less than 0.5%

TABLE IV: Type of Fraternity College Seniors
Would "Feel Most At Home In"

	NON-JEWISH SENIORS	JEWISH SENIORS	NON-JEWISH SENIORS ATTENDING A COLLEGE WHERE FRATERNITIES OR SORORITIES ARE PRESENT WHO	
			ARE MEMBERS	ARE NOT MEMBERS
Number of Respondents	918	91	405	344
One that was completely restricted to Gentiles	22%	0%	31%	17%
One that was completely restricted to Jews	0	12	1	0
One that admitted Jews occasionally but was always at least 90% Gentile	18	0	23	14
One that admitted Gentiles occasionally but was always at least 90% Jewish	0	8	0	1
One that freely admitted both Jews and Gentiles and that usually contained a considerable number of each	57	79	44	64
Don't know and no answer	3	1	1	4

although not a majority of fraternity members. Twenty-two per cent of Gentile seniors would "feel most at home in" (a euphemism for "would prefer to join") a fraternity or sorority restricted solely to Gentiles; 12 per cent of the Jewish seniors would prefer a fraternity or sorority restricted to Jews. Since the exclusion of Jews from Gentile fraternities and Gentiles from Jewish fraternities is the usual rule on American campuses, it is encouraging that this status quo finds so few defenders who frankly admit they prefer it that way. While the percentages of fraternities and non-fraternity seniors who say they would feel more at home in a fraternity that did *not* discriminate must undoubtedly be discounted, there is still a definite indication from the findings that the fight by the Phi Kappa Psi chapter at Amherst for the right to pledge a minority group member finds growing spiritual support among American undergraduates.

Because of the important educational and prestige-giving role of campus "student activities" any discrimination in the distribution of opportunities to participants to attain distinction in these activities should be a matter of concern to educators. In this study two types of hypothetical situations involving discrimination were presented to students who were asked their opinions on the course of action to be followed. The first situation was one in which there were two candidates for election to the board of the local college newspaper, one of whom was a Jew, the other a Gentile. The student was told to assume that both were equally well qualified for the position and asked if he would have "any preference" as to which he would prefer to see elected. If he had a preference he was asked which he would prefer. If he reported no preference, he was then pushed a little farther by being asked, "Now suppose it meant that Jewish students would become a majority of the board if the Jewish candidate were elected. Do you think you would then have a preference for one of the candidates or not?"

TABLE V: Attitudes of Non-Jewish Seniors Toward the Election of a Jew to the Editorial Board of the Local College Newspaper

Number of Seniors Questioned		918
Would prefer Gentile be elected		36%
In any case	17%	
Only if Jews would be in minority	19	
Would have no preference		57
Would prefer Jew		1
Don't know and no answer		6
		100%

As Table V shows, about six out of ten of the seniors report that they would have no preference as between the Jewish and the Gentile candidates, even though the election of the Jew would give his religious group a majority on the board. Another two out of ten would be willing to see the Jew elected if it would not mean a Jewish majority. But 17 per cent of the non-Jewish seniors would oppose the election of a Jew to the board in any case.

The second student activity "situation" on which attitudes were tested was one involving the all-important institution of intercollegiate athletics. The question asked was, "Suppose six of the eleven best football players in college happened to be Jews. Do you think it would be a good idea to have them all play on the varsity team, or do you think it would be better on the whole not to have as many Jews as that on the team?" The results are shown in Table VI. It appears that an overwhelming majority of the non-Jewish seniors would like to see the college field its best football team, regardless of what racial or ethnic group contributed a majority of the members. A good many seniors specifically stated that they wanted the best football team they could get, and it may be that the discrimination issue has become as unimportant in college athletics as in professional sports, at least so far as the spectator is concerned. The con-

TABLE VI: *Attitudes of Non-Jewish Seniors Toward Having Six Out of the Eleven Players on the Varsity Football Team Jews or Negroes*

	SIX OUT OF ELEVEN OF THE TEAM	
	JEWS	NEGROES
Total Seniors Questioned	918	918
Good idea to have all of them play	49%	47%
Better not to have that many on the team	7	13
Doesn't matter (a volunteered answer)	41	36
Don't know and no answer	3	4
	100%	100%

trast in the amount of anti-Jewish discrimination revealed in relation to majority control of the editorial board of the college newspaper (36 per cent) and majority membership on the football varsity (7 per cent) is possibly an indication both of the professionalization of college athletics (the identification of the players as gladiators rather than as fellow students) and of the strong desire of the undergraduates to see their team win games.

Two final questions were asked in order to explore the issue of discrimination in employment. The first was an attempt to find out whether college seniors were aware that such discrimination existed, the second to learn what, if anything, they thought should be done about it. The results are shown in Tables VII and VIII. Inspection of these tables leads to two conclusions: (1) most seniors know that

TABLE VII: *Attitudes of Non-Jewish College Seniors Concerning the Placement Chances of a Jewish Senior with Good Grades and a Good Extra-curricular Activity Record*

If the Jewish senior applied in an industry owned and operated chiefly by Gentiles, he could—	ANSWERS OF 918 NON-JEWISH SENIORS
Get a decent job there as easily as a Gentile classmate with the same personality and college record	20%
Get a decent job only after applying at many more companies than a Gentile	67
Never get a decent job in that industry at all	5
Don't know and no answer	8

discrimination exists, but (2) there is no consensus on what should be done about it. It is true that 45 per cent of the seniors would favor giving publicity to the situations where a non-discrimination policy has proved satisfactory, but this is a recommendation only the strong anti-Semite will quarrel with. Only 21 per cent are apparently in favor of a state fair employment practices law, and 13 per cent like the idea of "exposing" discriminators, presumably without any other penalty than public stigma. On the other hand, there are a few (13 per cent) who seemingly favor a permanent segregation policy in employment and many of these are willing to justify this position, in terms of the old myth about unchangeable human nature.

It would take many more questions than have been reported on so far, to yield a complete and well-rounded picture of college anti-Semitism, but perhaps at least a general over-all feeling for the situation as it exists today has been provided. The largest percentage of anti-Semitism shows up where relatively close personal contact is involved, as in college fraternity membership or in intermarriage,

TABLE VIII: What Non-Jewish College Seniors
Would Like to See Done About
Discrimination Against Jews in Employment*

	ANSWERS OF 918 COLLEGE SENIORS **
	%
Pass a law to prevent discrimination on the basis of religion in hiring people for jobs	21
Expose individuals and companies who practice religious discrimination in hiring people for jobs	13
Give publicity to the success many companies have had in getting Jews and Gentiles to work together congenially	45
Try to educate Jews to change their behavior so they will be less objectionable to non-Jews	9
Let Jews work for Jewish companies and Gentiles work for Gentile companies	2
It's useless to try to do anything because human nature can't be changed, and you'll only stir up more trouble between Jews and Gentiles	11
None of them	5
Don't know	1

(*)   The actual question asked was: "If Jewish students *do* have trouble getting jobs in certain industries in some parts of the country, which, if any, of the things shown on this list would you like to see done about it?" (Card was then shown respondent with the alternatives in the table above.)

(**)   Percentages add to more than 100 because some respondents gave more than one answer.

but there is some fear of Jewish "control" over the editorial board of the college newspaper and some worry over the economic power that Jews are alleged to wield in the U. S. A. Nowhere, however, are the persons with anti-Semitic attitudes in the majority, and usually they are a fairly small (5–20 per cent) minority. Even though the methods of investigation employed probably tend to minimize anti-Semitism somewhat, this is still not as discouraging a finding as some may have expected. One may lament the residue of discrimination still existing and yet take comfort in the fact that *most* college students either now have democratic attitudes, or else are ashamed to confess that they do not have them. When the college figures are later compared with the results from a national cross section, the college picture will appear even more heartening.

ANTI-SEMITISM AMONG SUB-GROUPS OF COLLEGE SENIORS: College seniors are not a completely homogeneous group, any more than is the general population. There are men students; there are co-eds; there are students from the Northeast, and the Far West; there are Protestant students and Catholics and Jews. How do these various sub-groups of college seniors feel on the issue of anti-Semitism? Are the anti-Semites located in one particular section of the collective student body, or are they spread evenly in all groups?

TABLE IX: *Anti-Semitic Attitudes of Men and Women Non-Jewish Seniors*

	MEN	WOMEN
Number of Respondents	569	349
% who would prefer not to work side by side with Jews	6%	3%
% who would prefer not to have Jews move into their neighborhood to live	10	9
% who would prefer not to have Jews as guests in their home	4	3
% who would prefer not to have one of their near relatives marry a Jew	26	24
% who would prefer to send a child of theirs to a college which either excludes Jews entirely or admits them on some different and more exclusive basis than Gentiles	10	9
% who would prefer to join a fraternity (sorority) that was always *at least* 90% Gentile	39	42
% who would prefer to have a Gentile elected to the college newspaper board instead of an equally qualified Jew	36	36
% who would prefer not to have six of the eleven players on the college football team be Jews, even though they were better than the Gentiles who would take their places	7	7

Inspection of the rather complicated Table IX yields some answers to these queries. In the first place, there seems to be very little difference in anti-Semitism by sex. Men students and women students do not differ by more than three percentage points on any of the questions for which the sex tabulation is available. The sometimes offered hypothesis that women are more snobbish and exclusive than men, and consequently more anti-Semitic, finds no support from the data of this study. If anything, the results point slightly in the opposite direction so far as college women are concerned.

Religion is also an unimportant differentiating factor in college anti-Semitism. Some of the percentage differences between Protestants and Catholics shown in Table X are a little larger than any of those between men and women, but the differences do not form any consistent pattern. Protestant students appear to be significantly less willing than Catholics to approve intermarriage between one of their near relatives and a Jewish person, and Protestants are also less willing to see Jews in the fraternities they themselves join. Catholics, on the other hand, are less aware of employment discrimination against Jews.

There is a fairly definite *regional* pattern in the distribution of students' anti-Semitic attitudes. The Far Western campuses exhibit consistently less anti-Semitism on all the questions included in the study, and in some instances the differences are quite large. The only instance where Far Westerners show a fairly high anti-Semitic percentage, and at the same time approach closely the other regions, is on the issue of fraternity membership. National fraternity regulations may be a factor here, but at any rate there is a considerable vote (36 per cent) of Far Westerners for a fraternity that does not have more than 10 per cent Jews.

Just as Far Western students tend to be less anti-Semitic than the rest of the student population, Southern students tend to be more anti-Semitic. Since the actual numbers of Jewish students are low on both Far Western and Southern campuses, the clear-cut differences in the attitudes of the two regional groups seem to be a reflection to a considerable degree of differing cultural patterns in the two areas. Southern students as a group seem to be more concerned about keeping social distance between themselves and Jews, which may be a reflection of the traditional attitude of the "Old South." Many more of them profess to be worried about the economic and political power that the Jews are allegedly acquiring. But the anti-

TABLE X: Anti-Semitic Attitudes of Various Sub-Groups Among Non-Jewish Seniors

	SENIORS WHO ATTEND COLLEGE IN THE				SENIORS WHOSE RELIGION IS		FRATER-NITY MEMBERS	NON-FRATERNITY MEMBERS ON A CAMPUS WHERE THERE ARE FRATS
	NORTH-EAST	MID-WEST	SOUTH	FAR WEST	PROTES-TANT	CATHO-LIC		
Number of Respondents	240	300	250	128	539	286	405	344
% who think Jews are getting too much economic power in the U.S.*	23%	24%	29%	11%	**	**	**	**
% who think Jews are getting too much political power in the U.S.*	4	8	9	1	**	**	**	**
% who would prefer not to work side by side with Jews	3	3	9	3	5%	5%	4%	6%
% who would prefer not to have Jews as guests in their home	2	2	7	2	4	4	4	3
% who would prefer not to have Jews move into their neighborhood	10	9	11	8	10	11	10	9
% who would prefer not to have one of their near relatives marry a Jew	25	21	33	20	28	23	28	23
% who would prefer to send a child of theirs to a college which either excludes Jews entirely or admits them on some different and more exclusive basis than Gentiles	8	12	12	3	10	10	12	9

TABLE X—Anti-Semitic Attitudes of Various Sub-Groups Among Non-Jewish Seniors (Continued)

	SENIORS WHO ATTEND COLLEGE IN THE				SENIORS WHOSE RELIGION IS		FRATER-NITY MEMBERS	NON-FRATERNITY MEMBERS ON A CAMPUS WHERE THERE ARE FRATS
	NORTH-EAST	MID-WEST	SOUTH	FAR-WEST	PROTES-TANT	CATHO-LIC		
Number of Respondents	240	300	250	28	539	286	405	344
% who would prefer to join a fraternity (sorority) that was always *at least* 90% Gentile	39	38	46	36	44	39	54	31
% who would prefer to have a Gentile elected to the college newspaper board instead of an equally qualified Jew	42	31	45	22	37	40	39	38
% who would prefer not to have six of the eleven players on the college team be Jews, even though they were better than the Gentiles who would take their places	8	10	11	0	7	8	10	6
% who think a Jewish student can get a job in an industry owned and operated by Gentiles as easily as an equally qualified Gentile	18	21	23	17	19	24	—	—

(*) All seniors in sample; including 91 Jewish seniors. (**) Not available because ballot technique was used.

Semitism of Southern students is only a pale imitation of their anti-Negro prejudice. Almost three times as many would prefer not to see six Negroes on the football team as would object to six Jews on it and, whereas only 3 per cent would not like to entertain a Jew in their home, 45 per cent say they would not want to play host to a Negro.

The amount of anti-Semitism in the Northeastern and Midwestern college student bodies is generally intermediate between that found in the South and the Far West. Whether in spite of or because of the fact that Jewish student enrollment is heavily concentrated in Northeastern institutions, the average proportion of non-Jewish students holding anti-Semitic attitudes in that area is not consistently greater than the proportion of Midwestern students professing similar attitudes. Northeasterners are more willing to attend institutions that admit Jews on an equal basis with Gentiles, but are more resistant to seeing Jews become a majority on the board of the college newspaper.

Fraternity and sorority members tend to be somewhat more anti-Semitic than non-members on the same campuses, a discouraging fact if a not unexpected one. Since the fraternity and sorority groups make an effort to select potential campus leaders for membership, it is regrettable that this supposedly superior material is not freer from prejudice than it is. However, the nature of the fraternity as an exclusive social grouping probably tends to make its members more suggestible to the anti-Semitic prejudices that are going the rounds. Perhaps it is surprising that, under the circumstances, the fraternity men and the sorority women are as little more prejudiced than the non-members as they are.

DOES COLLEGE MAKE STUDENTS MORE ANTI-SEMITIC OR LESS?: It might be reasonably expected that a college education, since it is supposed to "open the mind" of the student, would make him less prejudiced. One way of measuring whether the college does actually have any such impact is to compare attitudes of freshmen and seniors. In the study reported in this chapter a national cross section of freshmen (who had just arrived on the campus) was included as well as the cross-section sample of seniors. The results of comparing their attitudes on the various anti-Semitic prejudice-revealing questions are shown in Table XI.

TABLE XI: *Anti-Semitic Attitudes of Non-Jewish Freshmen and Seniors*

	FRESHMEN	SENIORS
Number of Respondents	878	913
% who think Jews are getting too much economic power in the U.S.*	26%	23%
% who think Jews are getting too much political power in the U.S.	7	6
% who would prefer not to work side by side with Jews	5	5
% who would prefer not to have Jews as guests in their home	7	3
% who would prefer not to have Jews move into their neighborhood	9	10
% who would prefer not to have one of their near relatives marry a Jew	27	25
% who would prefer to send a child of theirs to a college which either excludes Jews entirely or admits them on some different and more exclusive basis than Gentiles	9	10
% who would prefer to join a fraternity (sorority) that was always *at least* 90% Gentile	38	40
% who would prefer to have a Gentile elected to the college newspaper board instead of an equally qualified Jew	41	36
% who would prefer not to have six of the eleven players on the college team be Jews, even though they were better than the Gentiles who would take their places	10	7
% who think a Jewish student can get a job in an industry owned and operated by Gentiles as easily as an equally qualified Gentile	19	20

(*) Includes Jews as well as non-Jews; total bases, Freshmen 993, Seniors 1,013

A mere glance at the table serves to dispose of the idea that the college exerts a clear-cut liberalizing influence in the area of religious prejudice. There are no such differences between the attitudes of the freshmen and the seniors as would support such a conclusion. What differences there are are relatively small and by no means always in the same direction. There does seem to be a very slight tendency toward lesser prejudice by seniors on a majority of the questions, but on the fraternity issue and the college admissions question, the trend is reversed. On the issue of discrimination against Jews in getting jobs, a question where factual information might presumably be acquired in college courses, the seniors are not significantly better informed than the freshmen. On the social distance questions the two classes think very much alike, but college students in general have so little resistance to associating with Jews (except for intermarriage) that there is not much left to be done by the college in this respect.

TABLE XII: Anti-Semitic Attitudes of Non-Jewish College Students in Various Fields of Study

	SOCIAL SCIENCE MAJORS		NATURAL SCIENCE MAJORS		HUMANITY MAJORS		BUSINESS AND COMMERCE MAJORS	
	FRESHMEN	SENIORS	FRESHMEN	SENIORS	FRESHMEN	SENIORS	FRESHMEN	SENIORS
Number of Respondents	50	116	104	110	151	197	102	108
% who would prefer not to have Jews move into their neighborhood	12%	10%	5%	9%	7%	10%	14%	11%
% who would prefer to send a child of theirs to a college which either excludes Jews entirely or admits them on some different and more exclusive basis than Gentiles	0	4	2	3	7	4	8	5
% who would prefer to have a Gentile elected to the college newspaper board instead of an equally qualified Jew	44	32	43	39	39	31	50	50
% who think a Jewish student can get a job in an industry owned and operated by Gentiles as easily as an equally qualified Gentile	22	13	17	25	23	21	19	25

One may speculate further as to the reasons for the general lack of impact of the college experience on anti-Semitic prejudice. Doubtless many students do not take courses in which the subject comes up. That the influence of classroom instruction on anti-Semitism may be important in some instances, however, is indicated by the results in Table XII. Senior majors in the social sciences and humanities are shown there to have less prejudice on one or two of the questions than those specializing in the natural sciences or in business and commerce, but the pattern is not entirely consistent. Furthermore there is apparently some slight tendency for the freshmen intending to major in social sciences and the humanities to be more prejudiced than the seniors who actually did major in them, but again the results do not all go one way and the samples are small for much generalization.

While one may, on the basis of these findings, give some credit to social science and humanities professors for the liberalism their students show, one cannot in any way conclude that natural science professors actually inculcate anti-Semitism. In addition to classroom impact, there are other elements in the campus culture that may negate influence of the classroom, or in the absence of any classroom influence be the most important elements in shaping the attitudes of students. The campus often has fraternities with "restrictions." It has also word-of-mouth gossip and campus folkways. Some students coming from areas where Jews are present in only small numbers may make their first acquaintance with anti-Semitism when they reach college. For every student whose prejudice is decreased by what he learns in the classroom, there may be another who acquires an anti-Jewish bias through the discovery that it is a conventional attribute of the fraternity man or is a characteristic of the roommate whom chance selects for him.

From another point of view the most important finding in the freshman-senior comparison is not the lack of change in attitudes from the first to the fourth year of college, but rather the generally low level of prejudice with which freshmen start their college careers. It may be that the major job of education in the field of anti-minority sentiment has already been done by the high school before students reach college, and that the only prejudiced students left are the bitter-enders with whom education has already proved ineffective. The facts at hand do not serve to prove or disprove this hypothesis, but it is certainly a possible one in the light of the data from the study.

ARE COLLEGE STUDENTS MORE OR LESS ANTI-SEMITIC THAN AMERICANS GENERALLY?: Since college students are frequently referred to as society's leaders of the future it is important to know whether they are ahead or behind the country as a whole in their attitudes toward the Jewish minority. By comparing the results of the national study done a year ago[2] for the Anti-Defamation League with the results of this year's study of college students it is possible to throw some light on the relative frequency of anti-Semitic attitudes among the two groups. Table XIII gives the comparative data on the seven questions that were identical in the two studies.

TABLE XIII: Comparison of Anti-Semitic Attitudes
of College Seniors and the General Adult Population

	SEPT. 1948 (ALL ADULTS 21 YEARS & OVER)	SEPT. 1948 (ALL ADULTS WITH A COLLEGE EDUCATION)	OCT. 1949 COLLEGE SENIORS
% who think Jews are getting too much economic power in the U.S.	38	*	23
% who think Jews are getting too much political power in the U.S.	19	*	6
% who would prefer not to work side by side with Jews	14	16	5
% who would prefer not to have Jews as guests in their home	15	14	3
% who would prefer not to have Jews move into their neighborhood	22	32	10
% who would prefer not to have one of their near relatives marry a Jew	48	52	25
% who would prefer to send a child of theirs to a college which either excludes Jews entirely or admits them on some different and more exclusive basis than Gentiles	29	27	10

*Not available because ballot technique was used.

A glance at the table reveals the clear-cut and consistent differences between college seniors and adults, both adults generally and adults with a college education. The college seniors are less anti-Semitic right down the line, and differences are so large that they could hardly be upset by any changes that have taken place in the attitude of the general population in the period between 1948 and 1949.

The explanation for the differences is harder to arrive at than the facts of the differences themselves. Since, as we have seen, college seniors do not differ significantly from college freshmen, it does not appear to be the college experience itself that makes the seniors so much more liberal than adults generally. The casual factors more probably lie in the processes that select college freshmen out of the general population. The freshmen tend to come from families above average in income, but this does not seem to account for their relative lack of bias, for upper income persons are not the less prejudiced because of their economic status, as we learned in the preceding chapter. The freshmen presumably also have higher scholastic aptitude than people in general, and this is a plausible explanation despite the fact that there is no data available to show that anti-Semitic prejudice varies with intelligence. Finally there is the possibility that the low-prejudice index of college freshmen is a function of their youth, since we do know that anti-Semitism is greater in the older age groups than in the younger. The trouble is that the percentage of anti-Semitism in the 21–34 age group, the only "younger" group for which data are available, is still much higher than that for the college freshmen.

The fact remains that college young people do show much less anti-Semitism than college graduates of greater age, and that may indicate an encouraging trend. Whether the trend—if it is one—is more due to modern primary and secondary education or to factors operating outside the schools in the general culture is a question. But certainly no clear case has been presented from the findings of this study to show that the college has itself made a significant contribution in decreasing anti-Semitism.

Chapter 9. May the Best Man Win

AMERICAN SPORTSMEN take pride in believing that their field is singularly free of prejudice and discrimination. "May the best man win," is the proud principle—and that means regardless of race or creed, say the spokesmen of the sports world.

Most people suppose that this great democratic principle is actually practiced in American sports. But there is an undercurrent of feeling that some prejudice, particularly racial prejudice, is present though carefully concealed or camouflaged.

The Anti-Defamation League decided to determine, if possible, the precise situation in 1949. If American sports are free from discrimination, this fact should be documented and made part of the record. Sports people are entitled to the credit of public acknowledgement.

In preparing this survey of democracy in sports, the Anti-Defamation League used the most effective available techniques of investigation and evaluation. The ADL interviewed scores of sports officials and athletes, amateur and professional. It solicited information from the nation's most authoritative sportswriters and experts. In professional sports, league and team presidents were asked for statements of policy and fact, which were then checked against the evidence of independent investigation. Private clubs—their rules, membership and practices—were carefully studied.

Thoughtful consideration made it clear that this survey would have to limit itself to a select number of professional and amateur areas; the others did not lend themselves to collection of precise data. The fields chosen in professional sports included baseball, basketball, football, hockey, and boxing. In amateur sports it was resolved to limit the inquiry to bowling, yachting clubs, tennis clubs, golf clubs, Y's, and private sports clubs.

As one factor in the research, it was decided to ascertain the actual number of Jews and Negroes in the selected sports. The ADL recognized, however, that this type of statistic is not conclusive in itself. Major league ice hockey, for example, had no Jewish players in 1949. But the game had only three players born in the United States; the rest came from Canada or Europe. This is not evidence of discrimination against persons born in the United States. The circumstance of climate alone has made Canada the major source of America's ice hockey players.

Other games require space and playing conditions not easily available in large urban centers where many Jews live; Jews do not participate in these sports in any great numbers. But in bowling the fact that there are no Negroes entered in tournaments sanctioned by the American Bowling Congress *is* significant. Neither climate nor lack of facilities combine to keep the Negro from bowling. Here statistics are significant of the Bowling Congress' stern refusal to permit "non-Caucasians" to participate in its approved tournaments. The same kind of discrimination does not obtain against Jews in ABC bowling.

1. BASEBALL: Baseball, long called America's national game, is also considered its most democratic sport. A fan does not go to a ball park just to see a game. He goes to be part of the crowd; to roll up his sleeves; to talk facts and gossip about the players with his grandstand neighbor. Baseball recruits its fans from all socio-economic strata of American society. The fans have treated the game well. Baseball is rich in tradition and rich in dollars.

How democratic is baseball? How democratic are the men who annually reap their incomes, and sometimes their fortunes, from the game?

The reserve roster of the sixteen major league clubs listed five Jews in a total of 640 players in December 1949—less than 1 per cent. These were Sid Gordon of the Boston Braves, Cal Abrams of the Brooklyn Dodgers, Al Rosen of the Cleveland Indians, and Myron Ginsberg and Saul Rogovin of the Detroit Tigers. One major league coach was also Jewish.

The same roster had ten Negro players. These were Sam Jethroe of the Boston Braves, Dan Bankhead, Roy Campanella, Don Newcombe, and Jackie Robinson of the Brooklyn Dodgers, Monte Irvin and Henry Thompson of the New York Giants, and Larry Doby, Luke Easter, and Satchel Paige (since released) of the Cleveland Indians.

In the research, the president of every major league club was asked for a team roster, the number of Jews and Negroes on it, and the team's policy regarding discriminatory conduct on the part of its members.

Eleven of the sixteen replied. The answer of Fred M. Saigh, president of the St. Louis Cardinals, seems to express the total point of view:

"Real Americans do not keep track of whether their employees are Negroes or Jewish. It just never occurs to us to ask or make a point of it. We don't care whether our employees are Negro, Jew, Catholic or Protestant, or otherwise, so long as they can fill their jobs and act as good Americans."

P. K. Wrigley, President of the Chicago Cubs, was more specific:

"Neither I nor anybody else connected with the club could possibly tell you which of the approximately 350 players under contract to the Cubs organization are of the Jewish faith. No player is ever asked any questions as to religion, and the only question relating to ancestry is a space for 'nationality' on the record card that each player fills out when he comes into the organization. Many of the players simply write in 'American' and many others don't fill in anything. We do not insist on an answer, as the only thing we are really interested in is the boy's ability to play baseball. As to Negro players, there are currently five players under contract in the Cubs organization whose color indicates that they are Negroes. . . . We have no regulations concerning prejudicial or discriminatory conduct on the part of players as there have never been any problems of this nature."

The remaining clubs which answered in a similar vein were: Philadelphia Phillies, Pittsburgh Pirates, Brooklyn Dodgers, Boston Braves, Washington Senators, St. Louis Browns, New York Yankees, New York Giants, and Cleveland Indians.

Despite their small number in major league baseball, there have been outstanding Jewish players. Johnny Kling was a great catcher in the early part of the century. Since then there have been players like Andy Cohen, Hank Greenberg, Buddy Myer, Harry Danning, Morrie Arnovich, Goody Rosen, Al Schacht, and Moe Berg.

More than 100 sports authorities—writers, commentators, players, etc.—in every section of the United States, were asked by the ADL whether Jewish aspirants faced any obstacles in professional baseball. The opinion of the experts was that the Jewish would-be ball player encountered no difficulties by reason of his faith; that his success in the game depended solely upon his ability.

The only widely reported incident involving charges of anti-Semitism in baseball in 1949 concerned Sid Gordon, then playing with the New York Giants. Gordon was probably the outstanding Jewish player of the year. In June he suddenly became the object of beanballs and riding from the St. Louis Cardinals' bench. Giant Manager Leo Durocher called the matter to the attention of the press and for a while a Giant-Cardinal feud blazed, at least in newspaper headlines.

The New York *Post* editorially attacked the Cardinals for their "personal comments on Sid Gordon's religion" as well as for riding Jackie Robinson when he first came to St. Louis. The *Post* added that "the St. Louis crusade is a tiresome and sickening aspect of what is still generally called the American game."

New York *Daily Mirror* sports columnist Dan Parker called for action on the part of Baseball Commissioner A. B. Chandler to squelch the reviling of a player because of his race, creed, or color. "Sid Gordon of the Giants," Parker reported, "has been subjected to this despicable form of jockeying for some time."

Gordon himself refused to comment on the attacks made against him. However, in a report to the Anti-Defamation League, J. Roy Stockton, sports editor of the St. Louis *Post-Dispatch*, presented another version which might explain Gordon's taciturnity.

"Manager Eddie Dyer of the Cardinals told me Gordon was his friend and that the Cardinals had not attacked him verbally because he was a Jew. . . . I know that dugout 'jockeying' is vicious and that no opportunity is overlooked to ride a man. . . . A dugout may apply epithets to a Jew one day, call another man a Dago, Swede, Limey, Mick, or Kraut the next. I don't think they gave Gordon any more than they'd give any other good ball player who was hurting the opposition by virtue of his skill. And I do know that the rank and file Cardinals admire Gordon as a player and like him personally."

Stockton then quoted New York writers as saying that someone had deliberately given the newspapers the story of the Cardinal attacks by telling a press conference that "the big story of the day had been overlooked" and then letting the Gordon story be drawn out.

In the light of the Sid Gordon incident, the ADL queried the sixteen major league baseball clubs—as it did all professional basketball, football, and hockey clubs—on whether they had provisions in their regulations forbidding prejudiced or discriminatory conduct by *players*. None thought it necessary.

There was no proof of discrimination against Jews on the part of club owners or managers. The Gordon incident is clearly not characteristic of any pattern in organized baseball. In the hard quest for pennant money and increased attendance, baseball clubs have drawn upon players who can hit best, pitch best, field best, without much regard for religion or nationality background. Major league clubs are always located in the large urban centers needed to support them. Usually, many members of minority groups live in these areas and constitute a good percentage of the potential number of spectators. Sometimes it is considered good business to hire a player of a minority creed or color.

Harold Ribalow, in his book, *The Jew in American Sports*, told of the case of Wally Moses who did not make the major leagues for several years because he was *not* Jewish. Moses was mistakenly regarded as Jewish because of his name, and several managers, therefore, welcomed the chance to sign him up; they wanted a minority representative on their teams. Moses, who knew the motive, had to say, "I'm not Jewish; sorry, but I'm not." The managers shied away from him. It took Wally Moses several years of outstanding minor league play to convince the baseball world that he was big league material, even if he was not a Jew.

Though no case of religious discrimination can be made against organized baseball, there were *individuals* in the game who have shown prejudice against Jews from time to time.

Major league baseball was involved in an unwritten agreement to bar Negroes from playing, until Jackie Robinson was invited to join the Brooklyn Dodgers in 1947. Because of the great number of Negro-American fans, and in recognition of the skill of Negroes playing in their own leagues, baseball management found it worth while to grant admittance to other Negroes—but still in limited numbers.

The threat that prejudiced white players would refuse to play with or against a team with Negroes in the line-up was completely dissipated and acceptance was hearteningly rapid by 1949. Robinson and the Negroes who followed him were subjected to all kinds of discrimination and prejudice, but usually not by people directly associated with the game. For example, when the Brooklyn Dodgers traveled to Cincinnati, Robinson, Campanella and Newcombe lived at the Netherlands-Plaza Hotel with the rest of their teammates. But they were compelled to take their meals in their rooms or else go to another part of town to find a non-Jim Crow restaurant.

In St. Louis, Negro ball players were not permitted to sleep in the same hotel as the rest of their teams. But Cardinal Manager Dyer and Robinson got along splendidly; it was the prejudiced patterns of the St. Louis *community* that restricted the college-trained Dodger star.

Patterns of segregation were broken throughout the South when the Dodgers played Robinson in a series of exhibition games in the spring of 1949. Many protests, including some from the Ku Klux Klan, and threats of legal action were made. There was a great hue and cry. But the games were played, with Negroes participating, and there were almost no incidents at the ball parks. The games were well attended, too.

The record of professional baseball is clean on religious discrimination; trail-blazing in terms of Negro participation. Two factors enter into this: the universal popularity of the game, which militates against discrimination stemming from social snobbery; the huge financial investment in the sport which puts club owners on guard against outraging the sensibilities of any large section of fandom.

2. BASKETBALL: For years basketball was considered by many an easterner's game, and as often as not, a "Jewish" game. From Nat Holman to Harry Boykoff, the history of the sport is studded with Jewish players, coaches, and managers.

The prominence of Jews in basketball has actually been the subject of some astonishing articles seeking to prove that Jews are so constructed that they can best stand the tension and strain of the game.

In his book, *Farewell to Sports*, reprinted in 1945, Paul Gallico absurdly concluded: "The reason, I suspect, that [basketball] appeals to the Hebrew with his Oriental background is that the game places a premium on an alert scheming mind and flashy trickiness, artful dodging, and general smartaleckness."

Mr. Gallico's shallow thought has been pretty well disproved by the status of basketball today. The sport has been adopted by colleges throughout the country; men of all faiths and colors have demonstrated the ability to play the game well. It attracts more spectators annually than any other sport.

The largest number of basketball fans, however, are followers, not of the professional game, but of college teams. Collegiate basketball ranks high in popularity among American sports fans. This survey did not examine the college area at all; for it recognized that the administration of the game on the campus would be controlled by the same attitudes which governed other campus activities. In a measure, Chapter 7, "Cracking the Quota," deals with this aspect of the problem.

Jewish players, in the past, were prominent on the professional and amateur basketball courts of America for one probable reason—which has nothing to do with "Oriental background." Basketball requires little space and little equipment; it is a game primarily for crowded cities. Most Jews in the United States live in large cities and sports-lovers among them found the game of basketball within convenient reach.

Professional basketball in 1949 had come a long way from the peach-basket game invented by Dr. James Naismith about sixty years ago. It is a big-league sport, now dominated by a new organization, the National Basketball Association founded in August 1949. The NBA consists of seventeen teams: Baltimore Bullets, Boston Celtics, New York Knickerbockers, Philadelphia Warriors, Syracuse Nationals, Washington Capitols, Chicago Stags, Fort Wayne Pistons, Minneapolis Lakers, Rochester Royals, St. Louis Bombers, Anderson Duffy Packers, Denver Nuggets, Indianapolis Olympians, Sheboygan Redskins, Tri-City Blackhawks, and Waterloo Hawks.

At the time this survey was made (September–December 1949), there were in all 206 players on the teams in the Association. Eight players, less than 4 per cent, were known to be Jews. So were several Association officials and coaches. In response to ADL questionnaires, several teams without Jewish players cited Jews on former rosters.

In 1949 there were yet no Negroes in the National Basketball Association. But individual teams seemed to have been honest in recent attempts to hire Negro players. The Chicago Stags tried to place Don Barksdale under contract; he refused, according to press reports, because he was engaged with his own team. It was also reported that the New York Knickerbockers wanted to hire Nathaniel Clifton, but his team, the Harlem Globetrotters, refused to sell him. Tom Blair, an outstanding Negro basketball player in New England in 1948, tried out for the Boston Celtics in 1949. According to Celtic President Walter A. Brown, he wasn't quite good enough to make it.

Two famed Negro athletes and Olympic stars, Fritz Pollard, now a member of the Chicago Commission on Human Relations, and Ralph Metcalfe, now on the Illinois Athletic Commission, declared that prejudice against Negroes in basketball in 1949 was substantially broken down in the East. The Middle West was still behind but Pollard and Metcalfe believed Negroes would break through remaining barriers soon.

The National League, a minor group in professional basketball, had one all-Negro team in 1949, the Renaissance Five, from Dayton, Ohio. Other clubs in that League have also used Negro players.

ADL data revealed that the National Basketball Association did not prohibit discrimination. Perhaps if the Association had created a code providing affirmatively a policy of non-prejudice, Negroes would have participated in its games.

3. FOOTBALL: Despite the constantly growing popularity of professional football, the college game continues to be dominant. As a matter of fact, during the brief ten-week collegiate season it wins more concentrated interest from Americans than any other sport during the year. However, the interest in professional football cannot be minimized.

The League's survey of American sports in 1949 touched upon collegiate football only in terms of the Roper survey, reported in Chapter 8. The League believed that the social attitudes of college educators would apply equally to college sports as it did to other aspects of academic life.

In the 1949 football season there were two major professional associations. The National Football League had ten teams: Chicago Bears, Chicago Cardinals, Detroit Lions, Green Bay Packers, Los Angeles Rams, New York Bulldogs, New York Giants, Philadelphia Eagles, Pittsburgh Steelers, and the Washington Redskins. Of 320 players in the League, four were known to be Jews; four were Negroes.

The second association, the All-American Football Conference, had seven teams: Baltimore Colts, Brooklyn-New York Yankees, Buffalo Bills, Chicago Hornets, Cleveland Browns, Los Angeles Dons, and San Francisco Forty-Niners. Of 224 players, twelve were Negroes. The number of Jews could not be determined.

Two of the greatest play-callers and passers of professional football have been Jews. One of them is Sid Luckman who marked his tenth year as a star player with the Chicago Bears in 1949. Another is Benny Friedman who played with Chicago, Cleveland, and Brooklyn twenty years ago. Marshall Goldberg, as a college player, made the All-America team when he was with the University of

Pittsburgh Panthers. He played with the Chicago Cardinals for several years and in 1949 was a coach for that team.

The Green Bay Packers, since its organization, has always had at least one Jewish player a season and sometimes three or four. It has never had Negroes. E. L. Lambeau, coach and manager of the Packers in 1949, offered the Anti-Defamation League his reasons why:

> The climate in the fall of the year in Wisconsin is not too pleasant from November 1 until the end of the season and I know from experience in talking with good Colored prospects that they were sort of reluctant to play in our northern country when they had opportunities to go with clubs situated in a warmer climate.

Until 1946, the National League had no Negroes at all except for men who played many years before, men like Paul Robeson, Duke Slater, and Joe Lillard.

The All-America Conference entered the field in 1946 to dispute the monopoly of the National League. The new group welcomed Negro players, which was probably the reason the older Conference dropped its previous undeclared ban. The Los Angeles Rams signed Kenny Washington in 1946. By 1949 some of the most popular professional football players were Negroes—including Buddy Young of the Brooklyn-New York Yankees and Marion Motley of the Cleveland Browns.

It is noteworthy that none of the thirty-seven communities surveyed by the ADL reported the receipt of any complaints of prejudice in connection with the 1949 professional football season.

4. HOCKEY: The major professional hockey association is the National Hockey League. It consists of six teams, the Boston Bruins, the Chicago Black Hawks, the Detroit Red Wings, the Montreal Canadiens, the New York Rangers, and the Toronto Maple Leafs. The game is played almost exclusively by Canadians. Of 114 men in the League, only three were born in the United States.

The data accumulated in the research on this sport revealed that there were no Jewish players in the National Hockey League in 1949 although there had been several in previous years. There have never been Negroes in the League.

In the past, Alex Levinsky starred for many years with the Chicago Black Hawks. Max Labovich played briefly with the New York

Rangers but soon went back to amateur status with the Toledo Buckeyes in the Eastern Amateur League.

The American Hockey League, a minor league, was headed by Maurice Podoloff, a Jew, who was also president of the National Basketball Association. In that league there was one Jew, Hy Buller, of the Cleveland Barons.

In 1948 the Rangers brought Herb Carnegie, a Negro, to their training camp. He did not meet requirements of skill and was offered a contract with the American League team in New Haven. Carnegie, a Canadian, refused the minor league offer. For a short while the Rangers also had a Chinese member, Larry Kwong.

5. BOXING: International repercussions resulted from a punch in the jaw landed the night of June 19, 1936. The puncher was Max Schmeling who that night upset all boxing form by knocking out Joe Louis, then riding high as an unbeatable contender for the uneasy crown of James J. Braddock.

In Nazi Germany, Schmeling was declared a national hero; Hitler cabled congratulations to him in New York. Joseph Goebbels ordered phonograph records made of the fight announcements and had them rebroadcast throughout Germany.

The unexpected victory short-circuited the flow of Nazi propaganda. A German magazine, with government approval, proceeded to publish a glowing biography of Schmeling's American manager. The Hitler government knew that the manager, Joe Jacobs, was Jewish. For the occasion, at least, that fact was overlooked.

When, two years later, Louis had a return bout with Schmeling, the American knocked him out in the first round, sending him to a hospital. The Nazi super-race theory was demolished again. But not in Germany; not a single German newspaper carried a report of the fight. Schmeling returned to Germany to live in obscurity and disgrace until he turned up as an over-age private in the Nazi glider forces during the war.

The acclaim accorded Schmeling when he beat Louis is characteristic of boxing. And the sport gives this acclaim not to a successful boxer; it often gives it to the race, religion, or ethnic background from which he is derived. For one reason or another, physical prowess is still used as a criterion for judging a whole people's caliber.

Both Jews and Negroes have contributed much to the annals of the ring. It was a Jew, Daniel Mendoza, who founded the modern school of fighting in England in the late eighteenth century. Since then there has been Joe Choynski who knocked out a great fighter like Jack Johnson and drew with Jim Jeffries who outweighed him by almost fifty pounds. There have been men like Benny Leonard, Abe Attell, and Barney Ross, to name a few of the champions among hundreds of Jewish fighters.

Boxing has often been accused of being a corrupt, vicious game where a manager or promoter will risk the health and even life of a fighter for the sake of a good gate. It *is* a tough game, a bloody one, but Jewish participation in it has done some good in shattering the malicious stereotype of the Jew as incapable of physical combat.

A noted editor once said, "Benny Leonard has done more to conquer anti-Semitism than a thousand textbooks have done." If true, Negro champions have not always won the same benefit for their people in the fight against Jim Crowism. Some caricatures of the Negro portray him with an exaggerated amount of savage physical superiority; his skill in boxing unfortunately sometimes has been used to reinforce the stereotype. The great quest for "a white hope," when Negro Jack Johnson won the heavyweight championship, was evidence of an attitude that the Negro was some sort of non-American and unfit to be a champion.

There was not nearly as much talk of that nature in the many years that Joe Louis held the championship. This may have been because of Louis' sportsmanlike conduct, in and out of the ring. Or it may have been because of a greater enlightenment on the part of sportswriters, fans, and participants alike.

Did Jews and Negroes have difficulty in getting ahead in the prize ring? According to the scores of experts questioned in the ADL survey, Jews experienced no difficulty at all. Many of the most prominent managers and promoters as well as boxers and fans have been Jewish. Tex Rickard, a famous promoter and the man who made boxing into a big business, recognized the value of the large number of Jewish ring fans, when he said, "Give me a Jewish fighter who can be built up into a challenger and I'll show you the man who can bring back the million dollar gate."

Prejudice against Jews in boxing was rarely displayed within the profession itself. But boxing is a primitive type of game and its fans are sometimes caught up in a frenzy of atavism. Ringside catcalls and the abuse of the they-can't-hurt-us partisan were often directed against the Jewish boxer who had to contend with cries of

"Kill the Kike" as well as the fists of his opponent. In this same circumstance, however, it was also "kill the Mick," or "the Polack," or
"the nigger"—as Roy Stockton said of baseball.

In short, the Jew and other boxers who represent minority groups
suffered the same type of abuse, resulting from ignorance as much
as bigotry. Unfortunately, the Negro boxer additionally suffered
from the frequently-reported assertion that his race has "crowded
the field."

Despite the common knowledge of racial and religious abuse by
boxing fans, no ADL or co-operating Community Council reported
receipt of any complaints during 1949. Perhaps it is in the unfortunate nature of the boxing bout to accept expressions of racial and
religious bigotry with indifference. Boxing, it appears, sometimes
brings out the worst in the spectator.

6. BOWLING: Bowling, in one sense, is an honest game among
American sports. Through its powerful American Bowling Congress,
in 1949, it continued to discriminate against Negroes—brazenly and
openly. It also discriminated against Chinese, Japanese, Indians,
Filipinos, and anyone else outside of the pale of "Caucasian." It did
not discriminate against Jews.

The American Bowling Congress was founded in 1895 and
chartered in 1903 by the State of Illinois. In 1949 it was a big business with a membership of more than 700,000. In one tournament
season the ABC had receipts and income of $1,700,000. It was proud
of its growth and boasted that it controlled almost every bowling
alley in the country. Its officers called bowling the all-American
game. One of its elaborate brochures described bowling as "the
greatest social leveler on earth."

Yet, during its entire life, the ABC has clung to its "Caucasian
rule" in its constitution, limiting its membership to "the white male
sex."

The ABC has enforced its rules by clamping down on alley operators who permitted non-whites to bowl. It did this by becoming
stringent about alley specifications, which it controlled, and by
threatening to burden errant owners with great expense for repairs.
The ABC also wielded the threat of revoking "sanction" from a
bowling team or league if it permitted non-Caucasians to bowl. Once
or twice in recent years a non-white played on a team but as soon
as that team came close to prize money the ABC cracked down with

its "no sanction" threat. Without such approval, no bowling teams' scores are officially recognized.

In 1949 the ABC met its most serious opposition to the maintenance of a discriminatory clause. Led by the United Automobile Workers, several agencies, including the Anti-Defamation League, organized a National Committee for Fair Play in Bowling. The National Fair Play Committee and its regional counterparts, holding their own tournaments throughout the country from time to time, encouraged alley owners to break free from ABC shackles, and tried to alert the general public to the danger to democracy inherent in ABC practice.

In 1949 the ABC held its annual tournament in Convention Hall in Atlantic City, starting February 12 and continuing for two months. Many groups, headed by the New Jersey State CIO, joined in protesting the "non-Caucasian" rule. They exerted themselves to persuade the ABC to change its policy, even to the extent of bringing charges against it on the grounds that the ABC constitution denied equality of opportunity in employment and violated the state's Fair Employment Practices Law.

Just before the convention started the ABC yielded and set up a subcommittee to hear the protests of the Fair Play in Bowling group. It turned out, however, that the subcommittee had no power to make recommendations; it couldn't even submit a report, it said, to the directors.

Finally, at the convention, the Rev. Charles Carow of the Brooklyn Youth Organization, for the fourth consecutive year, offered an amendment changing the "whites only" clause. He was voted down as before, but for the first time three or four *delegates* arose to support him.

Jim Crow bowled a strike in Atlantic City in 1949. But the opposition to the ABC's practices was getting bigger all the time. During the year the AMVETS and the American Legion joined in decrying ABC policy. Mayor Zeidler of Milwaukee, home town of the ABC, expressed concern about letting it use the Milwaukee municipal auditorium when and if the group requested it for a convention.

Until the discriminatory clause is removed the situation regarding Negroes will continue to be exemplified by San Francisco, a non-Jim Crow city. The Urban League there reported that, because of the ABC rule, Negroes were excluded from all tournament play and that practically all bowling alleys in the city, with the exception of one in a Negro district, were closed to Negroes.

7. GOLF: Golf—like tennis and yachting—is generally considered a gentleman's game. And private golf clubs in 1949 were rife with "gentleman's agreements."

Private golf clubs are important to the player. Often they are the only kind accessible. Club and association membership is frequently a prerequisite for tournament play. A private course usually gives a player more time, better instruction and fairways, and more opportunity to develop skills than does a municipal or public course.

Clubs are important, too, because an amateur golfer who wants to play in national tournaments cannot give his game incidental time. That's a fact accepted by most sports authorities. A Sunday afternoon golfer cannot possibly make the grade; he must live and study his game constantly to get ahead in competition. Often the "amateur" player is, *in effect*, subsidized by his club.

Private golf clubs are important and their policies, in the great majority of cases, are rankly discriminatory against Jews, Negroes, and members of many of America's other minority groups.

In its research for this section of the survey, the ADL asked its twenty-six regional offices and eleven Community Councils to ascertain the membership admission policies of two prominent golf clubs in each of their respective areas. The ADL then directed a letter to those clubs whose policies were reported to be discriminatory, asking whether it was true that racial or religious standards were employed in the selection of members.

In terms of democratic admissions policies concerning Jews, four general types of private golf clubs were found:

1. Clubs that close their doors completely to Jews.
2. Clubs that allow Jews to enter on a quota system or for reasons of great skill.
3. Clubs that accept members without regard for religion.
4. Clubs that are predominantly or exclusively "Jewish."

The reports indicated that the first two types constituted the great majority. The fourth type, the "Jewish club," has grown up in recent years as a defense against discriminatory policies of other clubs. Aside from cities with municipal courses, in many communities it was found that the Jewish club alone afforded facilities to Jewish golfers.

Because of the stringent restrictive policies in the Los Angeles area—where non-Jewish clubs such as the Los Angeles, Wilshire, Bel Air, and Lakeside Country Clubs exist—the Hillcrest Country Club grew up. It is one of the largest and best in the country. The Hillcrest had no provisions for barring non-Jews, but no non-Jews ever joined. Several non-Jews applied in 1949—among them James Roosevelt and comedian Danny Thomas. The membership met and unanimously agreed to accept qualified applicants regardless of religion.

The Bonnie Briar Country Club in Larchmont and the Pelham Country Club in Pelham Manor, New York, openly admitted their policies of exclusion of Jews. Their membership application blanks did not ask for religious affiliation but an applicant had to be proposed by one member, seconded by another and then passed on by a membership admissions committee. Rarely was a Jew invited or proposed in this type of club, and if he was, he had no chance at all of acceptance.

The Sand Point Golf and Country Club in Washington State had the unique distinction of excluding Jews both from its golf course and from buying real estate. Its property included a number of dwelling places which could not be rented or sold to Jews because of a restrictive covenant.

In the Portland, Oregon, community, there is the Tualatin Country Club, a Jewish-owned and operated organization. Other than this one, virtually no golf club in the area accepted Jewish membership.

A report from Cincinnati told of this condition:

There are two Jewish country clubs—the Losantiville Country Club and the Crest Hills Country Club. The Cincinnati Country Club and the Camargo Club are probably the two most exclusive non-Jewish clubs, with Maketewah and Kenwood Country Clubs and the Hyde Park Golf and Country Club close behind. There are a handful of Jews in a few of these five clubs, in some none at all. The usual devices are used to restrict membership. Operating much like fraternities—with nothing in the rules and regulations—the blackball and the whisper prove sufficient.

A club in San Francisco had a quota system and then abandoned it in favor of a policy of complete non-acceptance of *new* Jewish members. This club still has about twenty-five Jewish members. All their memberships dated back to before the war. At that time the German Consul Fritz Wiedemann was admitted as a member. Several Jewish members protested and the club formulated its new policy: no more Jews to be accepted. Another club in San Francisco maintained a generous quota system; the other important clubs in the vicinity had strict quotas or did not admit Jews at all.

In four cities in one area—Indianapolis, Evansville, Terre Haute, and Michigan City in Indiana—there were separate Jewish golf clubs. The other clubs in the vicinity had either a quota system or no Jews at all. Some of the few Jewish members of these clubs dated their association back twenty years or more, but in 1949 their sons were often excluded when they applied—the quotas were tighter than they had been twenty or thirty years ago.

The pattern is followed throughout the country. There were sixty-five private golf clubs in the Philadelphia area. Five of them are considered Jewish, the Philmont, Ashbourne, Green Valley, Rydal, and White Manor Country Clubs. These clubs each had several non-Jewish members too. The others all practiced varying degrees of discrimination.

Frequently, as in Washington, D.C., Jews were allowed to use the links as guests of club members but were themselves excluded from membership. There were two clubs in Washington with a primarily Jewish membership—their existence was used as a rationalization for the restrictive policies of most of the other clubs.

According to a *Fortune Magazine* survey conducted by the Elmo Roper organization in 1947, the southern and southwestern parts of the United States had less prejudice against the Jew than most parts of the country. But even the South and Southwest practiced the same type of exclusion in golf.

In March 1949 two men traveled to Virginia Beach, Virginia, with the intention of registering at the Cavalier Hotel and playing golf at the adjacent Princess Ann Golf Course. A hotel employee told them that the Cavalier furnished hotel guest cards which would permit them to play golf at the course. The two men, who were Jewish, asked the desk clerk for cards. He said that there was no such arrangement and the Cavalier offered no guest cards.

The men went out to the golf course. They were refused admission and informed that they needed guest cards from the hotel to play. The men, realizing they were being exluded by a crude deception, left in disgust.

In order to protect themselves many golf clubs which sponsored tournaments in the past ran them on invitation basis. In this fashion they avoided the religious and racial issue. Other golf clubs decided they were merely social organizations. Thus they succeeded in barring from membership those who come from minority groups.

Municipally owned golf courses are usually free of discrimination against Jews; but they are not free of discrimination against Negroes. Even where patterns of segregation are not in effect, the Negro finds the world of golf undemocratic.

In Cleveland in 1949, two Negroes lost a suit in Common Pleas Court asking for the right to play at the Lakeshore Golf Club in Bratenahl. The golfers claimed they had been denied playing privileges at the club in July, after its incorporation as a private course; they had played there when it was public. The judge ruled that a private club has the right to limit the use of its course to its members. In January 1950, however, the Ohio Court of Appeals reversed the lower court and, in holding that the golf club was not "private," granted an injunction against its practice of discrimination.

In April 1949 five Negro leaders in Miami, Florida, appeared at the Miami Springs Golf Course and requested permission to play. The matter was taken up with the City Manager, O. P. Hart, and, not that day but soon after, Negroes were allowed to play on the course one day a week—an obviously unsatisfactory arrangement to the men. Negro golfer Joseph Rice filed a mandamus suit seeking to force Superintendent H. H. Arnold to sell him a ticket on another day of the week.

The suit was lost in the Dade County Circuit Court on the ground that the City of Miami had the right to allot one day to Negroes (to play on the municipal course) under the general policy of segregation.

The problem of the Negro who wants to take up golf as a sport is far more than a mere matter of cost, an excuse sometimes offered in explaining why there were no Negroes in the sport. Even if he had the money, he could not play on most private clubs and many public courses.

The Professional Golfers' Association of America most openly discriminated against the Negro. It has been under fire for several years for the provision of its constitution which, it was openly stated to the Anti-Defamation League by PGA President Joe Novak, "limits membership in our association to those of the Caucasian race."

The PGA also insisted that entrants in any tournament it sponsors must be the professional of a recognized golf club. No Negro and few Jews have ever achieved such positions.

Recently in New York, the Gotham Golf Club, a Negro-organized group, held its second annual tournament. Some of the best Negro golfers in the country entered the tournament. First-rate courses rejected the contest. Properly "respectable" clubs did not relish the thought of having Negro golfers on its fairways. Despite the quality of the play, the tournament had to be held at a course of secondary championship caliber, the only one open to it, on Staten Island.

The Gotham Golf Club tournament did not reciprocate the discrimination; its entry list was wide open. White golfers as well as Negroes were eligible. In the dark, undemocratic sport of golf, the Gotham Golf Club contest was a beacon of hope.

The significant fact that stood out in bold relief from all the data accumulated about racial and religious prejudice in golf, is that the practice of discrimination was virtually iron-clad—with hardly a word to that effect in the written rules.

8. TENNIS: The business of becoming a top-rank tennis player involves much more than native ability to play the game. When a promising player is discovered on the public courts or playing at a small club, the practice has been, if the player has no independent means, for an "angel" to sponsor him and to see that he becomes affiliated with a club that can afford him expert instructions. Pancho Gonzales, a twenty-one-year-old Mexican-American who recently won the United States Lawn Tennis Association men's singles championship for the second year in a row—the most coveted crown in tennis—had an "angel." So did Frankie Parker, another tennis champion who, by society tennis standards, also came from the wrong side of the tracks.

All major tennis competition in the United States is held under the sanction of the United States Lawn Tennis Association which consists of thirteen regional associations and about one thousand individual clubs. Players were ranked by the USLTA which, it was reported, made its selections solely on the basis of ability. It was these ranking players who usually played in major tournaments.

Most of the important contests sanctioned by the Association are held at the West Side Tennis Club at Forest Hills. In 1949 these tournaments were played there: the Davis Cup Challenge Rounds, the United States Lawn Tennis Association women's singles, men's singles, and mixed doubles.

On the basis of the information obtained in the research for this section, the Anti-Defamation League believes that the West Side Tennis Club, "the capital of the tennis world," has practiced a policy of discrimination. It has been generally known and understood that exceedingly few Jews and no Negroes ever become members of the West Side Tennis Club. The Los Angeles Tennis Club, another powerful group in the USLTA, has practiced the same type of discrimination.

The net effect of this denial of membership has been that a promising player could not obtain instruction from the professionals attached to the club.

The same practice of discrimination is enforced by many other ranking tennis clubs throughout the United States. The ADL used the same research technique here as it did in connection with golf clubs, surveying two prominent tennis clubs in each of thirty-seven communities.

The fact that tennis clubs discriminate against members of minority groups did not necessarily prevent them from reaching the top ranks of the tennis world. Because of his Mexican background Pancho Gonzales was subject to discrimination by some clubs. He surmounted it. Jewish tennis players Seymour Greenberg and Irving Dorfman also became prominent despite their lack of affiliation with any of the snobbish tennis clubs.

Dr. Reginald Weir is a top Negro tennis player. He has played in three white tournaments, pioneering for Negroes. But he usually has been forced to compete in tournaments for Negroes only, which have been held under the auspices of the American Tennis Association, the national ruling body of Negro tennis. As in golf, there were tennis clubs organized by minority group members and used predominantly by them. This, of course, was the defense mechanism again, and often the only way by which minority group members were able to acquire skills in their chosen sport.

Many players, members of minority groups, are discouraged from making tennis their careers simply because they are unable to obtain the expert instruction required for a player of championship caliber.

Many tournaments are open affairs; anyone who qualifies by virtue of skill can compete despite lack of club affiliation. Technically, it was possible for a Jewish tennis player not affiliated with the West Side Tennis Club to participate in a tournament sponsored by it.

In the case of smaller tennis clubs, the survey showed that the patterns of discrimination against Jews were as strong as they were in golf. Tennis clubs used the quota system to restrict the number of Jewish members, and frequently excluded Jews completely. As in golf, in many areas Jewish tennis players were forced to start their own clubs if they were to play at all.

The Jackson Heights Tennis Club and the Seminole Tennis Club, both in Queens, New York, were officially non-sectarian in membership. In practice, at least in recent years, they excluded Jews completely. In order to join either of these clubs, a prospective member had to know two members of the club and be sponsored by one, seconded by the other.

Among other clubs that practiced similar methods were the Philadelphia Rifle Club, Merion Cricket Club, the Cynwyd Club, and Germantown Cricket Club in the Philadelphia area. Another club in the same area, the Idle Hour Tennis Club, had three Jewish members. None of these clubs had Negro players.

The Irvington Tennis Club in Portland, Oregon, has long had a policy of discrimination. In 1949, however, it accepted Jews as playing members if they had exceptional skill. This qualification was not required of non-Jewish applicants.

The Seattle (Washington) Tennis Club, while it had several Jewish members, generally was known to be discriminatory.

In tennis "the best man" wins—if he is free, white, and gentile.

9. YACHTING:

Is yachting an exclusive sport, a way of life filled with midnight champagne parties? Not always—even granting that most yachtowners are wealthy, that yachting is an expensive sport. But many yacht club members do not have boats of their own; they are men who like to indulge their taste for the seas and lakes in one of the most aesthetic and arduous of all sports. They join a club to share in the operation and racing of yachts, to share in its athletic and social life.

Swank? Yes.

Discriminatory? Yes.

Yachting, as discussed here, means sailboating rather than power boating. In 1949 its one national association was the North American Yacht Racing Union, located in New York City. This is the only permanent legislative and governing body of national scope; through it racing and measurement and rules have become standardized. The Union has an appeals committee to which protested decisions are submitted for the purpose of interpreting rules. In May 1949 the Union had 1147 individual members. It was composed of 164 yacht clubs and the seventeen most important yacht associations in the country.

In answer to an ADL survey inquiry, the corresponding secretary of the Union, Lt. Commander Ernest Stavey, made a statement extremely limited in meaning and application:

"The North American Yacht Racing Union has never promulgated any rules or regulations concerning racial or religious discrimination in the membership policies of individual, sustaining, member yacht clubs, or member association."

The North American Yacht Racing Union does not itself sponsor any racing competition. This is done either by regional yachting associations or by individual yacht clubs. Some of the more important races, such as the New York to Bermuda Yacht Race, the Annapolis Yacht Race, and the Miami to Nassau race, are held under the auspices of individual yacht clubs. A contestant, to qualify, has to belong to a "recognized" yacht club. Recognition is given only by the regional yachting association. As a general rule regional associations, including the Yacht Racing Association of Long Island Sound which sponsored many leading races, do not recognize Jewish yacht clubs.

The various regional associations may arbitrarily refuse to recognize any club within their jurisdiction. Even if a Jewish yacht club can meet the wharfage, membership, and other standards set by a regional association, the association may abitrarily refuse recognition. There is no appeal from this ruling.

As part of the attempt to assay the extent of discrimination by yacht clubs, the ADL directed a letter in November 1949 to the 34 clubs constituent to the Yacht Racing Association of Long Island Sound; this communication asked each club whether it used racial and religious criteria in judging applications for membership. Significantly, by the year's end *only one* of these clubs—the Plando Field and Marine Club—replied, stating that it had no racial or religious qualifications for or barriers against membership.

As a matter of fact, the Yacht Racing Association of Long Island Sound did *not* accept the Jewish clubs. But it still recognized two clubs, the Knickerbocker and Orienta Yacht Clubs, which informally have become classified as Jewish because more than half of their members are Jews. These clubs were accepted by the association before their membership was opened to Jewish applicants. Recognition has continued.

The outstanding club in the country is probably the New York Yacht Club. It occupies a pre-eminent position in the field and its membership consists of many prominent yachtsmen. In 1949 it had no known Jewish members.

Some major yacht clubs have accepted one or two outstanding

Jewish personalities as members—but only one or two. For example, the Manhasset Bay Yacht Club accepted Bernard Baruch and his family. The mere fact that one or two of its members were Jewish has not resulted in the club's loss of recognition. But if a club is predominantly Jewish when application to an association is made, recognition is almost certain to be withheld.

An association is rated according to its club membership and the importance of the races it annually sponsors. In tournament racing, a general rule is that a participant must belong to a recognized club to qualify for an association tournament. In some international competitions, such as the New York to Bermuda Race, if a Jew is a prominent yachtsman, the fact that he was not affiliated with a recognized yacht club may be overlooked. But in other types of competition, such as the Miami to Nassau Race, the rule is rigidly enforced by the governing body. In still another competition, such as the one sponsored by the Storm Trysail Club, the policy varies from year to year depending on the whims and composition of the club committee on eligibility.

The devices for excluding Jews from yacht clubs are simple. Usually, a yachtsman does not apply directly for membership; he awaits an invitation. In the rare event that a Jew is invited, he goes through the routine of submitting an application for the approval of an admissions committee. Sometimes the reason for rejection of his application is given. "No facilities for new members." Sometimes the more direct statement is made that the applicant does not have "social acceptability." Sometimes, there is just the "blackball"—and no reasons are divulged.

The social life of a Jewish yachtsman admitted to a recognized yacht club varies greatly when using the courtesy facilities of other clubs. Sometimes he faces hostility; sometimes there is at least some outward sign of social acceptance.

A few yacht clubs accord Jews the privilege of mooring even though they do not accept them for membership. A prominent New York Jewish yachtsman was permitted to moor his yacht at a Mamaroneck club which does not accept Jews. He paid rental and storage fees, but he was not allowed to use club house facilities.

More often, even the use of mooring facilities are denied Jewish yacht-owners. A new yacht club, the Bahia-Mar in Fort Lauderdale, Florida, had docking facilities to rent. Its advertising in 1949 was headed, "GOOD NEWS FOR YACHTSMEN LOOKING FOR A 'BREAK' THEY'VE NEVER HAD BEFORE!" The kind of "break" it offered may be indicated in this statement of the captain of a yacht owned by a prominent sportsman of Woonsocket, Rhode Island, who is of the Jewish faith.

One Sunday, November 13, 1949, we pulled into Fort Lauderdale, and tied up at our assigned berth at the Bahia-Mar. After being in dock one hour, I was asked to come to the main office.

Mr. Hershner, the manager, said, "Let's lay our cards on the table. Is your owner Jewish?" I told him "Yes." He said, "I'm sorry, You can't tie up here." We discussed the situation while I tried to find out who was behind the set-up and why they were operating on this basis.

Mr. —— was not aboard at the time, but his uncle, Dr. ——, and two other relatives were. . . . I told them about it and we pulled out and berthed in Hollywood, Florida.

I think they are only going to hurt themselves and lose out in the end. . . . They have 400 berths but there are only 70 odd boats berthed there.

The fact that Bahia-Mar was constructed on land owned by the City of Fort Lauderdale posed a significant legal question as to the use of public property for discriminatory purposes. The yacht club's application blank pointedly asked: "Church affiliation or denomination?"

The Lido Island Yacht Club in California sought membership from among all the residents of the Balboa area when it first opened. However, Jews who applied were told that they could not be accepted because the club had reciprocal arrangements with other clubs along the coast and that Jewish members of the Lido Island club would be barred from using the facilities of these other clubs, all of which have restrictive policies.

Summarizing the survey data about yachting, these appeared to be the general rules concerning clubs and associations.

1. Most yacht clubs belonging to recognized associations do not admit Jews for membership. If a club was recognized before the membership became partially Jewish, it retained recognition.

2. The few clubs that have admitted Jews for membership admitted only one or two "prominent" ones under a strict quota system. This has not impaired the club's recognition by its association.

3. Clubs whose membership has been predominantly Jewish have not gained recognition.

10. ATHLETIC CLUBS: The nation's top athletic association is the Amateur Athletic Union which sets standards and records achievements in many amateur sports. These include track, field, and swimming events. The AAU sanctions meets held by athletic clubs and associations.

The AAU, in recent years, has consistently attempted to eliminate discrimination in any form, according to Col. Harry D. Henshel, Sr., an authority on amateur sports in the United States. If any type of AAU competition is scheduled in a region where Negro athletes are not allowed to participate, either the sponsoring organization has to change its policy or the locale of the meet has to be changed, he said.

Col. Henshel pointed out in an Anti-Defamation League interview that Negroes could participate against whites in AAU competition, particularly in track and field meets, in most Southern cities. He ascribed this change of policy to pressure brought by the AAU and to the fact that several track meets were taken away from the South because of anti-Negro policies.

There is no known evidence of discrimination on the part of the Olympic selections committee which often consist of AAU officials. Members of minority groups are frequently starred on American Olympic teams. The consternation of Adolf Hitler when Negro track star Jesse Owen repeatedly won major events at the 1936 Olympic games held in Berlin is a case in point.

But the data accumulated by the ADL from all corners of the country revealed that some athletic clubs whose tournaments were held under AAU sanction have been guilty of outright discrimination. As with golf and tennis clubs, the ADL sampled the membership policies of prominent private athletic clubs—thirty-one of them in twenty-eight cities; twenty-four were reported to be discriminating against Jews.

One of the most important clubs in the country, the New York Athletic Club, has rarely if ever accepted Jews or Negroes as members. There is no exclusion clause in its constitution but after an applicant has been recommended, his background is circulated to all members in the club's house organ. Members are invited to make comments which are then reviewed by the membership committee. Persons refused membership are never told why.

Although the New York Athletic Club discriminates, it sponsors teams which often compete against teams containing minority group members. The major event of each year under the club's sponsorship has been an invitation track meet held at Madison Square Garden. Minority group members participated in this meet, but under the colors of various other organizations.

Throughout the country, smaller athletic clubs discriminated to about the same degree as golf and tennis clubs. Many of these are social clubs more than amateur athletic groups; they provide gym facilities and swimming pools for a member and his family. Many of them follow the pattern of the Laurelhurst Beach Club in Washington State and the Pasadena Athletic Club and the Pacific Coast Club in California, which do not accept Jewish members.

Private clubs follow about the same tactics for excluding members of minority groups as tennis, golf, yachting and athletic clubs do. These include:

1. Failure to invite Jews to meetings or functions.
2. Use of the blackball.
3. Ignoring application blanks.
4. Inclusion of slight religious activity in club activity.
5. Refusal of application blanks.
6. Failure to notify when membership is open or failure to invite when new membership is desired.

A major factor which led to the exclusion of minority group members in 1949 was their own acceptance of discriminatory patterns. Men and women of many racial, religious, and ethnic groups, resigned to the fact that they were not wanted, hesitated or refrained from even trying to join clubs which were known to discriminate. The Anti-Defamation League conducted thousands of independent inquiries to complete this survey; the identities of hundreds of groups that discriminated were learned. Yet, aside from several incidents reported here, there were few cases of persons attempting to violate the "gentlemen's agreements."

Sports in America may be divided into three categories: professional, college, and amateur-social sports. Each is ruled by a different set of standards, resulting in differing codes of conduct.

Professional sports are operated as commercial enterprises; the rules that apply in business govern professional games which have a mass market. Those who run sports have long since learned that if they do *anything* which alienates whole sections of the people, they simply reduce their own incomes. By and large, the American people frown on undemocratic prejudice and discrimination. Hence sports management must, of necessity, avoid it.

There is a sports-world doggerel to the effect that: "It's not the winning or the losing that matters, it's the way you play the game." If the saying ever had any acceptance among amateurs, it certainly no longer does among professionals: a player's etiquette on the field is incidental to home runs, touchdowns, and final scores.

However, there is ample evidence that professional sports management is happy to go in the direction toward which public sentiment has led it. Whatever discrimination does exist in professional sports is not typical of policy or planning on the part of sports entrepreneurs themselves. Instead, it represents the social climate of a region. The major exception to the general rule of fair play in professional sports is the Professional Golfers' Association which maintains a policy of discrimination against non-Caucasians. Another group, the American Bowling Congress, touching both the professional and amateur levels, officially discriminates against Negroes. In 1949 determined campaigns were waged to break down the barrier raised by this organization.

College sports, not covered in detail in this chapter, are governed by social ethics which are somewhat different from the professional game. The Elmo Roper study of Anti-Semitism in American Colleges (Chapter 8) gives some evidence of the attitudes toward Jews in varsity sports. The study showed that 36 per cent of the non-Jewish seniors of the sample would prefer not to elect a Jew to the editorial board of their college newspaper, but only 7 per cent of the seniors said they would dislike having a Jewish majority on the varsity football team. *Ninety per cent said that it didn't matter if the majority of the players were Jewish or Negro so long as they were the best players.*

Amateur sports which are an integral part of a community's social activities have a wholly different set of values from professional and collegiate sports. Tennis, yachting, golfing, etc., are largely dominated by the social attitudes of people who can afford sports as an expensive social diversion. Games which attract a select few are more easily burdened by the snobbery of its participants. The resulting discrimination is of a piece with restrictive covenants in homes, the barring of minorities in resort hotels, and other exclusion of certain groups from social and civic community affairs.

Unfortunately, some middle-class, social-athletic organizations have imitated the snobbery of the social-athletic bluebloods. Where such clubs take on the aspect of quasi-public institutions—holding themselves out as open to the general public—they will be subject to the ever-increasing press of civil rights legislation and court action leveled at restrictive realty covenants and at discrimination in resort accommodations.

Amateur-social sports are as far removed from the principles of democracy as the sandlots are from major league baseball.

Chapter 10. Law—A Partial Answer

1. FEDERAL LEGISLATION: As it has so frequently in the past, the United States Senate, on February 28, 1949, became embroiled in a struggle to end the threat of filibuster by a determined minority. Behind the desperate effort to prevent members from speaking ad nauseam was the real issue—the civil rights program placed before the 81st Congress by President Truman. Three weeks later the effort to limit debate was lost, and it became sadly clear that the federal civil rights program would inevitably be shelved for the year 1949— as it was on the morning of October 3.

That, in brief, is the story of the year's long drawn out fight for federal civil rights legislation. The sorry failure to obtain even one statute in an entire congressional session at this stage in American history is not just a matter of standing still; it is a step backwards. Only the fact that a campaign for the enactment of legislation, even an unsuccessful one, is in itself of great educational value, mitigates the defeat to some degree.

Congress' failure to enact any civil rights legislation stands in sharp contrast to the earnest pleas of President Truman, to the platform commitments of the two major parties and to the significant civil rights advances made in a number of states. The sober judgment of Washington observers was that the first session of the 81st Congress in the civil rights field scarcely bettered the "do-nothing" record of its predecessor. While the account of a congress cannot, of course, be closed until the last day of the last session, it would be naïve to ignore the disappointments in the first session and the difficulties it created for the second.

Friends and foes of the civil rights program are in agreement on one point: both assume that the civil rights bills, *if brought to a vote,* would pass. The fanatic opposition, therefore, is resolved to prevent any democratization of the Senate rules which would deprive them of their decisive weapon—the filibuster. In the name of freedom of debate, the strategy of the reactionary Southern bloc is to retain the filibuster so as to prevent civil rights legislation from coming to a vote.

Supporters of the civil rights program launched a thoughtful attack on the ineffective Senate cloture rule. They sought an amendment that would give a majority of the Senate the power to control its own deliberations. They argued that freedom of debate was meaningless without a corresponding ultimate freedom to vote. They insisted that the Senate rules should not permit a small group of willful men to talk a bill to death.

The decisive test came in March. The stubborn Southern bloc was filibustering a motion to consider a resolution which provided for a new Senate rule on ending debate. The Administration forces filed a cloture petition to shut off the filibuster and bring the motion to a vote. The Southerners argued the position was out of order, claiming that cloture could be applied only to bills and resolutions, not to motions to take them up for consideration.

Vice-President Alben Barkley ruled that the cloture petition was in order. He held that the body *could* limit debate on the motion to modify the filibuster rule. Barkley's decision was simple and clear-cut. It paid due deference to the plain meaning of plain language, to technical precedent, to the intention of the 1917 Senate that first adopted the cloture rule, and finally to the common sense necessity of interpreting the existing rule so that it did not produce legislative paralysis. In appealing the Vice-President's decision to the whole Senate, the die-hard Southerners found an ally in Senator Arthur Vandenberg who attempted to justify his own contrary decision on a similar point the year before when he presided over the Senate. The Vandenberg logic was that the Senate could shut off debate by a two-thirds cloture vote when it was debating a bill of vital importance (on which, presumably, senators would want to be heard at some length); but when the Senate calendar of vital measures was being deliberately blocked by "talkathons" on preliminary motions or maneuvers, the Senate was impotent to shut off debate! Barkley was overruled by a vote of 46–41.

This disappointing blow to the civil rights program was followed by another, even more serious. The cloture rule was amended. Instead of the former requirement of a two-thirds approval of those voting to impose cloture, the new rule adopted now required the approval of two thirds of all the members of the Senate, i.e., sixty-four senators, to curb a filibuster. The new rule was called a "compromise" because it was made applicable not only to bills but also to motions to take up bills—except motions to change the rules, which are still subject to unlimited debate.

The new "compromise" on cloture hangs like the sword of Damocles over the whole federal civil rights program. There are very few congressional observers who are prepared to say that the inevitable Southern filibuster against effective civil rights legislation can be broken under a rule which requires sixty-four affirmative votes.

This backward step taken in the Senate quite overshadowed the forward-looking and historic action by the House in the first days of its session. By a vote of 275–142, the House cut down the autocratic power enjoyed by its Rules Committee, which, in the past, could virtually pigeonhole any measure by simply denying it "a rule." The House gave the several committee chairmen an opportunity to by-pass the Rules Committee and bring their committee-approved measures directly to the floor for a vote.

The House, in the past, has taken the lead on civil rights legislation. In the first session of the 81st Congress, however, the House moved slowly. Perhaps the defeat of the Senate's attempt to curb filibusters discouraged more expeditious action. Another important consideration, however, may have been the desire to postpone the crucial test votes as long as possible so that they would remain fresh in the voters' minds for the November 1950 congressional elections.

The House, for the fifth consecutive time in five sessions of Congress, passed an anti-poll tax bill (H.R. 3199) which would outlaw the requirement of the payment of a tax as a condition of the right to vote in any federal election, primary or regular. The vote was again overwhelming: 273–116. The Senate took no action.

The FEPC bill, which civil rights groups and the Administration made the focal point of their drive, was placed on the calendar of both houses. In the House, the Education and Labor Committee voted it out favorably, 19–6, on July 21. The Senate Committee on Education and Public Welfare reported the bill without recommendation. Hence, at the end of 1949 the FEPC bill was ready for immediate consideration in the 1950 session of the Congress.

The anti-lynching bill received no consideration in the House. The Ferguson Anti-Lynching Bill, S. 91, was reported favorably by the Senate Judiciary Committee. That bill had been denounced, however, by the National Association for the Advancement of Colored People as a toothless bill which could become a "blueprint for legalized lynching."

The drive to amend the Displaced Persons Act of 1948 involved more than humanitarian issues. One of its main objectives was to wipe out the discriminatory provisions of the 1948 Act and provide an unprejudiced basis for admission of DPs into the United States. Provisions of the DP Act of 1948 which are regarded as discriminatory are those which require (1) that at least 30 per cent of the DPs admitted should be persons previously engaged in agricultural pursuits, and (2) that at least 40 per cent of the visas issued under the Act should be available exclusively to DPs whose place of origin or country of nationality has been annexed by a foreign power. This latter provision in effect favors nationals or natives of the Baltic states who are Protestants.

The fight in the House centered around the hearings in the Judiciary Sub-Committee. The bill that emerged compromised away a number of important demands of the Administration and humanitarian groups, but at least H.R. 4567 erased the more flagrant blots from the existing law. It passed the House overwhelmingly in an unrecorded voice vote.

In the Senate, the DP program ran into a campaign of obstructionism spearheaded by the chairman of the Judiciary Committee, Pat McCarran of Nevada. McCarran's shabby maneuvers included the introduction of a demagogic bill that would have increased the number of DP immigrants from the Administration's proposal of 400,000 to 500,000. (The bill, of course, was hedged around with restrictions that made the 500,000 figure purely academic.) McCarran's chief tactic was to delay the hearings on the House-enacted bill, then to solicit testimony from obscure representatives of obscure organizations in opposition to the bill, and finally to insist that further "investigation" was needed to make sure that "dangerous elements" among the DPs would not be smuggled into the United States.

In the closing weeks of the first session, Administration leaders and liberal Republicans moved to discharge the Senate Judiciary Committee and bring the bill to the floor. Faced with that threat, the Committee, in the absence of Senator McCarran, voted the bill out without recommendation. On the Senate floor, the bill was filibustered by McCarran's allies, Senators Harry P. Cain of Washington and William N. Langer of North Dakota. Their counter-motion to send the bill back to committee was passed by a vote of 36–30. Attached to this motion was a direction to report out a bill by January 25, 1950.

Relatively unnoticed, but nonetheless important as signaling a liberalization in America's naturalization policy toward Asiatics, was the passage by the House of H.J. Res. 238 which would make persons of Asiatic and Pacific origin who are legally resident here, eligible for naturalization. On the Senate side, the bill was reported favorably by the Judiciary Committee and placed on the Senate calendar but was "passed over" at the request of Senator Richard B. Russell of Georgia. The Judd Bill, H.R. 199, which would for the first time grant annual immigration quotas to certain Asiatics and Pacific peoples, was passed by an overwhelming vote in the House. No action was taken on the bill by the Senate Judiciary Committee.

On June 16, 1949, President Truman submitted to the Senate for ratification the Convention on the Prevention and Punishment of the Crime of Genocide, which had been adopted by the General Assembly of the United Nations on December 9, 1948. This Convention declared genocide—the deliberate physical or biological destruction of a racial, ethnic, religious or national group—to be a crime under international law and obligated the states participating in the Convention to provide for punishment of its perpetrators. The punishment would extend to instigators and accomplices, whether they were constitutionally responsible rulers, public officials or private individuals.

In his message of transmittal urging Senate ratification, the President characterized the Convention as "an effective international instrument outlawing the world-shocking crime of genocide." The Convention was referred to a sub-committee of the Senate Foreign Relations Committee headed by Senator Brien McMahon of Connecticut, which planned to hold hearings in the second session. By the end of 1949 five nations—Australia, Norway, Ethiopia, Iceland, and Ecuador—had ratified the Convention. It can become effective only after twenty nations have ratified it.

2. COURT DECISIONS: The constitution contains no detailed blueprint of the nature and extent of the civil rights it guarantees to the American people. The function of defining those rights, therefore, has fallen to the United States Supreme Court.

A decision[1] of the Court in 1896 opened the door for the various states to maintain lawfully the apparatus of segregation. In 1949, however, the Supreme Court undertook to review three cases which may result in closing the door to state-sanctioned segregation.

In contrast to the pessimism which pervades civil rights groups on the legislative front, anti-discrimination forces await with eagerness the decisions of the Supreme Court in the three lawsuits. Each challenges the doctrine that segregation is not necessarily discrimination. In each, the Court is asked by Negro appellants to reject the separate-but-equal doctrine first stated by the Supreme Court more than fifty years ago in Plessy *v.* Ferguson. The rule established in this old case is that segregation of Negroes does not deny them equal protection provided that the facilities granted them are "substantially equal" to those available to white persons.

The first case, Henderson *v.* U. S.,[2] involved the validity of a railroad regulation of the Southern Railway, approved by the Interstate Commerce Commission, compelling racial segregation in interstate railroad dining cars. The regulation provides that one table in each dining car must be reserved exclusively for colored passengers and all other tables must be reserved exclusively for white passengers. The Court is asked to rule that this regulation violates both the Fifth Amendment to the Constitution and Section 3 of the Interstate Commerce Act which makes it unlawful for any carrier to subject any traveler to "any undue or unreasonable prejudice or disadvantage. . . ."

Ironically enough, the complainant in the case who was denied dining car service solely because of his color, was a field representative of the wartime federal FEPC traveling, in his official capacity, from Washington, D. C., to Birmingham, Alabama. Although a nominal defendant in the case, the government, acting through Solicitor General Philip B. Perlman, with the approval of Attorney General J. Howard McGrath, has filed a vigorous and eloquent brief asking the Court to invalidate the Interstate Commerce Commission order approving the regulations. The brief also attacks the separate-but-equal doctrine, calling for a repudiation of the Plessy decision.

The other two cases involve the right of a state to segregate students in its universities on the basis of race. In one case,[3] the plaintiff was denied admission to the University of Texas School of Law on the ground that a separate law school is provided for Negroes. In the other case[4] the plaintiff, though admitted to the University, is excluded from the classroom and compelled to sit outside the doorway. The state contends that he was as near to the instructor as most members of the class and could hear and see the teacher as well as anyone in the class.

If the Supreme Court holds that segregation is unconstitutional, it will be a death blow to the practice in interstate commerce and state institutions.

3. STATE LEGISLATION: Although civil rights progress on the federal legislative level in 1949 was virtually nil, the picture was brighter in the area of state legislation where a number of civil rights statutes were enacted. Unfortunately, there were not nearly as many as was hoped for. And the serious defeats which came in some states after long and difficult struggle are discouraging. It is worthwhile to review the state-wide achievements for 1949 in each field of "traditional" discrimination.

DISCRIMINATION IN EMPLOYMENT

Mrs. X answered an ad in a Los Angeles newspaper asking for a secretary. She had an interview with the manager of the firm and was hired. At the end of the conversation, she was asked to fill out an application form. Mrs. X, looking at the form, said: "This form asks for my religion. I am ——. Does that make any difference?" The manager replied, "Yes, it does. We have no ——s employed in this office and want to keep it that way."

Discrimination in employment is, in a sense, the most serious aspect of religious and racial intolerance. If the job opportunities of the minority groups are considerably poorer than those of the majority, their economic and social status must inevitably fall below the level of the majority. This fact, in turn, tends to create in the majority a feeling of superiority. A further consequence is discrimination in other fields—education, housing, and so forth.

By the beginning of 1949, four states—New York, New Jersey, Massachusetts, Connecticut—had passed effective legislation against unfair employment practices. These so-called FEPC laws give state agencies the power to eliminate discriminatory practices by employers through persuasion and conciliation or, if such efforts at mediation fail, by cease-and-desist orders.[5]

At the end of 1949, the number of states with enforceable FEPC laws had doubled. The new ones are Washington, Oregon, New Mexico and Rhode Island.[6]

However, educational, civic and legislative campaigns for the enactment of effective laws against job discrimination were conducted in many more states. Unsuccessful campaigns were waged in Pennsylvania, Michigan and Indiana. In Colorado and Ohio FEPC bills were passed by the lower Houses but failed hopelessly in the upper Houses. In Illinois the bill was narrowly defeated in the Senate by two votes as a result of sharp pressures upon the senators by powerful business and employers groups.

Opponents of the proposed legislation argue stubbornly that such laws interfere with the right of management to hire qualified employees. Advocates contend that their only purpose is to prevent irrelevant religious and racial considerations by management in the selection of employees. They point out that no remedy or redress is available to an American denied the equal opportunity to earn a living simply because of his color or creed. If such an injustice occurs in a state *with* FEPC legislation, complaint can be made to the state agency charged with enforcement of the fair-employment-practice law; the agency after verifying all the facts would first attempt to settle the matter by informal mediation and conciliation—as provided for in all FEPC laws; if such attempts prove useless the agency would then hold formal hearings, take evidence, and issue an order requiring the employer to hire the complainant or compensate him for the injury. In actual practice, however, mediation and conciliation, short of legal force, have been effective in most cases.

FEPC laws enacted in Washington, Oregon, New Mexico and Rhode Island follow the same general pattern set by previous FEPC legislation. The authors of the new laws, of course, had the advantage of the experience gained from the actual operation of the earlier statutes; they embodied improvements.

One weakness in the first FEPC laws is the comparatively short time allowed within which complaints have to be filed. In New York and New Jersey it is ninety days after the discriminatory action has taken place. Massachusetts and Connecticut provide for a six-month period of limitation. Rhode Island provides for a period of one year; Oregon and New Mexico fix *no* period of limitation.[7]

Another helpful innovation in the Rhode Island law is a provision permitting the filing of complaints by "any organization chartered for the purpose of combatting discrimination or racism or . . . of promoting full, free or equal employment opportunities." This makes it possible for civic-minded organizations to seek redress in behalf of persons who, because of fear of reprisal or lack of funds, are unwilling to appear as complainants. (Other FEPC laws give certain state officials—Attorney General, Industrial Commissioner or the Fair Employment Practices Commission—the right themselves to initiate complaints. But experience proves that state authorities sometimes are reluctant to start proceedings.)

The FEPC law of Rhode Island is superior to those in the seven other states in a number of other respects. It has by far the broadest definition of unfair employment practices. Under the law in Rhode Island, it is illegal for an employer *knowingly* to use the services of employment agencies, training schools, etc., which practice racial or religious discrimination. This provision is aimed at employers who deliberately use the facilities of schools or agencies which they know in advance will not refer to them applicants from particular minority groups. The same law expressly prohibits an employment agency, training school, etc., from servicing an employer whose request indicates directly or indirectly that he will not grant full and equal job opportunities to all applicants regardless of race, religion or national origin.

The Rhode Island law has one other important advantage. It prohibits employers, employment agencies *and labor organizations* from using application forms or keeping personnel records which show race, religion or national origin.

The city of Richmond, California, passed an ordinance against employment discrimination—the seventh city in a non-FEPC state which has adopted such a measure without waiting for statewide legislation.[8] Like the ordinance enacted the year before in Phoenix, Arizona,[9] the Richmond regulation applies only to the city (as an employer) and to those employers under contract to the city. Like Phoenix, too, it creates no special agency to enforce the ordinance; instead, it makes violation a misdemeanor punishable by fine and imprisonment.

New Jersey, which took a major step forward in extending its anti-discrimination law, in enacting it, accepted a half step backward. It passed the so-called Freeman Law,[10] which discontinued the power of the administering agency to create local advisory boards and conciliation councils. It also eliminated the duty of its administrators and the courts to interpret the law liberally.

Two states, in order to enforce constitutional prohibitions against racial or religious discrimination in *state* employment, enacted laws prohibiting the asking of questions regarding color and faith. New York passed a bill[11] barring any query about birthplace from civil service applications. California did the same in connection with questions about race or religion.[12]

Progress in the United States in the struggle for greater legal protection against racial and religious discrimination in employment was unmistakable in 1949.

DISCRIMINATION IN HOUSING

Dear Sir:

In answer to your ad in the Sunday *Republican* concerning a home to rent, I am, or rather, my husband and I would consider renting ours. Mr. ——— has been very ill for 4 weeks, and the doctor says he must go to a warmer climate, to gain his health back. But rather than go into detail, I would suggest, if you have not already secured a place, to drop out to Bradley Rd. and talk with us. It's a brand new home, 5 rooms all on one floor, 3 bedrooms, oil-heat and two car garage.

Come on Sumner Avenue to Allen St., continue on Allen, past Wenks Greenhouse's Bradley Road is just beyond 1st street on left. Yellow-ranch type home.

Sincerely,

Mrs. ———

P.S. Neighborhood code does not permit me to rent or sell to anyone who is Hebrew. (Strictly Gentile)

Pandit Nehru, were his identity unknown, would have been forced into a ghetto had he tried to find living quarters when he arrived in the United States in October 1949. Sun Yat Sen, were he alive, could not purchase a house in at least one part of virtually every city in our nation. *Entire* sections of most American towns would be indifferent to an apartment rental to a former bank swindler who is white, while barring a George Washington Carver who is not. And in every corner of the country there are neighborhoods, sometimes even whole communities, where the founder of Christianity, because he was a Jew, would be unwelcome.

Discrimination in housing in our great democracy is shamefully widespread. The undemocratic contagion afflicts large numbers, and victimizes Negroes, Mexicans, Puerto Ricans, Chinese, Japanese, Spanish-Americans, Catholics, Jews and many others.

The lamentable consequences of housing segregation on the life of the community were well described in a bill introduced in 1948 in New York State. Segregated racial areas, it warned, "resulted in many social evils . . . extreme overcrowding and deterioration of segregated areas . . . creation of de facto segregated schools, recreational facilities and other public services although such segregation is prohibited by law . . . decline of neighborhood standards . . . concentration of vice and unsocial practices in segregated areas . . . concentration of minorities in segregated areas . . . mutual distrust and fear between the residents of the segregated areas and the majority racial groups . . . conflicts, tensions, disharmonies, race riots and a general increase in crime and unsocial practices."[13]

Since 1945 a number of states[14] have passed legislation outlawing discrimination in public or publicly assisted housing projects erected for veterans, low income groups or for slum clearance. Pennsylvania, Wisconsin and Connecticut were among the states enacting laws[15] of this kind in 1949.

The law enacted in Connecticut is the first in the United States to establish an administrative procedure to combat discrimination by way of conciliation and, if necessary, by a cease-and-desist order enforceable through the courts. Such a procedure will probably prove to be much more effective than the usual court action.

The new Connecticut law also makes any act of discrimination a criminal offense punishable by fines up to $100 and imprisonment up to thirty days. The statute does not force the victim to choose between administrative proceedings and the initiation of criminal proceedings. The remedies may be pursued simultaneously.

Connecticut therefore represents a departure in the efforts to prevent patterns of discrimination and segregation in public housing projects.

Bills covering various aspects of housing discrimination were introduced in several states during 1949 but failed of enactment. In New York three measures were introduced under the sponsorship of the New York State Committee on Discrimination in Housing. One would have created a temporary state commission to study discrimination in housing and to make recommendations to the legislature. Another would have declared discrimination illegal in publicly assisted housing. A third would have prohibited lending organizations from discriminating in the granting of mortgages on residential property. All three measures died in committee.

On December 16, 1949, the New York City Council adopted a local law prohibiting discrimination in private redevelopment housing projects assisted by the city.

Discrimination in housing was not the subject of 1949 state legislation except as it concerned *publicly* built projects. Improvements in the law were mostly due to enlightened decisions by the courts in the last two years.

One of the common devices used to exclude members of some nationalities, races or religions from a neighborhood, is the "restrictive covenant." This is an agreement by property owners never to sell or rent their property to, or permit it to be occupied by, members of the excluded groups. The covenant *perpetuates* a pattern of exclusion in the area covered.

Under the law in the United States,[16] up to 1948 any property owner who was party to a restrictive covenant could enforce it against violators by court action; the court could order a forbidden purchaser or tenant to surrender possession of the restricted property. In other words, the authority of the state was used to maintain inviolate the undemocratic practice.

In 1948 the United States Supreme Court changed the law. It held in two cases[17] that had come before it for review that the power and authority of state courts could no longer be used to enforce restrictive covenants. To permit them to do so, the court said, would be in violation of the 14th Amendment which guarantees the equal protection of the laws to all. In two companion cases the Supreme Court ruled that federal courts were also forbidden to enforce such covenants.[18]

The malicious device which had kept neighborhoods untenanted by minorities had suddenly lost most of its effectiveness. The Supreme Court, to be sure, did not declare in the decisions that restrictive covenants were void or illegal; only *unenforceable* by court action. But now they are effective only so long as all partners to the agreement and their successors abide by them. If an owner violates the covenant, his neighbors can no longer get the help of the court to force compliance.

Some real estate interests and others reacted violently to the decision. Lawyers tried hard to find loopholes. In one case[19] they sought a state court decision that if the purchaser knew in advance that the property was restricted, he was bound by it. The Maryland Court of Appeals said no, that nobody could be precluded from invoking his constitutional rights guaranteed by the 14th Amendment. The Court opinion concluded:

The decisions of the Supreme Court of the United States, construing the United States Constitution and its Amendments are binding on this Court, and once definitely made, as in this case, must be followed by us. We are not at liberty to decide to the contrary, or to attempt to whittle away the effect of such decisions by holding that some of the statements made are dicta. If the Supreme Court did not mean what it said, or said more than it should, or what it should not have said, the responsibility is its and not ours.

Another effort to avoid the Supreme Court decision was made in Missouri. Actions were brought against Negro buyers and white sellers of homes in which money damages were sought for breaches of these covenants. The Supreme Court of Missouri, the state's highest judicial tribunal, held that the plaintiffs had a right to collect damages.[20] It gave as its reason that the United States Supreme Court did *not* say the prejudiced provision was, in and of itself, void. Opponents of the undemocratic device believe that if the litigation reaches the nation's highest court, the Missouri judgment will be reversed.

In an attempt to help correct the widespread un-American abuse in housing, the federal government in December 1949 announced a new policy regarding mortgage insurance issued by the Federal Housing and Veterans Administrations. Beginning in February 1950 the FHA would no longer insure mortgages on property which would thereafter be burdened with racial or religious restrictive covenants. To insure against tricks, the regulations compel the borrower to pledge that he will not attach the undemocratic provision to his property during the life of the government insurance contract. If he does, the mortgage can fall due and payable immediately.

The Veterans Administration, too, announced that it would issue similar regulations in the near future, in connection with mortgage loans to veterans which it insures under the G.I. Bill of Rights.

There are other ways of barring fellow Americans from buying or renting homes where they would like to live. A large property-holding corporation, for example, decides to keep its realty possessions "exclusive." So long as such projects are truly and purely private, existing law provides no remedy against such residential snobbery.

In many cases, however, the multimillion dollar properties are not private in the true sense. The larger a project, usually the more dependent it has been on the co-operation of state and municipal authorities. The erection of large city developments, in many cases, would have been impossible if the authorities had not assisted by condemning property needed for the project, by closing streets, and by special tax exemptions. This co-operation between private enterprise and municipal authority reaches a point where the description of the project as private ceases to be accurate. Typical of this is Stuyvesant Town in New York City, where alleged discriminatory practices against Negroes provoked litigation in the New York courts.

Stuyvesant Town is a redevelopment company totally owned by the Metropolitan Life Insurance Company. It was formed pursuant to the Redevelopment Companies Law of 1942. (This law recognizes the substandard housing conditions in the state as beyond the remedial ability of private enterprise; it emphasizes the need for government co-operation with privately-owned redevelopment companies. City governments are given authority to approve proposed redevelopment plans and to assist redevelopment companies in the operation and supervision of projects. Cities are also authorized to help such projects with tax exemption, eminent domain and transfer of public streets.)

Stuyvesant Town is an enormous project, a city within a city. It occupies eighteen city blocks and contains a population of 25,000 people. All tenants are white; the Metropolitan Life Insurance Company, from the very beginning, adopted a policy of excluding Negroes. The company contended that, as a private enterprise, it is free to select tenants at its discretion. It pointed out that the Redevelopment Companies Law (different in this respect from various state laws on public housing) contains no clause prohibiting discrimination on account of race, religion or national origin.

With the assistance of the National Association for the Advancement of Colored People and the American Jewish Congress, a suit was brought by Negro veterans asking the court to enjoin Stuyvesant Town from refusing to consider applications from Negroes. The veterans argued that the project is not a private enterprise, could not have been undertaken without the active co-operation of the state and the city of New York, and therefore, as a quasi-official entity, is prohibited from discriminating.

The trial court dismissed the action on the ground that Stuyvesant Town is a private project and not bound by the 14th Amendment. The Court of Appeals—the highest state tribunal—on July 19, 1949, by a majority of 4 to 3 affirmed the decision.[21] In a forceful dissent, Judge Stanley Fuld wrote:

As an enterprise in urban redevelopment, Stuyvesant Town is a far cry from a privately built and privately run apartment house. More, its peculiar features yield to those eligible as tenants tremendous advantages in modern housing and at rentals far below those charged in purely private developments. As citizens and residents of the City, Negroes as well as white people have contributed to the development. Those who have paid and will continue to pay should share in the benefits to be derived. Stuyvesant Town in its role as chosen instrument for this public purpose may not escape the obligations that accompany the privileges accorded to it.

The unsuccessful plaintiffs petitioned the United States Supreme Court for a review of the case on the ground that the decision of the Court of Appeals is in conflict with the 14th Amendment. The matter is pending.

DISCRIMINATION IN PLACES OF PUBLIC ACCOMMODATION

Mr. —— called the ———— Hotel at ———— Springs, Pennsylvania, asking the hotel clerk whether a room could be reserved for him for a specified date. The answer was in the affirmative. The hotel clerk then asked for the name. When he heard the name, he said "Oh, if you are of the Jewish faith, I am very sorry but we cannot take you. We only have selected clientele."

The incident reported above is not an isolated case. Hotel and resort operators throughout the United States express their anti-Semitic policy of discrimination in advertisements and folders: "White Christians Only," "Restricted Clientele," "Selected Clientele," "Congenial Surroundings," "Protestant Churches Nearby," etc.

A number of states have legislation directed against racial and religious discrimination by hotels, restaurants, theaters, amusement halls, public conveyances and other enterprises which offer their facilities to the general public; these are known in the law[22] as "places of public accommodation." Statutes against discrimination by such places declare the right of an individual to the full and equal enjoyment of their facilities and advantages; they impose civil and criminal sanctions upon violations. In some states the publication of discriminatory advertisements is also declared illegal.

Civil rights statutes are not always effective in eliminating "public accommodation" discrimination. Enforcement of these laws has been entrusted to the local judiciary. In criminal and in civil actions the decision usually has rested with jurors who were frequently reluctant to convict the owner of a business for doing something which, in their view, did not involve any moral turpitude. Also, under ordinary trial court rules it is difficult to prove the charge that the refusal of a hotel to accommodate a guest is due to racial prejudice rather than the unavailability of a room.

The Report of the President's Committee on Civil Rights, published in 1947,[23] confirmed the shortcomings of the existing machinery:

> The civil suit for damages and the misdemeanor penalty have proved to be inadequate sanctions to secure the observance of these laws. Additional means, such as the revocation of licenses, and the issuance of cease-and-desist orders by administrative agencies are needed to bring about wider compliance. We think that all of the states should enact such

legislation, using the broadest possible definition of public accommodation [page 171].

The first two states to act on the recommendation were New Jersey and Connecticut. Each passed legislation[24] in 1949 giving administrative state agencies authority to handle charges of discrimination in places of public accommodation by persuasion and conciliation or, if such attempts at mediation fail, by cease-and-desist orders.

Both New Jersey and Connecticut permitted the traditional remedy of court action to remain on their statute books. However, there is an important difference in the laws of the two states: in New Jersey a complainant must make a choice between instituting court litigation or filing a complaint with the Division Against Discrimination; in Connecticut, the remedies are not mutually exclusive. It is still too early to estimate the effectiveness of these two laws which really embody a new approach to the problem of discrimination by places of public accommodation. Success will depend upon two factors: the willingness of aggrieved persons to initiate administrative proceedings, and the diligence of the agencies charged with the responsibility of administering the law.

Another interesting development in legislation against discrimination in places of public accommodation is the Anti-Bias Sign Ordinance passed in June 1949 by the City Council of Miami Beach, Florida. It prohibits places of public accommodation, resort or amusement within the city from posting or displaying any advertisement or notice that they discriminate against any religious or racial group. Violations are made punishable by fines and imprisonment.

Apart from its practical importance, the ordinance is interesting for its history: In May 1947 the Miami Beach City Council unanimously adopted an ordinance banning the display of discriminatory signs and advertisements. In July 1947 a court test resulted in a ruling that the city lacked the power to enact such an ordinance; it was declared invalid. In May 1949 the Florida state legislature passed an enabling act authorizing the city of Miami Beach to pass an ordinance against discriminatory signs. In the following month the City Council, now having the necessary authority, re-passed the ordinance.

THE POLL TAX

In seven Southern states—Alabama, Arkansas, Mississippi, South Carolina, Tennessee, Texas and Virginia—large portions of the

Negro population are prevented from taking part in elections because of their inability to pay the poll tax. One argument advanced against a federal anti-poll tax law is that Southern states which still require a payment prerequisite to voting, themselves would repeal such laws. What happened in 1949?

One of the seven states took some action during the year. Tennessee enacted laws exempting various groups—women, veterans, and the blind—from the poll tax; it eliminated the payment as a requirement for voting in primary elections; it decreased the number of years in which citizens must pay. But the Constitution of Tennessee makes the poll tax mandatory. A proposal to call a convention to amend this provision and authorize the legislature to repeal the law was defeated by the voters in the November elections.

Attempts in other states to wipe out the poll tax were also futile. In Alabama and Arkansas bills were introduced in the legislatures that failed or were withdrawn. Virginia and Texas rejected constitutional amendments in their November elections.

In 1946 Alabama amended its constitution to provide that only persons who could "understand and explain" every article of the federal Constitution could register to vote. In January 1949 a Federal District Court, finding that the amendment had been enacted to prevent Negroes from voting, declared it to be in violation of the 15th Amendment and, therefore, unconstitutional. Two months later the United States Supreme Court affirmed the decision.[25]

In 1949, too, a Federal District Court in South Carolina issued a permanent injunction ordering the Democratic Party to open its books of enrollment for the party's primary to all persons entitled to vote under the constitution and laws of South Carolina, regardless of race, color or creed. In May 1949 a United States Court of Appeals affirmed the decision.[26]

The state of Georgia tried in 1949 to disenfranchise the 120,000 registered Negro voters by a legislative device; Governor Herman Talmadge had promised to end alleged "bloc voting" by Negroes. Early in the year his legislature passed a law[27] that required *all* voters to re-register and pass a new literacy test—the idea being to rule out Negroes on the test. But the attempt has boomeranged. The task of re-registering the *entire* Georgia electorate, including those in the tremendous rural areas, is proving virtually impossible and, as a result, many white voters may not participate in the 1950 elections.

LYNCHING

The legislature of Texas in 1949 enacted a law against lynching. The statute[28] defines lynching as acts of violence by a mob; it provides that every person who is part of a mob is punishable by death or imprisonment for not less than five years if the violence results in the death of a person, or by imprisonment from one to ten years if no death results from the mob's action.

Although this statute did introduce a new crime into the law of Texas, the crime of lynching, the acts it defines as lynching are already subject to punishment. The penal code of Texas contains provisions against murder, other kinds of homicide, assault and offenses against public peace; these provisions could cover any of the acts constituting lynching under the new statute. The effect of the new act, therefore, is only to supplement the punishment for certain unlawful deeds.

DISCRIMINATION IN STATE MILITIAS

Seven states passed laws in 1949 directed against racial and religious discrimination and segregation in their state militias.[29] They followed the lead of New Jersey which, in its new constitution adopted in 1947, provided that "no person shall be denied the enjoyment of any civil or military right . . . nor be segregated in the militia . . . because of religious principles, race, color, ancestry, or national origin" (Article I, Sec. 5).

Connecticut, Wisconsin, Illinois and Massachusetts made the change effective immediately. New York, Pennsylvania and California, however, ruled that the corrections be made "with due regard . . . to the time required to effectuate changes without impairing the efficiency or morale of the militia."

In July 1948 a Presidential Executive Order[30] declared that there shall be equality of treatment and opportunity for all persons in the armed services of the United States without regard to race, color, religion or national origin. This order contained the clause which obviously served as the pattern for the legislators of New York, Pennsylvania and California.

In Minnesota Governor Youngdahl issued an executive order decreeing that "there shall be equality of opportunity and treatment for all, including Negro citizens, who shall serve in the military and naval forces of the state without segregation into separate units." The order permits no postponement of its execution.

ANTI-MASK LEGISLATION

Anti-mask laws enacted during 1949 in the state of Alabama and in more than a score of Southern municipalities were not the first attempts by the South to thwart the Ku Klux Klan by destroying its hooded secrecy. Many previous laws on the statute books, still in effect, similarly were intended to disable the Klan and they included the wearing of masks as one of the facts constituting a criminal offense. For example, Sec. 1131 of the Criminal Code of South Carolina provides that it shall be unlawful for a group assembled under any pretext whatsoever, while wearing a mask, to assault or intimidate any person.

Most of these old statutes have one common defect. To obtain a conviction the prosecution must prove to the satisfaction of a Southern jury a specific intent on the part of the defendants to intimidate the victim or to deprive him of his rights. It is not surprising that these laws are dead letters, there have been practically no successful prosecutions under them.

The new concept in anti-mask laws introduced by anti-Klan Southerners—with the aid of the Southern office of the Anti-Defamation League, in Atlanta—provides for a law which bans the wearing of masks or hoods generally, without regard to the purpose for which such covering is worn. (Exceptions are made, of course, for the wearing of masks or hoods for clearly proper purposes, such as a masquerade ball, etc.)

Southern communities which have enacted this more effective type of anti-mask law include:

GEORGIA: Wrightsville, Macon City, Atlanta, Columbus, Gainesville, Valdosta, Swainsboro, Augusta, Moultrie, Albany, Iron City, Cedartown.

FLORIDA: Tallahassee, Miami, Miami Shores, South Miami, Miami Beach, Coral Gables, Atlantic Beach, Bartow, Tarpon Springs.

TENNESSEE: Knoxville, Nashville, Morristown.

NORTH CAROLINA: Charlotte.

Such were the 1949 accomplishments and setbacks in American law in the field of civil rights. By comparison with other recent years, it was true and substantial progress; the over-all picture was heartening. The men and women who sat in America's legislative halls, on its court benches and in its administrative offices understood that there was work to be done; they knew, too, that the people were behind them in the effort. This nation knows that a long uphill legislative climb still confronts it, before it may claim to the world that it has perfected its legal machinery to insure human equality.

A Final Word

WE HAVE DWELT at length upon discrimination against Jews and other minorities in several major areas of American life, and upon the anti-Semitism which besets and corrodes the democracy. Reciting this meaningful story was, at best, an unpleasant task.

The facts put together between the covers of this volume stress the unwholesome racial and religious prejudices and undemocratic discriminations in the United States. They are but blemishes which disfigure an otherwise healthy body politic. Were we to end this book having recited merely the weaknesses in the democratic fabric, it would be like the doctor describing the blemish to the patient and then turning his back upon the illness without even a suggestion for cure.

There are no panaceas. Strengthening democratic life in America is not the responsibility of any single group or any individual, but the responsibility of every citizen who would enjoy the benefits and the freedom that America gives. On every level of social and communal enterprise men and women in the conduct of their daily affairs must remain aware of the need to protect their democratic heritage. Wholesome attitudes must be instilled into the hearts and minds of all the people. Attention must be focused on flagrant violations of justice and fair play, and public opinion mobilized behind the forces struggling to forge this nation into a better likeness of the ideals upon which it was founded.

Years of study of this complex problem lead us to the conclusion that there are three fundamental forces which can be called into effective counterplay against prejudice—law, education, and community action. Woven together they become extraordinarily powerful; alone, each is insufficient. And when used simultaneously to complement one another they tend to become indistinguishable. Education generates a community's social action, frequently resulting in the enactment of legislation. At the same time, legislation itself is frequently a potent educative force.

In the use of these forces it is not enough to rest with the expression of well-meaning generalities. It is necessary to deal with realities. The targets must be delineated. Lip service to the concept of equality is not enough. There must be an insistence upon such specifics as elimination of discriminatory practices in housing, in education, in employment, in voting and in the use of public accommodations.

A secure and free people who have adequate opportunity to fulfill themselves and to lead happy lives will reject those who spread hatred. On the other hand, exhortation will have little effect in breaking down racial and religious hostility while men are frustrated or while they are afraid. There can be no freedom from discrimination in employment until there is full employment. There can be no freedom from discrimination in higher education until there are adequate facilities for all capable of higher education. There can be no freedom from discrimination in housing until there are ample housing facilities for all. Where there is scarcity and men compete desperately for the basic necessities of life, the minorities—and eventually the majority—will be at the mercy of those who stir up hatred and fear.

Racial and religious bigotry cannot thrive in an economically and democratically healthy society.

Footnotes

Chapter 4

1. *The Anti-Defamation League and Its Use in the World Communist Offensive.*

Chapter 5

1. New York *Post* 4/28/49.
2. *Cong. Rec.* 1/31/49 p. 746.

Chapter 6

1. Daniel Katz and K. W. Braly, "Racial Stereotypes of 100 College Students," *Journal of Abnormal & Social Psychology,* Vol. 28, pp. 280–290 (Oct. 1933).
2. *Public Attitudes Toward Minorities,* Opinion Research Center, University of Denver, 1948. See also Don Cahalan and Frank N. Trager, "Free Answer Stereotypes and Anti-Semitism," *Public Opinion Quarterly,* Vol. 13, pp. 93–104 (Spring 1949).
3. *Fortune,* Vol. 19, p. 104 (April 1939).
4. *Attitudes Toward Jews in the United States,* Office of War Information, Division of Surveys Report, No. 29, Oct. 1942.
5. *Fortune,* Vol. 28, p. 14 (Nov. 1943); Elmo Roper, *A Study of Anti-Minority Sentiment in the United States,* p. 3, New York, Sep. 1948.
6. Emory S. Bogardus, "Measuring Social Distances," *Journal of Applied Sociology,* Vol. 9, pp. 299–308 (March–April, 1925).
7. Emory S. Bogardus, "Changes in Racial Distances," *International Journal of Opinion and Attitude Research,* Vol. 1, pp. 55–62 (Dec. 1947).
8. Roper, *op. cit.,* p. 17.
9. J. P. Guilford, "Racial Preference of a Thousand American University Students," *Journal of Social Psychology,* Vol. 2, pp. 179–204 (May 1931).
10. Psychological Corporation, *What Is Good and Bad Americanism?* New York, Nov. 1946.
11. Roper, *op. cit.,* p. 64.
12. *Fortune,* Vol. 35, p. 32 (Oct. 1948).
13. *Opinion News,* Vol. 10, No. 4, p. 6.
14. Roper, *op. cit.,* pp. 44–45. A 1946 Gallup question yielded a similar 40 per cent who were in favor of a plan to "require each nation to take in a given number of Jewish and other European refugees, based upon the size and population of each nation."
15. In 1939 83 per cent of a Roper national sample were opposed to opening the doors to a larger number of immigrants than were then admitted under our immigration quotas.
16. *On Getting Into College,* American Council on Education, Washington 1949; *Inequality of Opportunity in Higher Education,* The New York Commission on the Need for a State University, Albany, 1948;

College Admission Practices With Respect to Race, Religion, and National Origin of Connecticut High School Graduates, Connecticut State Inter-racial Commission, Hartford, 1949.

17. *Higher Education,* A Supplement to *Fortune* for September 1949, p. 13.
18. Roper, *op. cit.,* p. 70.
19. Raymond Franzen, *A Study of Anti-Semitic Prejudice Among Middle Class New Yorkers,* unpublished mss, Sept. 1946, p. 10.
20. Raymond Franzen and Louisa Franzen, *Studies of Anti-Semitic Prejudice,* unpublished mss, June 1949.
21. *Public Attitudes Toward Minorities,* Opinion Research Center, University of Denver, 1948.
22. Daniel J. Levinson and R. Nevitt Sanford, "A Scale for the Measurement of Anti-Semitism," *Journal of Psychology,* Vol. 44, pp. 339–370 (April 1944). T. W. Adorno, Else Frenkel-Brunswik, Daniel Levinson, R. Nevitt Sanford, *The Authoritarian Personality,* Harper and Brothers, February, 1950. *Studies in Prejudice,* sponsored by American Jewish Committee, edited by Max Horkheimer and Samuel H. Flowerman.
23. The results of these studies were obtained from the American Jewish Committee, through the cooperation of Dr. Samuel Flowerman. By that time the Committee's newly formed Department of Scientific Research had become well established. It examined these previous studies and because of many shortcomings in the design and execution of the studies, decided to abandon this type of investigation, concentrating instead upon intensive studies in various communities, using more highly developed instruments, which include a number of dimensions of anti-Semitism.
24. The sample used in the A.J.C. studies was one described as representing the non-Jewish "voting population" of the United States, but both the design of the sample itself and the lack of rigor with which the design was administered would be criticized by most public opinion research experts today. Interviewing apparently took place in parks and public places rather than on doorsteps, which raises some question about how economic level controls were administered. There were also some considerable variations from study to study in the percentage of people found in various geographic, age, city size, and other subgroups within the sample, giving rise to questions about the rigor with which the sampling design was executed.
25. *Fortune,* Vol. 32, No. 2, p. 258 (Feb. 1946).

Also see:
Bruno Bettelheim and Morris Janowitz, *Dynamics of Prejudice,* Harper and Brothers, January, 1950. *Studies in Prejudice,* sponsored by American Jewish Committee, edited by Max Horkheimer and Samuel H. Flowerman.

Chapter 7

1. *Factors Affecting the Admission of High School Seniors to College,* A Report by Elmo Roper for the Committee on a Study of Discriminations in College Admissions (American Council on Education); 1949.
2. *Higher Education for American Democracy,* Vol. 2: *Equalizing and Expanding Individual Opportunity* (President's Commission on Higher Education); 1947.
3. *Inequality of Opportunity in Higher Education.*

4. *Factors Affecting the Admission of High School Seniors to College*, A Report by Elmo Roper for the Committee on a Study of Discriminations in College Admissions (American Council on Education); 1949.
5. *College Admission Practices With Respect to Race, Religion and National Origin of Connecticut High School Graduates.*
6. ADL Annual Survey for 1948; Doubleday & Co., 1949.
7. *Education Directory, Higher Education, Part 3, 1948–49;* Federal Security Agency, U. S. Office of Education.
8. Ibid.
9. 109 U.S. 3.
10. Chart analyzing State Laws concerning discrimination in education is available upon request from the ADL.
11. Laws of 1949, Chapter 11.
12. Laws of 1949, Chapter 726.
13. 163 U.S. 537.
14. Pitts v. Board of Trustees, 84F. Supp. 975.
15. Corbin v. County School Board of Pulaski County, 177 F. 2d 924.
16. Missouri ex rel. Gaines v. Canada, 305 U.S. 337.
17. Sipuel v. Board of Regents of the University of Oklahoma 332 U.S. 631.
18. Johnson v. Board of Trustees of University of Kentucky 83F. Supp. 707.
19. Oklahoma Session Laws, 1949, pp. 608–9.
20. See Chapter X, p. 197.
21. McCready v. Byrd, Baltimore City Court ruled October 10, 1949; case now before Maryland Court of Appeals.
22. See Chapter X, p. 197.
23. Laws of 1949, Chapter 186.
24. Laws of 1949, Chapter 433.
25. Westminster School District v. Mendez, 64F. Supp. 544 and 161 F. 2d 774; Dayton Board of Education v. State ex rel Reese, 114 Ohio St. 188; Crawford v. District School Board 68 Ore 388.
26. Webb et al v. School District No. 90 (#37,427).
27. Illinois School Appropriation Act of 1949.

Chapter 8

1. Theological seminaries were excluded. For a more detailed description of the sampling techniques see, Elmo Roper, *A Study of Anti-Minority Sentiment in Colleges,* unpublished, New York 1949.
2. Elmo Roper, *A Study of Anti-Minority Sentiment in the United States,* prepared for the Anti-Defamation League of B'nai B'rith, New York, 1948.

Chapter 10

1. Plessy v. Ferguson 163 U.S. 537.
2. On appeal from a decision of the Federal District Court in Maryland (80 F. Supp. 32).
3. Sweatt v. Painter. Certiorari granted by Supreme Court on November 7, 1949 (70 S. Ct. 139).
4. McLaurin v. Oklahoma State Regents for Higher Education—On appeal from Federal District Court in Oklahoma (87 F. Supp. 528).

5. Indiana and Wisconsin have laws providing for fair employment practices commissions, with the right to mediate disputes but with no right to issue enforceable orders; these two states are not listed among those with "effective" FEPC legislation.

6. Session Laws of Washington, 1949, Chapter 183; Oregon Laws, 1949, Chapter 221; Session Laws of New Mexico, 1949, Chapter 161; Laws of Rhode Island, January Session, 1949, Chapter 218I.

7. The law of Washington follows Massachusetts and Connecticut in providing for a six-month period of limitation.

8. The other cities are Chicago, Milwaukee, Cincinnati, Minneapolis, Philadelphia and Phoenix.

9. See ADL Annual Survey for 1948, pp. 74, 75.

10. Laws of 1949, Chapter 11. Extended the law to educational institutions and public accommodations.

11. Laws of 1949, Chapter 384.

12. Statutes of 1949, Chapter 1578.

13. Assembly Bill No. 130, introduced by Assemblyman Bernard Austin.

14. The laws passed before 1949 are listed in the ADL Annual Survey for 1948, pp. 21 and 22.

15. The Housing and Redevelopment Assistance Law of Pa. (Act No. 493). Wisconsin: Laws of 1949, Chapter 592. Connecticut: Public Act No. 291.

16. Except in Minnesota where, in 1919, a law was passed which declared void discriminatory clauses contained in instruments affecting real estate.

17. Shelley v. Kraemer and McGhee v. Sipes (334 U.S. 1).

18. Hurd v. Hodge and Urciolo v. Hodge (334 U.S. 24).

19. Goetz v. Smith and Saunders v. Philips (62 Atl. 2nd 602; cert. den. 69 S. Ct. 938).

20. Weiss et al v. Leaon et al. Case No. 41134, September Session 1949; S. Ct., Missouri.

21. Dorsey v. Stuyvesant Town Corp. 87 NE 2nd 541.

22. ADL Annual Survey for 1948, Appendix I.

23. "To Secure These Rights," Simon and Schuster.

24. New Jersey: Laws of 1949, Chapter 11. Connecticut: Public Law No. 291.

25. Davis v. Schnell, 81 F. Supp. 872; 69 S. Ct. 749.

26. Brown v. Baskin, 80 F. Supp. 1017; aff'd 174 F. 2nd 391.

27. Voters Registration Act (Georgia Laws, 1949, No. 297).

28. Laws of Texas, 1949, Chapter 582.

29. Connecticut: Public Act No. 8; Wisconsin: Laws of 1949, Chapter 76; Illinois: Revised Statutes, 1949, Chapter 129, Section 2; Massachusetts: Laws of 1949, Chapter 398; New York: Laws of 1949, Chapter 497; Pennsylvania: Public Law No. 568; California: Statutes, 1949, Chapter 948.

30. Executive Order No. 9981.

APPENDIX : *MODEL FAIR EDUCATIONAL PRACTICES ACT*

SECTION I: DECLARATION OF POLICY

It is hereby declared to be the policy of this state that the American ideal of equality of opportunity requires that our education system should develop the fullest potentialities of the individual and prepare him for responsible citizenship, and that persons otherwise qualified be admitted to educational institutions without discrimination based on race, color, religion, ancestry, or national origin, except that, with regard to religious or denominational educational institutions, persons otherwise qualified shall have equal opportunity to attend therein without discrimination because of race, color, ancestry or national origin. The right of all persons within the state to obtain all the accommodations, advantages, facilities and privileges of any educational institution covered by this Act without discrimination based on race, color, religion, ancestry or national origin, subject only to conditions and limitations applicable alike to all persons, and subject also to the right of religious or denominational educational institutions to grant preference on the basis of religious affiliation, is hereby declared to be a civil right.

SECTION II: DEFINITIONS AND EXEMPTIONS

a. For purposes of this Act "educational institution" means any institution devoted in whole or in part to instruction or training which is subject to visitation, examination, or inspection by the State Department of Education or which accepts applications for admission from the public generally. The term includes, but is not limited to secretarial, business, vocational, trade, and technical schools and academies, colleges, universities, and professional schools. The term does not include any educational institution which is, in its nature, distinctly private, is not supported in whole or in part by public funds or by contributions from the general public, and which does not accept applications for admission from the public generally.

b. The term "discriminate" includes "segregate".

c. Religious or denominational institution means an educational institution which is operated, supervised, or controlled by a religious or denominational organization, and which has certified to the State Department of Education that it is a religious or denominational educational institution.

d. Nothing in this Act shall be deemed to prevent a religious or denominational educational institution from selecting its students exclusively from adherents or members of such religion or denomination, or from giving preference in such selection to such adherents or members.

SECTION III: UNFAIR EDUCATIONAL PRACTICES

It shall be an unfair educational practice for an educational institution:

a. To use a quota system based on race, color, religion, ancestry or national origin in the admission of students, or otherwise to follow a policy of limiting admission of, or denying admission to, students because of their race, color, religion, ancestry, or national origin.

b. To exclude or otherwise discriminate against any person seeking admission as a student to such institution because of his race, color, religion, ancestry, or national origin.

c. To make or cause to be made any written or oral inquiry concerning the race, color, religion, ancestry or national origin of a person seeking admission or to make any other inquiry or investigation which the State Department of Education by regulation has determined facilitates discrimination, except that a religious or denominational educational institution may inquire whether applicants for admission are adherents or members of such religion or denomination.

d. To discriminate in the use of its facilities, accommodations, advantages, or privileges, against any student or group of students because of his or their race, color, religion, ancestry, or national origin.

e. To penalize any of its students or employees or any applicant for admission because he has testified, petitioned, or assisted in any proceeding under this Act.

f. To fail to preserve for a period of at least three years any and all records, documents, notations, and other data dealing with or pertaining to the admission, rejection, expulsion or suspension of students; or to refuse to make such records, documents, notations and data available at all times for the inspection of the Associate Superintendent in Charge of Fair Educational Practices.

SECTION IV: CERTIFYING OF RELIGIOUS AND DENOMINATIONAL INSTITUTIONS

An educational institution operated, supervised, or controlled by a religious or denominational organization may, through its chief executive officer, certify in writing to the State Department of Education that it is so operated, controlled, or supervised, and that it elects to be considered a religious or denominational educational institution, and it thereupon shall be deemed a religious or denominational institution for the purposes of this Act.

SECTION V: OFFICE OF FAIR EDUCATIONAL PRACTICES

a. There is hereby created in the State Department of Education an Office of Fair Educational Practices, to be headed by an Associate Superintendent in Charge of Fair Educational Practices. The Associate Superintendent in Charge of Fair Educational Practices shall be appointed by the Governor, with the approval of the upper house of the state legislature.

b. Whenever the Associate Superintendent in Charge of Fair Educational Practices has reason to believe or whenever it is charged by an aggrieved person or by his parent or guardian or by an organization which has as one of its purposes the combatting of educational discrimination or the promotion of equal educational opportunities, that an educational institution has engaged in an unfair educational practice, the Associate Superintendent shall cause an investigation to be made to determine whether any unfair educational practice has been committed. The Associate Superintendent shall have the power to subpoena witnesses, compel their attendance, administer oaths, take testimony, and require the production of evidence relating to the matter under investigation by him.

c. If the Associate Superintendent shall determine that proper cause exists for a finding that an unfair educational practice has been engaged in, he shall attempt, by informal methods of persuasion, conciliation, or mediation, to induce the elimination of the unfair educational practice. He shall not disclose what takes place during such informal efforts at persuasion, conciliation, or mediation, nor may he offer in evidence in any proceeding the occurrences during such informal efforts.

d. If the Associate Superintendent is unable to induce elimination of an unfair educational practice by informal methods, he shall issue and cause to be served upon the educational institution alleged to have engaged in such practice a complaint setting forth the unfair educational practice charged, together with a notice of public hearing before a hearing officer designated for that purpose by the Superintendent of the State Department of Education, at a place therein fixed to be held not less than twenty days after service of such complaint. Any complaint issued pursuant to this section must be issued within three years after the alleged unfair educational practice was committed.

e. The institution complained against shall have the right to answer the original and any amended complaint, and to appear at such hearing by counsel, present evidence, and examine and cross-examine witnesses.

f. The hearing officer shall have the power to subpoena witnesses, compel their attendance, administer oaths, take the testimony of any person under oath, and require the production of evidence relating to the matter in question before him. The testimony taken at the hearing shall be under oath and shall be reduced to writing and filed with the State Department of Education.

g. After the hearing is completed, the hearing officer shall file an intermediate report with the Superintendent of the State Department of Education which shall contain his detailed findings of fact, conclusions and the reasons therefor, upon the issues in the proceeding, and his recommendations as to the final disposition of the proceeding. A copy of the hearing officer's report shall be made public and shall be served on the parties to the proceeding. Any party to the proceeding may, within twenty days after such service, file with the Superintendent exceptions to the findings, conclusions, or recommendations, or to any other part of the record or proceeding, with a brief in support thereof, or may file a brief in support of such findings, conclusions, or recommendations.

h. If, upon all the evidence, the Superintendent of the State Department of Education shall determine that the educational institution which is the subject of the charges made in the proceeding has engaged in an unfair educational practice, the Superintendent shall state his findings of fact and conclusions of law, and shall issue and cause to be served upon such educational institution a copy of such findings and conclusions, and an order requiring such educational institution to cease and desist from unfair educational practices and to take such action as will, in the opinion of the Superintendent, best effectuate the purposes of this Act.

i. If, upon all the evidence, the Superintendent shall find that the educational institution which is charged with an unfair educational practice has not engaged in any such practice, the Superintendent shall state his findings and shall issue and cause to be served on all the parties to the proceeding a copy of such findings and conclusions, and an order dismissing the complaint.

SECTION VI: JUDICIAL REVIEW AND ENFORCEMENT

a. Whenever the Superintendent has issued an order as provided in this Act, he may apply to the appropriate court of record for the enforcement of such order by a proceeding brought in that court of general jurisdiction within the judicial district including any county wherein the educational institution charged with an unfair educational practice is located. The Superintendent shall file with the court a transcript of the record of the hearing before its hearing officer, and the court shall have jurisdiction of the proceeding and of the questions determined therein, and shall have power to make an order annulling or confirming, wholly or in part, or modifying the determination reviewed. The order of the appropriate court shall be subject to review by the higher courts of the state in accordance with the regular appellate procedure of the state, in the same manner and with the same effect as provided on an appeal from a final judgment made by the court without a jury. The findings of the Superintendent as to the facts shall be conclusive, if supported by substantial evidence on the record considered as a whole.

b. Any party to the proceeding aggrieved by a final order of the Superintendent may obtain a judicial review thereof by an application to the court in accordance with the procedure provided in paragraph a of this section.

SECTION VII: PROMULGATION OF RULES AND REGULATIONS

The Superintendent of the State Department of Education may adopt, promulgate, amend, or rescind rules and regulations to effectuate the purposes and provisions of this Act.

SECTION VIII: EDUCATIONAL AND RESEARCH PROGRAM

The Associate Superintendent in Charge of Fair Educational Practices shall formulate and carry out, in cooperation with the Department of Education, a comprehensive program of education and research designed to eliminate and prevent the discrimination forbidden by this Act; and to issue such reports and such publications as in his judgment will tend to promote good will and prevent, minimize, or eliminate, discrimination in education because of race, religion, color, ancestry, or national origin.

SECTION IX: REPORT OF THE SUPERINTENDENT

The Superintendent of the State Department of Education shall make an annual report to the Governor and the legislature which shall include a resume of the nature and substance of the cases disposed of by public hearings, as well as recommendations for further action to eliminate discrimination in education, if he believes such is needed.

SECTION X: CONSTRUCTION

The provisions of this act shall be construed liberally for the accomplishment of the purposes thereof, and any law inconsistent with any provisions of this act shall no longer apply.

SECTION XI: APPROPRIATIONS

The sum of $ per annum, or so much thereof as may be necessary is hereby appropriated to the Department of Education for carrying out the provisions of this act.

CHART I

ORGANIZATIONS WITH ANTI-SEMITIC RECORDS

NAME	ADDRESS	LEADER	FOUNDED	GEOGRAPHIC CHARACTER
American Bilbo Club	Atlanta, Ga.	Ira Jett	May, 1949	local
American Anti-Communist League	St. Louis, Mo.	Gerald Smith	1948	national
Anglo-American Bible Study Group	Los Angeles, Cal.	Wesley Swift	1947	local
Anglo-Saxon Christian Association	Portland, Ore.	G. Fred Johnson	unknown	local
Anglo-Saxon Christian Congregation	Los Angeles, Cal.	Wesley Swift	1945	local
Anglo-Saxon Federation	Haverhill, Mass.	Howard B. Rand	1928	national
Anglo-Saxon Federation	Chicago, Ill.	Robert B. Record	early 1930's	local
Judge Armstrong Foundation	Ft. Worth, Texas	George W. Armstrong	Nov. 1945	national
Associated Klans of America	Atlanta, Ga.	Sam W. Roper	Sept. 1949	regional
Association of Georgia Klans	Atlanta, Ga.	Sam W. Roper	May, 1946	regional
William L. Blessing Organization	Denver, Colo.	William L. Blessing	1941	regional
California Anti-Communist League	Los Angeles, Cal.	Wesley Swift	June, 1949	regional
Christian Civic League	Albany, N. Y.	Rev. O. R. Miller	1910	local
Christian Evangelistic Anti-Vice Association	Lincoln, Neb.	Isaac Braxton Flint	1948	"national"
Christian Nationalist Crusade (Party)	St. Louis, Mo.	Gerald Smith	1946	national
Christian Patriots Anonymous	Los Angeles, Cal.	Stanley Leon	1949	local
Upton Close Organization	Washington, D.C.	Upton Close	Early forties	national
Constitutional Educational League	New York, N. Y.	Joseph P. Kamp	1937	national
Economics League	Buffalo, N. Y.	Jos. H. Stoffel	About 1936	local

ESSENTIAL NATURE	MEMBERSHIP	NATURE OF ANTI-SEMITIC ACTIVITY (AND OTHER)	OFFICIAL PUBLICATION	ESTIMATE OF ORGANIZATION
racist	60 (claimed)	Unsuccessful attempt to reorganize former "Columbians" movement. Became inactive by June, 1949	none	Influence negligible
"politico-economic"	none	Literature distribution	none	See Christian Nationalist Crusade, below
religious	Approx. 250 followers	Meetings	none	See Anglo-Saxon Christian Congregation, below
religious	100 maximum attendance at meetings	Meetings; literature distribution; (Bible classes)	The Reminder	Small; influence negligible
religious	200–300 followers	Meetings; political action, (radio b'cast)	none	Strongest anti-Semitic organization on West Coast
religious	300–400 in New England	Meetings; wide sale of publications	Destiny Magazine	Well-established with national supporters
religious	Approx. 200 followers	Meetings; literature distribution	Covenant Voice	Local and limited influence
"politico-economic"	none	Literature distribution; financial support to like-minded agencies	none	Important because of Armstrong's wealth
racist	See Association of Ga. Klans	See Association of Georgia Klans	none	Merger of Association of Georgia Klans and Knights of the KKK's of America
racist	About 10,000	Meetings; cross-burnings, etc.	none	Most powerful Klan faction; see Associated Klans of America, above
religious	unknown	Meetings; publications; sermons; (radio)	Showers of Blessing	Some local influence
"politico-economic"	Claims 17,000; unverified. Average mtg. attendance 450	Meetings	none	A Gerald Smith-Wesley Swift merger; see Anglo-Saxon Christian Congregation, above
"politico-economic"	unknown	Publication; (political action)	The Civic Bulletin	Small organization; little influence
"religious"	unknown	Distribution of religious tracts	none	Distributes large quantities of literature
"politico-economic"	Claims over three million; unverified	Meetings; publications; political action; speakers bureau	The Cross and the Flag	Important national group; successful financially; widespread literature distribution; no political party influence
"politico-economic"	unknown	Literature distribution	none	No influence
"politico-economic"	none	Speeches; publications; newspaper columns; (radio)	Closer-Ups	Important influence
"politico-economic"	none	Distribution of pamphlets; political action	none	Important pamphlet publisher
"politico-economic"	unknown	Meetings; (literature)	none	Small group; little influence. Sponsors Gerald Smith and Fred Kister

CHART I—(Cont'd)

NAME	ADDRESS	LEADER	FOUNDED	GEOGRAPHIC CHARACTER
Federated KKK, Inc.	Birmingham, Ala.	Wm. H. Morris	June 21, 1946	regional
Federation of Carolina Klans	Leesville, S. C.	Thomas L. Hamilton	Nov. 1949	regional
German-American Citizens League	Chicago, Ill.	Rudolph Hillebrand	Early forties	regional
Great Pyramid Club	Los Angeles, Cal.	Wesley Swift	Oct. 1946	local
Mordecai F. Ham Movement	Louisville, Ky.	Mordecai F. Ham	Early forties	regional
Institute of Arab-American Affairs	New York, N. Y.	Khalil Totah	Jan. 15, 1945	national
Iowa Anti-Communist League	Waterloo, Iowa	Stanley Baker	1948	local
Knights of the Ku Klux Klans of America	Montgomery, Ala.	Lycurgus Spinks	Aug. 23, 1949	regional
Ku Klux Klan of Florida, Inc.	Orlando, Fla.	A. B. Taylor	Sept. 1944	regional
Loyal American Group	Union, N. J.	Conde McGinley	March, 1947	local
Lutheran Research Society	Detroit, Mich.	Lawrence Reilly	Jan. 1946	local
Kurt Mertig Organization (Citizens Protective League)	New York, N. Y.	Kurt Mertig	unknown	local
Midwestern Political Survey Institute	St. Louis, Mo.	Gerald Smith	1946	national
National Blue Star Mothers of America	Phila., Pa.	Katherine Brown	1943	local
National Economic Council	New York, N. Y.	Merwin K. Hart	1931	national
National Patrick Henry Organization	Columbus, Ga.	Mrs. Jessie W. Jenkins	Dec. 1947	local
National Renaissance Party	Beacon, N. Y.	James Madole	Jan. 1949	local
National Security League	Dayton, Ohio	H. W. Binegar	Nov. 1948	local

ESSENTIAL NATURE	MEMBERSHIP	NATURE OF ANTI-SEMITIC ACTIVITY (AND OTHER)	OFFICIAL PUBLICATION	ESTIMATE OF ORGANIZATION
racist	Claims over 30,000; unverified	Meetings; cross-burnings, etc.	Uxtra	An important Klan faction
racist	unknown	In formative stage	none	Consolidation of Klansmen of North and South Carolina
"politico-economic"	unknown	Newspaper; (meetings)	Deutsch-Amerikanische Buergerzeitung	Small nationalist German group with mid-West sympathetic, pro-German, support
religious	About 400	Meetings	none	Very small treasury; influence limited. See Anglo-Saxon Christian Congregation, above
religious	none	Meetings; publication; (radio)	Old Kentucky Home Revivalist	Important impact because of radio following
"politico-economic"	unknown	Distribution of non-organizational literature; (publication)	Institute of Arab American Affairs Bulletin	Leading American pro-Arab propaganda agency
"politico-economic"	unknown	Meetings; literature distribution	none	One-man organization; no influence
racist	Claims 650,000; unverified	Meetings; cross-burnings, etc.	none	Active Klan faction; see Associated Klans of America, above
racist	unknown	Meetings; cross-burnings, etc.	none	Moderately important Klan faction
"politico-economic"	unknown	Meetings; publication	Common Sense	Minor group; little influence
religious	Claims 4000; unverified	Publications; (radio broadcasts)	Eleventh Hour	Influence limited
"politico-economic"	unknown	Meetings; political action	none	Nazi apologist, letter-writer and petitioner; small following
"politico-economic"	unknown	Literature distribution	none	See Christian Nationalist Crusade, above
"politico-economic"	75–100 based on mtg. attendance	Meetings; publications; political action	none	Small membership; little influence
"politico-economic"	unknown	Publications; political action; (radio programs)	Economic Council Letter	Important, effective, high level propaganda agency
racist	unknown	Publications	none	One-woman organization; virtually moribund
"politico-economic"	unknown	Publications	National Renaissance Bulletin	One-man organization; financially weak; little influence
"politico-economic"	unknown	Meetings; publication	Ohio Pioneer	Minor group, mainly composed of Gerald Smith supporters

CHART I—(Cont'd)

NAME	ADDRESS	LEADER	FOUNDED	GEOGRAPHIC CHARACTER
National Workers League	Detroit, Mich.	Russell Roberts	1938	local
Nationalist Action League	Phila., Pa.	W. Henry MacFarland, Jr.	July, 1948	local
Nationalist Unity Congress	Chicago, Ill.	Andrew B. McAllister	June, 1949	"national"
Nationalist Veterans of America	St. Louis, Mo.	Chris Schlather	Oct. 1949	national
New Thought Forum	Boston, Mass.	Mrs. Maude Moulton	unknown	local
Organized Americans of German Ancestry	Chicago, Ill.	Leonard Enders	Nov. 1946	local
Original Southern Klans, Inc.	Columbus, Ga.	E. G. Johnston	June, 1948	regional
Patriotic Tract Society	St. Louis, Mo.	Gerald Smith	May, 1948	national
Pro-American Information Bureau	Hinckley, Ill.	Andrew B. McAllister	1947	"national"
Protestant War Veterans of the U.S., Inc.	New York, N. Y.	Edward James Smythe	1937	"national"
Public Affairs Forum	Los Angeles, Cal.	Earl C. Craig	Jan. 1948	local
Racial Purity Committee	St. Louis, Mo.	Gerald Smith	1949	local
Paul & Luke Rader Organization	Minneapolis, Minn.	Paul & Luke Rader	May, 1928	local
Southern Knights of the Ku Klux Klan	Tallahassee, Fla.	Bill Hendrix	Jan. 1949	regional
O. C. Stadsklev Organization	Minneapolis, Minn.	O. C. Stadsklev	unknown	local
United Mothers of America, Inc.	Cleveland, Ohio	Ella C. Monreal	1941	local
Voters Alliance for Americans of German Ancestry, Inc.	New York, N. Y.	A. O. Tittman	1946	local
We, the Mothers Mobilize for America, Inc.	Chicago, Ill.	Lyrl Clark Van Hyning	Feb. 10, 1941	national
White Man's League	Atlanta, Ga.	Emory Burke	Nov. 1949	"regional"
Gerald B. Winrod Organization	Wichita, Kan.	Gerald B. Winrod	1927	national

SSENTIAL ATURE	MEMBERSHIP	NATURE OF ANTI-SEMITIC ACTIVITY (AND OTHER)	OFFICIAL PUBLICATION	ESTIMATE OF ORGANIZATION
"politico-economic"	unknown	Publications	none	Virtually moribund
"politico-economic"	75–100 based on meeting attendance	Meetings; publications; political action	National Progress	Minor group; little influence
"politico-economic"	unknown	Meetings; sale of literature	none	Minor group; little influence
"politico-economic"	unknown	Meetings	none	A Gerald Smith organization; see Christian Nationalist Crusade, above
"politico-economic"	unknown	Meetings	none	Minor group; little influence
"politico-economic"	About 50 based on meeting attendance	Meetings; booklets; (bulletin)	Bulletin Newsletter distributed sporadically	Minor group active in German-American circles; little influence
racist	unknown	Meetings; cross-burnings, etc.	Klansman	Klan faction of minor influence
"politico-economic"	none	Literature distribution	none	See Christian Nationalist Crusade, above
"politico-economic"	none	Literature distribution	none	Became inactive in June, 1949
"politico-economic"	unknown	Leaflet distribution	none	One-man organization; little influence
"politico-economic"	About 75 based on mtg. attendance	Meetings; political action	none	Minor group; little influence
racist	unknown	Political action	none	See Christian Nationalist Crusade, above
religious	From 25–300 based on meeting attendance	Sermons; publication; (radio broadcasts); (River Lake Tabernacle)	Sunshine News	Minor group; little influence
racist	About 200	Meetings; publication; political action	The Klansman	Comparatively important Klan faction
religious	100–200 based on meeting attendance	Sermons; publication; (radio) (Truth & Liberty Temple)	Truth and Liberty	Minor group; local influence
"politico-economic"	About 50	Meetings	none	Incorporated late in 1949 after being dormant for a number of years. Minor group; little influence
"politico-economic"	unknown	Meetings	none	Minor group active in German-American circles; little influence
"politico-economic"	unknown	Literature distribution	Women's Voice	Strongest women's organization in field
racist	none	Meetings	none	One-man organization; little influence
religious	70,000 to 100,000 subscribers	Publications; (radio); (Defender Publishers, Inc., Defenders of the Christian Faith, Defenders of the Theological Seminary)	Defender Magazine; Prayer Circle Letter	Well-organized and highly financed with considerable influence, especially in mid-West

LEADERS WITH ANTI-SEMITIC RECORDS

NAME	ORGANIZATIONAL AFFILIATION	ADDRESS	FOUNDED	GEOGRAPHIC CHARACTER
John B. Trevor	American Coalition of Patriotic Societies	Washington, D. C.	1929	national
Frederick Kister	American Renaissance Book Club	Chicago, Ill.	Sept. 1947	"national"
Austin J. App	Boniface Press	Philadelphia, Pa.	Jan. 1949	"national"
Millard Grubbs	Border State Chamber of Commerce & Education	Louisville, Ky.	1949	local
Rev. William T. Watson	Christian Medical Research League	Detroit, Mich.	Nov. 1948	"national"
Millard J. Flenner	Dayton Theological Seminary	Dayton, Ohio	Sept. 1947	local
Rev. William T. Watson	Florida Bible Institute	Tampa, Fla.	unknown	regional
Allan Zoll	National Council for American Education	New York, N. Y.	July, 1948	national
F. C. Sammons	West Virginia Anti-Soviet League	Huntington, W. Va.	Nov. 1949	regional

ESSENTIAL NATURE	SIZE	NATURE OF ANTI-SEMITIC ACTIVITY (AND OTHER)	OFFICIAL OR UNOFFICIAL PUBLICATION	ESTIMATE OF ORGANIZATION
"politico-economic"	unknown	Pamphlets (meetings)	none	Coalition of approx. 125 misc. organizations
"educational"	unknown	(Sale of books and pamphlets)	none	Minor group; little influence
"politico-economic"	none	(Pamphlets)	none	One-man organization; moderate influence
"politico-economic"	unknown	Literature distribution	none	One-man organization; little influence
"religious"	unknown	Meetings	none	Minor group; little influence
religious	small school	(School curriculum and speakers)	none	moderate influence; little prestige
religious	unknown	Meetings	none	Moderate influence; little prestige
"educational"	unknown	(Publications)	none	Moderately important and effective
"politico-economic"	unknown	Pamphlets	none	In formation; Gerald Smith followers

CHART II: PERIODICALS

NAME	ADDRESS	FOUNDED	PUBLISHER; EDITOR; ORGANIZATION	TYPE	CIRCULATION AND DISTRIBUTION	SUBSCRIPTION
American Commentator	Cedar City, Utah	November 1947	Stephen Nenoff	Irregular newspaper	National but limited	$4.00 per year
American Digest	Atlanta, Georgia	1939	Dewey Taft	Irregular newspaper	300	$3.00 per year
American World Intelligence	Chicago, Ill.	1947	Dr. C. S. Norborg	Bi-weekly newsletter	1,000; National	$10.00 per year
Beacon Light Herald	Atascadero, Calif.		William Kullgren	Monthly newsletter		$3.00 per year
Bible News Flashes	Faribault, Minnesota	1940	William D. Herrstrom	Monthly magazine	3,000; National	$1.00 per year
Boise Valley Herald	Middleton, Canyon City, Idaho		A. Cornell Boyd B. Cornell I. W. Cornell	Weekly newspaper	475	$2.00 per year
The Broom	East San Diego, Calif.	March 1931	C. Leon de Aryan	Weekly newspaper	2,500; National	$4.00 per year
Christian Veterans Political Counsel	Chicago, Illinois	December 1945	Frederick Kister; Christian Veterans of America	Irregular newsletter	Limited; National	Contributions
The Civic Bulletin	Albany, New York		Rev. O. R. Miller; Christian Civic League	Weekly & monthly newsletter		$.50 per year
Closer-ups	Washington, D. C.	July 1945	Upton Close	Semi-monthly newsletter	14,000–18,000; National	$15.00 per year
Common Sense (formerly Think Weekly)	Union, New Jersey	May 1946	Conde McGinley; Loyal American Group	Irregular newspaper		$2.00 per year
The Covenant Voice	Chicago, Ill.	November 1942	Robert B. Record; Anglo-Saxon Federation	Monthly newsletter	5,000; Local	Contributions

CHART II: PERIODICALS—(Cont'd)

NAME	ADDRESS	FOUNDED	PUBLISHER; EDITOR; ORGANIZATION	TYPE	CIRCULATION AND DISTRIBUTION	SUBSCRIPTION
The Cross and the Flag	St. Louis, Missouri	April 1942	Gerald L. K. Smith; Don Lohbeck; Christian Nationalist Crusade	Monthly magazine	Approx. 23,000; National	$2.00 per year
The Crusader	Jacksonville, Fla.	1921	Rev. Allen C. Shuler	Semi-monthly or irregular newsletter	5,000; National	$1.00 per year
Dayton Independent	Dayton, Ohio	1921	A. G. Silvey	Weekly newspaper	11,500; Regional	$1.00 per year
The Defender	Wichita, Kansas	May 1925	Gerald B. Winrod; Principal organ of various Winrod enterprises	Monthly magazine	70,000-100,000; National	$.50 per year
Destiny	Haverhill, Massachusetts		Howard B. Rand; Anglo-Saxon Federation of America	Monthly magazine	10,000-18,000; National	$3.00 per year
Economic Council Letter	New York City	Probably 1937	Merwin K. Hart; National Economic Council	Semi-monthly newsletter	10,000-140,000; National	$10.00 per year
The Eleventh Hour	Detroit, Michigan	1944	Lawrence Reilly; Lutheran Research Society	Monthly & Bi-monthly magazine	4,000; National	$1.00 per year
The Free Press	Redmond, Oregon	1940	Syd Pierce	Semi-monthly newspaper	300-1,000; National	$1.50 per year
The Guildsman	Germantown, Illinois	1932	Edward A. Koch	Monthly magazine	Limited; National	$.75 per year
Information for Americans	Cleveland, Ohio	1935	John P. Moran; League for Justice	Irregular newsletter	Local	None
The Individualist	Danville, Virginia		Guy C. Stephens	Irregular newsletter		$.25 for 24 issues

CHART II: PERIODICALS—(Cont'd)

NAME	ADDRESS	FOUNDED	PUBLISHER; EDITOR; ORGANIZATION	TYPE	CIRCULATION AND DISTRIBUTION	SUBSCRIPTION
Kingdom Digest	Fort Worth, Texas	September 1949	J. A. Lovell	Monthly magazine		$3.00 for 13 months
The Klansman	Jacksonville, Florida	September 1949	Jacksonville Klavern of KKK	Newspaper; only one issue published	Minute; local	None
The Klansman	Tallahassee, Florida	April 15, 1949	Bill Hendrix; Southern Knights of the KKK	Newspaper; only one issue published	Minute; local	None
The Letter	St. Louis, Missouri	April 1945	Gerald L. K. Smith; Nationalist News Service affiliated with Christian Nationalist Crusade	Monthly newsletter	Approx. 15,000; National	$3.00 per year
The Malist	Meriden, Conn.		Henry S. Sattler	Monthly magazine		$3.00 per year
The Methodist Challenge	Los Angeles, Calif.	1947	Robert P. Shuler; Bob Shuler, Sr.	Monthly magazine	16,309; National	$1.00 per year
National American	Bronx, N. Y.	September 1949	Raymond Burke; National Renaissance Party	Irregular newsletter		$.05 per copy
National Defense	Arcadia, Calif.	1928	A. Hoeppel	Monthly magazine		$2.00 per year
National Progress	Philadelphia, Pa.	1947	Henry W. MacFarland, Jr.; Nationalist Action League	Semi-monthly newsletter; discontinued in June 1949	500; Regional	$1.00 per year
National Renaissance Bulletin	Beacon, N. Y.	January 1949	James Madole; National Renaissance Party	Irregular newsletter		$3.00 per year
The Ohio Pioneer	Dayton, Ohio	November 1947	H. W. Binegar; National Security League	Irregular newspaper	Limited; regional	$1.00 per year

CHART II: PERIODICALS—(Cont'd)

NAME	ADDRESS	FOUNDED	PUBLISHER; EDITOR; ORGANIZATION	TYPE	CIRCULATION AND DISTRIBUTION	SUBSCRIPTION
Old Kentucky Home Revivalist	Louisville, Ky.		Mordecai F. Ham; Mordecai F. Ham Evangelist Assoc. Inc.	Semi-monthly newspaper		$1.00 per year
Patriotic Research Bureau	Chicago, Ill.	Approx. 1933	Elizabeth Dilling; Patriotic Research Bureau	Monthly newsletter; discontinued in August 1949	National	$3.00 per year
Prayer Circle Letter	Wichita, Kansas	Late 1930's	Gerald B. Winrod; Represents various Winrod projects	Irregular letter	25,000; National	Donations
The Protestant Newsletter (formerly Kings Gazette)	Costa Mesa, Calif.	1945	David Baxter	Monthly newsletter		$1.00 per year
The Reminder	Portland, Oregon	1932	Hugh C. Krum; Anglo-Saxon Christian Assoc. of the United States of America	Monthly magazine	2,000; National	$1.00 per year
Round Table News Flashes	Indianapolis, Ind.	April 1946	Archibald McKinnon	Irregular bulletin	400–500; National	$.10 per copy
The Rubicon	New York City	1941	Luigi Criscuolo	Monthly newsletter		$3.00 per year
Showers of Blessing	Denver, Colo.	November 1941	William L. Blessing; House of Prayer For All People	Monthly magazine	National	None
The Southern Gospel	River Junction Florida	July 1949	Rev. A. C. Shuler	Monthly newspaper; only two issues published	Minute; local	$1.00 per year
Sunshine News	Minneapolis, Minn.	1934	Luke Rader; River Lake Tabernacle	Weekly magazine	883; Regional	$1.00 per year

CHART II: PERIODICALS—(Cont'd)

NAME	ADDRESS	FOUNDED	PUBLISHER; EDITOR; ORGANIZATION	TYPE	CIRCULATION AND DISTRIBUTION	SUBSCRIPTION
Truth and Liberty Magazine	Minneapolis, Minn.	May 1944	C. O. Stadsklev; Truth and Liberty Temple	Monthly magazine	1,000; Regional	$3.50 per year
Ux-tra	Birmingham, Ala.	1949	Brett Brasfield; Federated KKK Inc.	Irregular newspaper; only one issue published	Regional	$1.00 per year
Williams Intelligence Summary	Santa Ana, Calif.	December 1948	Robert H. Williams	Monthly newsletter	3,000-15,000; National	$3.00 per year
Women's Voice	Chicago, Ill.	August 1943	Lyrl Clark Van Hyning; We, The Mothers Mobilize For America, Inc.	Monthly newspaper	10,000; National	$2.00 per year
X-ray	Muncie, Indiana	September 1937	Court Asher	Weekly newspaper	1,000; National	$2.00 per year

CHART III: BOOKS, PAMPHLETS AND LEAFLETS

TITLE	PUBLISHER OR SPONSOR	AUTHOR	FIRST APPEARANCE	NUMBER PRINTED & DISTRIBUTION METHOD
Alien Minorities and Mongrelization (Book)	Meador Publishing Co. Boston, Mass.	Marilyn R. Allen P.O. Box 2243 Salt Lake City, Utah	September 1949	3,000; Mail
In Defense of the Ku Klux Klan (Letter)	None	Marilyn R. Allen P.O. Box 2243 Salt Lake City, Utah	December 1949	Mail
Jewish Loans On Increase (Leaflet)	Anglo-Saxon Committee Burbank, Calif.	Unknown	1949	Mail
Money and The Tariff (Pamphlet)	Judge Armstrong Foundation Fort Worth, Texas	George W. Armstrong Fort Worth, Texas	September 1949	Mail
Zionist Wall Street (Pamphlet)	Judge Armstrong Foundation Fort Worth, Texas	George W. Armstrong Fort Worth, Texas	June 1949	Mail
Controversy of Zion (Pamphlet)	Christian Evangelistic Anti-Vice Association Lincoln, Nebraska	British Israel Assoc. of Greater Vancouver Vancouver, B. C.	Unknown	Mail
The Zionist State Versus The Kingdom of God (Pamphlet)	Christian Evangelistic Anti-Vice Association Lincoln, Nebraska	British Israel Assoc. of Greater Vancouver Vancouver, B. C.	Unknown	Mail
Chain-Ganged By The Jewish Gestapo (Pamphlet)	Gerald L. K. Smith St. Louis, Missouri	Emory Burke	Fall 1949	Mail
What Does Gerald L. K. Smith Stand For? (Card)	Christian Nationalist Crusade St. Louis, Missouri	Unknown	1949	Mail
High Treason and Conspiracy (Leaflet)	Unknown	Christian Patriots Anonymous	1949	Meeting
Israel's Fingerprints (Pamphlet)	Dr. Wesley Swift's Ministry Lancaster, Calif.	Bertrand L. Comparet	June 1949	Meeting

CHART III: BOOKS, PAMPHLETS AND LEAFLETS—(Cont'd)

TITLE	PUBLISHER OR SPONSOR	AUTHOR	FIRST APPEARANCE	NUMBER PRINTED & DISTRIBUTION METHOD
Food For Thought (Pamphlet)	Unknown	Marion Curtis 29 Lewis Tower Philadelphia, Penn.	July 1949	Mail
Why F.E.P.C. (Pamphlet)	Distributor: Upton Close Washington, D. C.	Marion Curtis 29 Lewis Tower Philadelphia, Penn.	January 1949	Mail
The Jewnited Nations—Headquarters For World Spies and Traitors (Leaflet)	O. E. Edstrom San Francisco, Calif.	O. E. Edstrom	January 1949	Approximately 2,000; Mail
The Reward For Stupendous Stupidity (Leaflet)	O. E. Edstrom San Francisco, Calif.	O. E. Edstrom	January 1949	Approximately 2,000; Mail
The World Church In Prophecy (Pamphlet)	Prophetic Bible Conference Bureau Hoisington, Kansas Distributor: Gerald B. Winrod, Wichita, Kansas	Dr. Edward Fehr	1949	Mail
The Crime of Our Age (Third Edition) (Pamphlet)	Organized Americans of German Ancestry Chicago, Ill.	Dr. Ludwig Fritsch 5121 N. New England Ave. Chicago, Ill.	1947	10,000; Mail, Meetings
The International Jew (Book)	Christian Nationalist Crusade St. Louis, Missouri	G. F. Green Herts, England	1949	Mail
If That Is What It Is, That Is What We Call It (Brochure)	The Hoosier Press Lafayette, Ind.	Ainsley E. Horney P.O. Box 529 Lafayette, Indiana	October 1949	Unknown
Civil Rights or State Sovereignty (Pamphlet)	National Patrick Henry Organization, Inc. Columbus, Ga.	Jessie W. Jenkins P.O. Box 985 Columbus, Ga.	September 1949	Mail
Frankfurter Recommended "Commie" Dupes (Leaflet)	None	Henry H. Klein 261 Broadway New York City	February 1949	Mail

CHART III: BOOKS, PAMPHLETS AND LEAFLETS—(Cont'd)

TITLE	PUBLISHER OR SPONSOR	AUTHOR	FIRST APPEARANCE	NUMBER PRINTED & DISTRIBUTION METHOD
If I Were Dictator of the United States (Leaflet)	None	Henry H. Klein New York City	November 1949	Mail
Jews Are Not Favored By God (Leaflet)	None	Henry H. Klein New York City	September 1949	Mail
Limit Excessive Private Fortunes Or Die En Masse (Leaflet)	None	Henry H. Klein New York City	February 1949	Mail
Petition For the Impeachment of Felix Frankfurter (Leaflet)	Non	Henry H. Klein New York City	June 1949	Mail
Potash And Oil Are Making a Deal, So The War In Palestine May Soon Be Over (Leaflet)	None	Henry H. Klein New York City	1949	Mail
Roosevelt, Frankfurter, Zionism, Communism and Standard Oil	None	Henry H. Klein New York City	June 1949	Mail
Our Jewish Aristocracy (Fifth edition March 1949) (Pamphlet)	Distributor: Women's Voice 537 S. Dearborn Street Chicago, Ill.	Arnold Leese England	Unknown	Mail
What Jews Can We Trust? (Letter)	None	George Van Horn Moseley Atlanta, Georgia	December 1949	Mail
Open Letter To Senator Arthur H. Vandenberg (Letter)	None	George Van Horn Moseley Atlanta, Georgia	May 1949	Mail
Facts Concerning The Community Chest You Should Know (Leaflet)	National Blue Star Mothers of America 5200 Warren Street Philadelphia, Penn.	Unknown	November 1949	Mail
Demand Freedom of Speech For Anti-Communist Forces in New York City (Leaflet)	National Renaissance Party 224 E. Main Street Beacon, N. Y.	Unknown	October 1949	Mail

CHART III: BOOKS, PAMPHLETS AND LEAFLETS—(Cont'd)

TITLE	PUBLISHER OR SPONSOR	AUTHOR	FIRST APPEARANCE	NUMBER PRINTED & DISTRIBUTION METHOD
Program of the National Renaissance Party (Leaflet)	National Renaissance Party Beacon, N. Y.	Unknown	April 1949	Mail
The Race Question and the Tolerance Racket (Leaflet)	National Renaissance Party Beacon, N. Y.	Unknown	June 1949	Mail
America Goes Communist (Pamphlet)	National Patrick Henry Organization, Inc. Columbus, Georgia	Unknown	June 1949	Mail
Abstract of Title to Palestine (Leaflet)	Unknown	Keen Polk 64 West 2nd Street Salt Lake City, Utah	1949	Mail
America's War Criminals (Leaflet)	Protestant War Veterans Washington, D. C.	Unknown	1949	Unknown
Jewish Terrorists in Palestine (Leaflet)	Protestant War Veterans Washington, D. C.	Unknown	1949	Unknown
Uphold the Constitution (Leaflet)	Protestant War Veterans Washington, D. C.	Unknown	March 1949	Mail
The World's Greatest Swindle (Leaflet)	Protestant War Veterans Washington, D. C.	Unknown	1949	Unknown
My Fight For the Right (Pamphlet)	Christian Nationalist Crusade, St. Louis, Missouri	Gerald L. K. Smith P.O. Box D-4 St. Louis, Missouri	1949	Mail
Israel—Her Racial Divisions and Geographical Wanderings (Pamphlet)	Publisher: Covenant Publishing Co., Ltd., London, England Distributor: Destiny Publishers, Haverhill, Massachusetts	Rev. Merton Smith	Unknown	Mail, Meetings
Master Alchemist of the Kingdom (Pamphlet)	Dr. Wesley Swift's Ministry, Lancaster, Calif.	Dr. Wesley Swift	June 1949	Meeting

CHART III: BOOKS, PAMPHLETS AND LEAFLETS—(Cont'd)

TITLE	PUBLISHER OR SPONSOR	AUTHOR	FIRST APPEARANCE	NUMBER PRINTED & DISTRIBUTION METHOD
Save America From The Horror of War (Leaflet)	Agnes Waters P.O. Box 3560 Washington, D. C.	Agnes Waters	May 1949	Mail
Statement of Mrs. Agnes Waters Against the Nomination of Dean Acheson For Secretary of State (Letter)	None	Agnes Waters Washington, D. C.	March 1949	Mail
Warning! International Plots In Making! (Letter)	None	Agnes Waters Washington, D.C.	February 1949	Mail
Leopards Cannot Change Their Spots (Leaflet)	None	John T. Wiandt Detroit, Michigan	Unknown	Mail
Open Letter to Los Angeles City Council (Letter)	Distributed at Christian Nationalist Crusade Meeting	Robert H. Williams Glendale, Calif.	August 1949	Meeting
Answering Mrs. Roosevelt (Manuscript)	Defender Publishers, Wichita Kansas	Gerald B. Winrod Wichita, Kansas	October 1949	Mail
Good and Bad Planning (Manuscript)	Defenders, Inc. Wichita, Kansas	Gerald B. Winrod Wichita, Kansas	July 1949	Mail
Suicide (Pamphlet)	Christian Nationalist Crusade P.O. Box D-4 St. Louis, Missouri	Mr. "X"	November 1949	Mail

Credits

THE Civil Rights Committee of the Anti-Defamation League of B'nai B'rith wishes to record its sincere tribute to its staff and co-operating agencies, without whose talents and devoted services the Committee's task could not have been completed. The persons who participated, in addition to those acknowledged previously, are:

NATIONAL STAFF DIRECTORS

Oscar Cohen   J. Harold Saks   Frank N. Trager

HEADQUARTERS STAFF

Nissen N. Gross	Sally R. Linett	Nessa Hurwitz
Dr. Leo Srole	Dr. Joseph L. Lichten	Arline Seitel
Hilda Weinstein	Dr. John Merlander	Nettie Cohen
Eleanor Belack	Doris J. Nelson	Shirley Feinberg
William G. Pinsley	Helene E. Auerbach	Betty Goetz
Samuel D. Freifeld	Mortimer Kass	Bernice Farber
Isadore Zack	Sandra Abramson	Anne Schoenbrun

REGIONAL DIRECTORS

Gilbert J. Balkin	Florida Regional Office
Brant Coopersmith	New Orleans Regional Office
Herman Edelsberg	Washington, D. C. Regional Office
Ben-Zion Emanuel	Illinois Regional Office
Theodore Freedman	Raleigh Regional Office
S. Thomas Friedman	Southwestern Regional Jewish Community Relations Council
Seymour Gorchoff	Ohio-Kentucky Regional Office
Louis B. Greenberg	Indiana Jewish Community Relations Council
Oscar Groner	New Jersey Regional Office
Fred Grossman	Pennsylvania Regional Office
George J. Harrison	Western New York State Regional Office
Stanley S. Jacobs	Washington State Regional Office
Mrs. Thelma Keitlen	Western Massachusetts Regional Office
Sol Kolack	New England Regional Office
Haskell L. Lazere	Michigan Regional Office
Sidney Lawrence	Jewish Community Council of Greater Kansas City
Arthur J. Levin	Atlanta Regional Office
Alexander F. Miller	Southern Office
Israel H. Moss	Eastern New York State Regional Office
P. Allen Rickles	Northern California Regional Office
David Robinson	Western Regional Office

A. Abbot Rosen — Midwest Regional Office
Sidney H. Sayles — Wisconsin Regional Office
Milton A. Senn — Southern California Regional Office
Louis E. Sidman — Mountain States Regional Office
Lester J. Waldman — Metropolitan New York Regional Office

COMMUNITY RELATIONS DIRECTORS

Harry I. Barron — Cleveland, Ohio
Leonard J. Brooks — Cincinnati, Ohio
Maurice B. Fagan — Philadelphia, Pennsylvania
Mrs. Lillian A. Friedberg — Pittsburgh, Pennsylvania
Arnold Harris — Newark, New Jersey
Boris Joffe — Detroit, Michigan
Simon Krakow — New Haven, Connecticut
Herman B. Levensohn — Hartford, Connecticut
Samuel L. Scheiner — Minneapolis, Minnesota
Myron Schwartz — St. Louis, Missouri
Louis J. Segel — Oakland, California

Anti-Defamation League of B'nai B'rith

Index

Talladega, Alabama, Ku Klux Klan activity in, 20, 21
Tallahassee, Florida, anti-mask ordinance, 33; Ku Klux Klan demonstration in, 22–23, 29
Talmadge, Gene, 19
Talmadge, Herman, governor of Georgia, 18–19
Tanner, Opal, secretary of Gerald L. K. Smith, 40

Taylor, A. B., in Ku Klux Klan, 28
Tennessee, anti-mask bill in, 34; Ku Klux Klan activity in, 20, 23
Tenney, Jack B., California State senator, and California Anti-Communist League, 40
Tennis, discrimination in, 183–85
Terminiello, Arthur, disagreement with Gerald L. K. Smith, 40
Terminiello case, 9–10
Terral, Vaughan, opposition to anti-mask bill in Georgia legislature, 33
They Want Your Child!, booklet by Allen Zoll, 77
Thomas, Danny, 180
Thompson, Henry, 167
"Tolerance Machine," Upton Close on, 59
Totah, Khalil, executive director of Institute of Arab-American Affairs, 78
Trends in anti-Semitism, 110–12
Trenton, Georgia, Ku Klux Klan activities in, 21
Trevor, John B., 71
True Americans, 25
Truman, Harry S., conference with Cecil Palmer, 72
Tulane University, Ku Klux Klan activity at, 19
Tulsa (Okla.) Women's Republican Club, Upton Close speech before, 59

Union, New Jersey, Ku Klux Klan activity in, 20
Union Carbide and Carbon Company, contributor to National Economic Council, 69
Union College, Schenectady, New York, 127
United Nations, in anti-Semitic press, 87
United States Court of Appeals, ruling on Joseph P. Kamp contempt case, 45
University of Kentucky, racial discrimination case at, 144
University of Michigan Medical School, action against discrimination in, 118
University of Minnesota Medical School, 118
University of Missouri, racial discrimination case at, 144
University of Oklahoma, racial discrimination case at, 144

Index by Harriet Thompson